Cinema, Media, and Human Flourishing

THE HUMANITIES AND HUMAN FLOURISHING

Series editor: James O. Pawelski, *University of Pennsylvania*

Other Volumes in the series

Philosophy and Human Flourishing
Edited by John J. Stuhr

History and Human Flourishing
Edited by Darrin M. McMahon

Literary Studies and Human Flourishing
Edited by James F. English and Heather Love

Religious Studies, Theology, and Human Flourishing
Edited by Justin Thomas McDaniel and Hector Kilgoe

Theater and Human Flourishing
Edited by Harvey Young

Cinema, Media, and Human Flourishing
Edited by Timothy Corrigan

Music and Human Flourishing
Edited by Anna Harwell Celenza

Visual Arts and Human Flourishing
Edited by Selma Holo

The Humanities and Human Flourishing
Edited by James O. Pawelski

Cinema, Media, and Human Flourishing

Edited by

TIMOTHY CORRIGAN

OXFORD
UNIVERSITY PRESS

Oxford University Press is a department of the University of Oxford. It furthers the University's objective of excellence in research, scholarship, and education by publishing worldwide. Oxford is a registered trade mark of Oxford University Press in the UK and certain other countries.

Published in the United States of America by Oxford University Press
198 Madison Avenue, New York, NY 10016, United States of America.

Library of Congress Cataloging-in-Publication Data
Names: Corrigan, Timothy, 1951– editor.
Title: Cinema, media, and human flourishing / Timothy Corrigan.
Description: New York : Oxford University Press, 2023. |
Series: The humanities and human flourishing |
Includes bibliographical references and index.
Identifiers: LCCN 2022021550 (print) | LCCN 2022021551 (ebook) |
ISBN 9780197624197 (paperback) | ISBN 9780197624180 (hardback) |
ISBN 9780197624210 (epub)
Subjects: LCSH: Motion pictures—Social aspects. | Happiness. |
Human beings—Philosophy.
Classification: LCC PN1995.9.S6 C4754 2023 (print) |
LCC PN1995.9.S6 (ebook) | DDC 302.23/43—dc23/eng/20220720
LC record available at https://lccn.loc.gov/2022021550
LC ebook record available at https://lccn.loc.gov/2022021551

DOI: 10.1093/oso/9780197624180.001.0001

1 3 5 7 9 8 6 4 2

Paperback printed by Marquis, Canada
Hardback printed by Bridgeport National Bindery, Inc., United States of America

Contents

List of Illustrations

Series Editor's Foreword

Imagine being invited to a weekend meeting to discuss connections between the humanities and human flourishing. You talk about ways in which the humanities can help us understand what human flourishing is—and is not. You explore how the humanities can help increase human flourishing. And you consider whether human flourishing is an absolute good, or whether it comes with certain limits and even potential dangers. How do you imagine the conversation playing out? What contributions might you make to the discussion?

The volumes in this series were borne out of just such a meeting. Or rather a series of such meetings, each gathering including some dozen scholars in a particular discipline in the humanities (understood to be inclusive of the arts). These disciplines include philosophy, history, literary studies, religious studies and theology, theater, cinema and media, music, and the visual arts. Participants were asked to consider how their work in their discipline intersects with well-being (taken to be roughly synonymous with human flourishing), along with a series of specific questions:

- How does your discipline conceptualize, understand, and define well-being?
- What does your discipline say about the cultivation of well-being? How does it encourage the implementation of well-being?
- In what ways does your discipline support flourishing? Do some approaches within your discipline advance human flourishing more effectively than others? Are there ways in which certain aspects of your discipline could more effectively promote well-being?
- Does your discipline contribute to well-being in any unique ways in which other endeavors do not?
- Are there ways in which your discipline can obstruct human flourishing?

As might be expected, the conversations in these meetings were rich and wide-ranging. Some of them headed in expected directions; others were more surprising. Each of them yielded opportunities to question assumptions and deepen perspectives. The conversations were rooted in disciplinary contexts and questions but yielded many generalizable insights on how to conceptualize human flourishing more clearly, how to cultivate it more effectively, and how to avoid negative consequences of understanding it in incomplete or overblown ways. I cannot properly describe or even summarize the richness of the discussions here, but I would like to point out a few of the highlights included in each of the resulting volumes.

Philosophy and Human Flourishing, edited by John J. Stuhr, addresses a number of fundamental questions. What is the value of discussing human flourishing in a world that in so many ways is decidedly not flourishing? In what ways is flourishing similar to and different from happiness? What is the role of morality in human flourishing? How does it relate to systemic privilege and oppression? To what degree is flourishing properly the concern of individuals, and to what degree is it a function of communities and societies? What are key factors in the fostering of flourishing? In addressing these questions, philosophers explore concepts such as mattering, homeostasis, pluralism, responsibility, and values, and consider the roles of individuals, educational institutions, and governments.

History and Human Flourishing, edited by Darrin M. McMahon, centers on the question, What is the value of history for life? This core question leads to a number of further inquiries. Is history only about the past, or does it have important implications for the present and the future? If the latter, then how can historical inquiry most effectively contribute to well-being? Does such inquiry currently focus in an imbalanced way on ill-being—on prejudices, class struggles, and wars? Such work is doubtless of great importance, not least by investigating how claims about happiness can serve as propaganda for continued oppression. But would hope for the future be more effectively kindled and concrete steps toward its realization more adeptly guided by increased attention to what has actually gone well in the past and what we can learn from it, or by more focus on how human beings have responded positively to adversity?

Literary Studies and Human Flourishing, edited by James F. English and Heather Love, focuses on the transformative power of literature. Scholars examine a range of topics, including the reparative possibilities of a literary encounter, the value of bibliotherapy and of therapeutic redescription, the genre of "uplit," and evolving methods for studying the activities and experiences of actual readers. A central question of this volume concerns the limits on transformations effected through literature. Several contributors worry that harnessing literary studies to the enterprise of human flourishing might lead readers merely to conform rather than to transform. To what extent might human flourishing serve as a palliative, enabling and encouraging readers to adapt to individual lives that lack moral depth and to social conditions that are rife with injustice, and thus obstruct the difficult and unsettling work of disruptive transformation needed for lasting individual and collective betterment?

Religious Studies, Theology, and Human Flourishing, edited by Justin Thomas McDaniel and Hector Kilgoe, explores ways in which individual and collective well-being can be increased through various religious perspectives and practices, including the Hindu concept of *sanmati* ("goodwill, wisdom, and noble-mindedness"), Buddhist meditation, and the cultivation of spiritual joy even while facing adversity. Scholars consider challenging questions concerning the proper contexts for learning *about* religion and for learning *from* religion, the right balance between the acknowledgment of suffering and the fostering of well-being, and the relationship between human flourishing and nonhuman worlds (including both natural and supernatural domains). A concern of some of these scholars is whether human flourishing entails a false universalism, one that seeks to reduce cultural diversities to one particular notion of what is desirable or even acceptable, and whether such a notion could be used to rate the value of different religions, or even ban religious practices (e.g., fasting, celibacy, or other ascetic austerities) that might be deemed misaligned with well-being.

Theater and Human Flourishing, edited by Harvey Young, considers the unique resources of theater and performance for imagining and enhancing well-being. Because theater involves both performers and audience members, it is inherently communal in ways many humanities disciplines and art forms are not. Theater allows groups of people—often strangers—to come together and experience the world in new ways. More than just an escape from ordinary life or a simple mirroring of reality, theater can provide opportunities for communal reimagining of the world, exploring new ways of thinking, feeling, and relating that can be experienced and then enacted to bring about a more flourishing future. Scholars examine connections between theater and human flourishing in more and less traditional spheres, looking at ways performance practices can be used to critique inadequate notions of human flourishing and to increase well-being in a wide variety of contexts, ranging from community theater to organizations serving soldiers with post-traumatic stress disorder (PTSD), and from oppressed groups to politically divided societies.

Cinema, Media, and Human Flourishing, edited by Timothy Corrigan, looks to film and a whole range of contemporary forms of digital media for what they can teach us about the nature of human flourishing and how it can be cultivated. These forms of communication have vast audiences and thus great power to support or subvert well-being. Contributors to this volume observe that human flourishing often seems to come piecemeal and as a hard-won result of conflict and struggle, and they explore ways in which well-being can be supported by collaborative practices for creating content, by the particular ways narratives are crafted, by certain genres, and by the various values that are embraced and transmitted. Contributors also consider how these popular forms can support individuals and groups on the margins of society by making more visible and sympathetic their struggles toward flourishing.

Music and Human Flourishing, edited by Anna Harwell Celenza, complements the commonly accepted and scientifically supported view that participating in music—as a listener, performer, or composer—can increase individual well-being. Instead of focusing on music as a performing art, this volume examines music as a humanities discipline, emphasizing the importance and value of music scholarship for fostering individual and collective human flourishing. How can music scholars (musicologists, ethnomusicologists, and music theorists) strengthen the effects of music on flourishing through a consideration of broader cultural, social, and political contexts? Contributors explore how processes of contemplation, critique, and communication within music scholarship can deepen the experience of music, resulting not just in the enhancement of individual well-being but in the more effective cultivation of wisdom and the greater realization of social justice.

Visual Arts and Human Flourishing, edited by Selma Holo, begins with the experience of artists themselves and the function of art in our society. If well-being is thought of as the happiness of self-satisfied complacency, then it would seem to be the antithesis of art, which is often disruptive, unnerving, and unsettling, asking viewers to question their assumptions and inviting them to see the world in new ways. But if well-being is understood more deeply as the flourishing that can arise from the full range of human experience, including the discomfort of contending forms of meaning and contested visions of reality, then it is difficult to think of it without art. Contributors to this volume consider the overwhelming personal necessity artists have to create, the role of well-being in art history, the increasing emphasis on human flourishing in architecture and public art, and salient questions of ethics, accessibility, and social justice in the context of art museums.

The Humanities and Human Flourishing, for which I serve as editor, is an interdisciplinary, capstone volume that contains contributions from the editors of the eight disciplinary volumes. After the disciplinary meetings were concluded, we gathered together to discuss what we had learned through the process. We considered both similarities and differences across the disciplinary discussions on human flourishing, identifying social justice and pedagogy as two common themes that emerged in the meetings. Like the other volumes in the series, this volume does not pretend to provide simple solutions or even unified answers to questions of how the humanities are or should be connected to the conceptualization and cultivation of human flourishing. Rather, it provides thoughtful questions and perspectives, distilled as it is from a deliberate process of extended engagement from diverse groups of scholars across eight different arts and humanities disciplines.

I would like to welcome you, the reader, to this book series. I hope you find it stimulating and even inspiring in its explorations into the complexities of the relationship between the humanities and human flourishing. And I hope you read across the volumes, as they are written in an accessible style that will yield valuable insights whether or not you have particular expertise in the discipline of the author whose work you are reading. To whatever degree you immerse yourself in this book series, though, I am sure of one thing: You will find it incomplete. As deep and as broad ranging as we tried to be in our explorations, none of the participants are under the illusion that the discussions and volumes brought it to a conclusion. We are keenly aware that a group of a dozen scholars, no matter how diverse, cannot speak for an entire discipline, and we realize that a focus on eight disciplines does not cover the entire domain of the humanities. Furthermore, our discussions and most of the writing were completed before the COVID-19 pandemic, which has made the nature and importance of flourishing all the more salient and has raised a host of new questions about well-being. Instead, we think of our work as an important beginning, and we would like to invite you to join the conversation. We hope a greater number and diversity of scholars, researchers, creators, practitioners, students, leaders in cultural organizations and creative industries, office holders in government, philanthropists, and members of the general public will bring their interests and expertise to the conversation, perhaps leading to new volumes in this series in the future. Investigations into human flourishing contribute to our knowledge and understanding of the human condition, and they have practical implications for the well-being of scholars, students, and societies. We hope our ongoing work together will enable the humanities to play a greater role in these investigations, effecting changes in scholarship, research, pedagogy, policy, and practice that will make them more supportive of human flourishing in academia and in the world at large.

Background and Rationale

For readers interested in more information on the background and rationale of this book series, I am happy to share further details on the perspectives, aims, and hopes that motivated it. A key catalyst for the development of this series was the dual observation that a growing number of individuals and organizations are focusing on human flourishing and that most of the headlines in this domain seem to be coming from the social sciences. Yale psychology professor Laurie Santos, for example, made the news when she developed a course on "Psychology and the Good Life"—and some 1200 students (nearly a quarter of Yale's undergraduate population) signed up for it.[1] As of this writing, her subsequent podcast, "The Happiness Lab," has reached 65 million downloads.[2] On an international scale, dozens of countries around the world have adopted psychological measures of subjective well-being as a complement to economic indicators, and a growing number of nations have embraced well-being, happiness, or flourishing as an explicit governmental goal.[3] The Organization for Economic Co-operation

[1] David Shimer, "Yale's Most Popular Class Ever: Happiness." *The New York Times*, January 26, 2018. https://www.nytimes.com/2018/01/26/nyregion/at-yale-class-on-happiness-draws-huge-crowd-laurie-santos.html

[2] Lucy Hodgman, and Evan Gorelick, "Silliman Head of College Laurie Santos to Take One-Year Leave to Address Burnout." *Yale News*, February 8, 2022. https://yaledailynews.com/blog/2022/02/08/silliman-head-of-college-laurie-santos-to-take-one-year-leave-to-address-burnout/

[3] https://weall.org/; https://www.ons.gov.uk/peoplepopulationandcommunity/wellbeing/articles/measuresofnationalwellbeingdashboard/2018-04-25; https://www.gnhcentrebhutan.org/history-of-gnh/; https://www.worldbank.org/en/news/feature/2013/10/24/Bolivia-quiere-replicar-el-indice-de-felicidad-de-Butan; https://u.ae/en/about-the-uae/the-uae-government/government-of-future/happiness/;

and Development (OECD), founded in 1961 to stimulate economic progress and world trade, has acknowledged the insufficiency of economic indicators alone for tracking progress. It launched its Better Life Initiative in 2011 to measure what drives the well-being of individuals and nations and to determine how countries can best support greater progress for all.[4] The United Nations publishes the World Happiness Report every year, releasing it on March 20, the UN International Day of Happiness.[5]

These are examples in the social sciences of what I have elsewhere called a "eudaimonic turn," an explicit commitment to human flourishing as a core theoretical and research interest and a desired practical outcome.[6] Over the last several decades, there has been a growing interest in human flourishing in economics, political science, psychology, and sociology, and in fields influenced by them, such as education, organizational studies, medicine, and public health. Perhaps the most well-known example of this eudaimonic turn in the social sciences occurred in psychology with the advent of positive psychology. Reflecting perspectives developed in humanistic psychology in the mid-twentieth century and building on increasing empirical work in self-efficacy, self-determination theory, subjective and psychological well-being, optimism, flow, passion, hope theory, positive emotions, and related areas, Martin Seligman and his colleagues launched the field of positive psychology. During a 1998 presidential address to the American Psychological Association, Seligman pointed out that mainstream psychology had become fixated on understanding and treating psychopathology. He argued that, although extremely important, healing mental illness is only part of psychology's mission. More broadly, he claimed, psychology should be about making the lives of all people better. He noted that this requires the careful empirical study of what makes life most worth living, including a deep understanding of flourishing individuals and thriving communities. Such study, he believed, would both increase well-being and decrease ill-being, since human strengths are both important in their own right and effective as buffers against mental illness. Known as "the scientific study of what enables individuals and societies to thrive,"[7] positive psychology has had a

[4] https://www.oecd.org/sdd/OECD-Better-Life-Initiative.pdf

[5] https://worldhappiness.report/

[6] James O. Pawelski, "What Is the Eudaimonic Turn?," in *The Eudaimonic Turn: Well-Being in Literary Studies*, ed. James O. Pawelski and D. J. Moores (Madison, NJ: Fairleigh Dickinson University Press, 2013), 3; and James O. Pawelski, "The Positive Humanities: Culture and Human Flourishing," in *The Oxford Handbook of the Positive Humanities*, ed. Louis Tay and James O. Pawelski (New York: Oxford University Press, 2022), 26.

[7] Constitution of the International Positive Psychology Association, Article 1, Section 2.

transformative effect on psychology and has deeply influenced many other fields of research and practice.

What role do the humanities play in all of this? What role could and should they play? How can the humanities help us conceptualize human flourishing more deeply, cultivate it more effectively, and critique it more insightfully? As a philosopher working in the field of positive psychology for more than twenty years, I have been concerned that there are not more voices from the humanities centrally involved in contemporary work in human flourishing. One of the core aims of this project and book series is to make a way for humanities scholars to play a larger role in this domain by inviting them to consider explicitly what contributions their work and their disciplines can make to the theory, research, and practice of human flourishing.

Historically, of course, human flourishing is at the root of the humanities.[8] The humanities were first defined and developed as a program of study by Renaissance scholars dissatisfied with scholasticism, which they perceived as leading to an overly technical university curriculum removed from the concerns of everyday life and unable to guide students toward human flourishing. They advocated, instead, a return to the Greek and Roman classics, reading them for insights and perspectives on how to live life well. Indeed, the Greeks and Romans had developed comprehensive programs of study (*paideia* and *artes liberales*, respectively) designed to teach students how to flourish individually and how to contribute to collective flourishing by participating effectively and wisely in civic life.

This emphasis on the understanding and cultivation of human flourishing that was so important to the Greeks and Romans was also of central concern to other philosophical and religious traditions that developed in the ancient world during what Karl Jaspers called the Axial Age.[9] Hinduism, Buddhism, Confucianism, Daoism, and Judaism, for example, along with the later Christianity and Islam, addressed the problem of human suffering and offered ways of promoting individual and collective flourishing. Although different in their cultural context and specific details, each of these traditions counseled against lives exclusively devoted to pleasure, wealth, power, or fame. They held that such lives only magnify suffering and that flourishing is actually fostered through a cultivation of virtue that allows

[8] Pawelski, "The Positive Humanities," 20–21; and Darrin M. McMahon, "The History of the Humanities and Human Flourishing," in *The Oxford Handbook of the Positive Humanities*, ed. Louis Tay and James O. Pawelski (New York: Oxford University Press, 2022), 45–50.

[9] Karl Jaspers, *The Origin and Goal of History* (Abingdon, UK: Routledge, 2011), 2.

for the transcendence of narrow, individual concerns in favor of a connection with the larger social world, the broader universe, or even the divine. Cultural forms such as literature, music, visual art, architecture, theater, history, and philosophical reflection were employed in the cultivation of virtue and the establishment of the broader and deeper connections valued for human flourishing.

Today, the humanities tend to be thought of less as a comprehensive program of study or means to cultivate virtue and more as a collection of academic disciplines. These disciplines are located largely within colleges and universities and are thus shaped by the values of these institutions. Much of higher education is driven more by the aim of creating knowledge than the goal of applying wisdom. To succeed in such an environment, scholars are required to become highly specialized professionals, spending most of their time publishing books and articles for other highly specialized professionals in their discipline. The courses they teach often focus more on the flourishing of their discipline than on the flourishing of their students, requiring students to learn *about* course content but not necessarily to learn *from* it. When human flourishing is addressed in the classroom, it is all too often done in a way that makes it difficult for students to apply it to their lives, and in many cases, it focuses more on obstacles to flourishing than on the nature and cultivation of well-being. It is important, of course, to understand and resist alienation, injustice, and malfeasance in the world and to expose corrosive ideologies that can permeate texts and other forms of culture. But it is also important to understand that flourishing is more than just the absence of languishing. And the argument has been made that "suspicious" approaches in the humanities need to be balanced by reparative approaches[10] and that critique needs to be complemented by a "positive aesthetics"[11] and a "hermeneutics of affirmation."[12] Meanwhile, students in the United States, at least, are reporting astonishingly high levels of anxiety, depression, and suicidality,[13] while at the same time coming under increasing economic

[10] Eve K. Sedgwick, "Paranoid Reading and Reparative Reading: Or, You're So Paranoid, You Probably Think This Introduction Is About You," in *Novel Gazing: Queer Readings in Fiction*, ed. Eve K. Sedgwick (Durham, NC: Duke University Press, 1997), 1–37.

[11] Rita Felski, *Uses of Literature* (Malden, MA: Blackwell, 2008), 22.

[12] D. J. Moores, "The Eudaimonic Turn in Literary Studies," in *The Eudaimonic Turn: Well-Being in Literary Studies*, ed. James O. Pawelski and D. J. Moores (Madison, NJ: Fairleigh Dickinson University Press, 2013), 27.

[13] Publications and Reports, National College Health Assessment, American College Health Association, accessed December 11, 2021, https://www.acha.org/NCHA/ACHA-NCHA_Data/Publications_and_Reports/NCHA/Data/Publications_and_Reports.aspx?hkey=d5fb767c-d15d-4efc-8c41-3546d92032c5

pressure to select courses of study that will directly help them find employment. Students who in the past might have followed their interests in the humanities are now more likely to major in STEM fields or to enroll in preprofessional tracks. Consequently, the number of students earning bachelor's degrees in the humanities is decreasing significantly.[14]

Would a eudaimonic turn in the humanities be helpful in addressing these obstacles of narrow professionalism, imbalanced focus, and student pressure? Would it help with what Louis Menand has called a "crisis of rationale" in the humanities, with scholars unable to agree on the fundamental nature and purpose of the humanities and thus unable to communicate their value clearly to students, parents, philanthropists, policymakers, and the general public?[15]Could the eudaimonic turn provide a unifying rationale in the humanities? Of course, there is a sense in which such a turn would actually be a eudaimonic *re*turn. This return would not be a nostalgic attempt to recover some imagined glorious past. The human flourishing historically supported by the humanities was significant, as mentioned above, but it was also very far from perfect, often embracing perspectives that supported unjust power structures that excluded many people—including laborers, women, and enslaved persons—from participating in flourishing and that enabled the exploitation of these individuals to the advantage of those in power. Tragically, our society suffers from some of these same injustices today. Instead of a glorification of a problematic past, which could well reinforce these injustices, a eudaimonic re/turn would invite us to focus our attention on perennial questions about human flourishing, building on wisdom from the past, but committing ourselves to a search for more inclusive answers that are fitting for our contemporary world.[16]

Not surprisingly, there is disagreement among scholars in these volumes, with some contributors endorsing the eudaimonic turn in the humanities and working to advance it and others putting forward a variety of concerns about the limitations and potential dangers of such an approach—and some even doing both. Scholars supporting a eudaimonic turn believe it could

[14] Jill Barshay, "PROOF POINTS: The Number of College Graduates in the Humanities Drops for the Eighth Consecutive Year," *The Hechinger Report*, November 22, 2021, https://hechingerreport.org/proof-points-the-number-of-college-graduates-in-the-humanities-drops-for-the-eighth-consecutive-year.

[15] Louis Menand, "The Marketplace of Ideas," American Council of Learned Societies Occasional Paper No. 49 (2001) http://archives.acls.org/op/49_Marketplace_of_Ideas.htm.

[16] Pawelski, "What Is the Eudaimonic Turn?" 17; Pawelski, "The Positive Humanities," 26; and McMahon, "The History of the Humanities and Human Flourishing," 45, 54.

revitalize the humanities by encouraging deeper investigations into the eudaimonic hopes that initially gave rise to their disciplines and the various ways in which contemporary work can support and develop these hopes. They believe these investigations could bring together scholars across the various humanities disciplines to create a common understanding and language for an examination of questions of human flourishing appropriate for our times. To be successful, such a project would not require complete agreement among scholars on the answers to these questions. On the contrary, diverse perspectives would enrich the inquiry, opening up new possibilities for human flourishing that are more equitable and widespread and that support the flourishing of the nonhuman world as well. Some contributors see significant potential in collaborating with the social sciences in their eudaimonic turn, a process that can be facilitated through the Positive Humanities, a new, interdisciplinary field of inquiry and practice focused on the relationship between culture and human flourishing.[17]

Scholars endorsing a eudaimonic turn in the humanities believe it could also inform, inspire, and support the work of museums, libraries, performing arts centers, and even creative industries (in music, movies, publishing, and other domains) to advance human flourishing more broadly in our society. They see a eudaimonic turn as also being of potential value to the millions of students who study the humanities each year. Without expecting humanities teachers and professors to take on therapeutic roles, they see considerable possible benefits in a pedagogical focus on how human flourishing can be understood and cultivated, with resulting courses intentionally designed to promote and preserve students' well-being and mitigate and prevent their ill-being.[18] Indeed, these scholars believe the volumes in this series might serve as useful texts for some of these courses.

Scholars with misgivings about a eudaimonic turn, on the other hand, raise a number of important concerns. Some contributors wonder whether human flourishing is a proper ideal in a world with so much suffering. Would such an ideal raise false hopes that would actually contribute to that suffering? Furthermore, are there more valuable things than human flourishing

[17] For more information on the Positive Humanities, see Louis Tay and James O. Pawelski, eds., *The Oxford Handbook of the Positive Humanities* (New York: Oxford University Press, 2022), especially the first three foundational chapters. Also, visit www.humanitiesandhumanflourishing.org.

[18] Furthermore, would students who perceive real life value in humanities courses be more likely to make room for them in their schedules, as suggested by the students who enrolled in Laurie Santos's course on "Psychology and the Good Life" in such large numbers? If so, could a side benefit of the eudaimonic turn be greater numbers of students signing up for courses in the humanities?

(e.g., ethics, the environment), and should flourishing be limited in favor of these greater goods? Is human flourishing inextricably linked to problematic ideological perspectives, perhaps ones that place too much emphasis on the individual and downplay or ignore issues of systemic injustice, or perhaps ones that serve the interests of a small number of persons in power and encourage everyone else to conform to the status quo? Is human flourishing a false universalism that might result in a failure to see and acknowledge deep cultural differences—or worse, that might see these differences as deviances that need to be suppressed and punished? Could an emphasis on well-being be employed to exploit individuals or groups of people, as notions of happiness have sometimes been used in the past? Are there other unexpected harms that might arise from a eudaimonic turn?

The unresolved tensions among the various chapters are part of what makes these volumes compelling reading. Are there ways to overcome concerns about the eudaimonic turn by clarifying its nature and aims, avoiding the dangers raised? Or will these concerns always persist alongside efforts to achieve individual and communal betterment through a theoretical and practical emphasis on flourishing? I welcome you, the reader, to join this discussion. What are your views on the perspectives expressed in these volumes? What points might you contribute to the ongoing conversation?

Process and People

I would like to conclude with a fuller account of the process by which the various volumes were created and an acknowledgment of the individuals and institutions who have made this book series possible. With the desire to give contributors ample time to reflect on how their work and their discipline relate to human flourishing, as well as to create opportunities to discuss these ideas with colleagues, we put into place an extended process for the creation of these volumes. After deciding on the eight disciplines in the arts and humanities we would be able to include in the project, we invited a leading scholar to chair the work in each of these disciplines and asked them to bring together a diverse group of some dozen noted scholars in their discipline.[19] For each group, we provided participants with some background

[19] For a full list of project participants, visit www.humanitiesandhumanflourishing.org.

reading[20] and asked them to prepare a draft essay on how their scholarly work informs the conceptualization and cultivation of human flourishing. Many participants chose to address the background reading—appreciatively, critically, or both—in their papers, although none were required to address it at all. We then circulated these drafts to the entire group in preparation for a three-day, face-to-face meeting, during which the disciplinary chair led a discussion and workshopping of the drafts. These disciplinary consultations, held in 2018 and 2019, were also joined by a junior scholar (usually a graduate student) in the field, one or two social scientists with work on relevant topics, and the Core Team.

Following these meetings, participants were asked to revise their drafts in light of our discussion, with the chairs serving as editors for the resulting disciplinary volumes. Given the nature of the project, I also read each of the contributions, providing comments along the way. From beginning to end, the process for creating and editing each of the volume manuscripts took well over a year and allowed for deep engagement with the subject matter and with other scholars. The disciplinary chairs and I were careful to emphasize that these discussions were intended to be robust and the writing authentic, with no foregone conclusions about the nature of human flourishing or the value of exploring it, and we were pleased by the range and depth of thinking undertaken by each group.

As mentioned above, after we held the eight disciplinary consultations, we held a ninth meeting where we invited the chairs of each of the disciplinary groups to present and discuss drafts of essays for a ninth, interdisciplinary volume sharing what they and their colleagues had learned through the process. We also invited a few humanities policy leaders, including past National Endowment for the Humanities Chairman William Adams, to join us and help think about the broader implications of this work.

[20] Martin E. P. Seligman and Mihaly Csikszentmihalyi, "Positive Psychology: An Introduction," *American Psychologist 55* (1) (2000): 5–14; Darrin M. McMahon, "From the Paleolithic to the Present: Three Revolutions in the Global History of Happiness," in *e-Handbook of Subjective Well-being*, ed. Ed Diener, Shigehiro Oishi, and Louis Tay (Champaign, IL: DEF Publishers, 2018); James O. Pawelski, "Defining the 'Positive' in Positive Psychology: Part I. A Descriptive Analysis," *The Journal of Positive Psychology 11* (4) (2016): 339–356; James O. Pawelski, "Defining the 'Positive' in Positive Psychology: Part II. A Normative Analysis," *The Journal of Positive Psychology 11* (4) (2016): 357–365; James O. Pawelski, "Bringing Together the Humanities and the Science of Well-Being to Advance Human Flourishing," in *Well-Being and Higher Education: A Strategy for Change and the Realization of Education's Greater Purposes*, ed. Donald W. Harward (Washington, D.C.: Bringing Theory to Practice, 207–216); and Louis Tay, James O. Pawelski, and Melissa G. Keith, "The Role of the Arts and Humanities in Human Flourishing: A Conceptual Model," *The Journal of Positive Psychology 13* (3) (2018): 215–225.

The compiling of the volumes was organized and overseen by the Humanities and Human Flourishing (HHF) Project at the University of Pennsylvania. HHF was founded in 2014 to support the interdisciplinary investigation and advancement of the relationship between the humanities and human flourishing. As the founding director of HHF, I am pleased that it has developed into a growing international and multidisciplinary network of more than 150 humanities scholars, scientific researchers, creative practitioners, college and university educators, wellness officers, policy experts, members of government, and leaders of cultural organizations. In addition to the disciplinary consultations described above and the resulting book series, we have published a number of conceptual papers and systematic reviews, developed conceptual models to guide empirical research, and created and validated a toolkit of measures. Designated a National Endowment for the Arts Research Lab, HHF has developed ongoing programs of research (including on art museums and human flourishing and on narrative technologies and well-being) to understand, assess, and advance the effects of engagement in the arts and humanities on human flourishing. We have published *The Oxford Handbook of the Positive Humanities* to help establish the Positive Humanities as a robust field of inquiry and practice at the intersection of culture, science, and human flourishing. For more information on HHF, including each of these endeavors as well as its current undertakings, please visit www.humanitiesandhumanflourishing.org.

I am deeply grateful to all the individuals and institutions whose collaboration has made this book series possible. I would like to begin by thanking Chris Stewart and Templeton Religion Trust for the generous grants that have underwritten this work. Thanks also go to the University of Pennsylvania for their robust institutional and financial support. (Of course, the views expressed in these volumes are those of the authors and do not necessarily reflect the views of Templeton Religion Trust or of the University of Pennsylvania.) I am grateful to the more than 80 contributors to these volumes for accepting our invitation to be a part of this work and bringing more depth and richness to it than I could have imagined. I am especially grateful to the chairs of each of the disciplinary groups for their belief in the importance of this work and their long-term dedication to making it a success. I also wish to express my appreciation for the hard work of the entire HHF Core Team, including Research Director Louis Tay, postdoctoral fellows Yerin Shim and Hoda Vaziri, Research Manager Michaela Ward, and especially Assistant Director Sarah Sidoti, who meticulously planned and oversaw each of the disciplinary consultations and used her expertise in academic publishing to help shape this book series in countless crucial ways. Most of the disciplinary consultations took place on the beautiful grounds of the Shawnee Inn & Golf Resort along the banks of the Delaware River. I am grateful to Charlie and Ginny Kirkwood, John Kirkwood, and all the folks at Shawnee for their gracious support and hospitality. Additionally, I am grateful to Jonathan Coopersmith and the Curtis Institute for donating space for the music group to meet, and to Bill Perthes and the Barnes Foundation for similarly donating space for the visual arts group. Thanks to the Penn Museum for a beautiful setting for the first day of our Chairs consultation and to Marty Seligman and Peter Schulman for donating further space at the Positive Psychology Center. Finally, I am grateful to Peter Ohlin and all the staff and reviewers at Oxford University Press for their partnership in publishing the volumes in this book series. I hope these volumes inspire further conversation, welcoming more people from a larger number of disciplines and a greater range of nationalities and cultural and ethnic backgrounds to inquire into what human flourishing is, how its potential harms can be avoided, and how its benefits can be more deeply experienced and more broadly extended.

James O. Pawelski
February 19, 2022

List of Contributors

Dudley Andrew is R. Selden Rose Professor Emeritus of Film and Comparative Literature at Yale where he moved in 2000 after thirty years at the University of Iowa. His first three books commented on film theory, and included a biography of *André Bazin*, whose thought he has broadcast in *What Cinema Is!*, *Opening Bazin*, and translations of Bazin's collected essays on subjects like new technologies, adaptation, and documentary. From the aesthetic and hermeneutic explorations of *Film in the Aura of Art* (1984), he turned to cultural historiography in *Mists of Regret* (1995) and *Popular Front Paris* (2005). An elected Fellow of the American Academy of Arts and Sciences and an appointed Commandeur de l'ordre des arts et des lettres, he is currently completing *Encountering World Cinema* and *A Very Short Introductoin to French Film*.

Timothy Corrigan is Professor Emeritus of English and Cinema Studies at the University of Pennsylvania. His work in Cinema Studies has focused on modern American and contemporary international cinema and documentary, adaptation studies, and documentary film and media. Books include *New German Film: The Displaced Image*, *The Films of Werner Herzog: Between Mirage and History*, *Writing about Film*, *A Cinema without Walls: Movies and Culture after Vietnam*, *Film and Literature: An Introduction and Reader*, *The Film Experience* (co-authored with Patricia White), *Critical Visions: Readings in Classic and Contemporary Film Theory* (co-authored with Patricia White and Meta Mazaj), *American Cinema of the 2000s*, *Essays on the Essay Film* (co-authored with Nora Alter), and *The Essay Film: From Montaigne, After Marker* (Oxford UP), winner of the 2012 Katherine Singer Kovács Award for the outstanding book in film and media studies. He has published essays in *Film Quarterly*, *Discourse*, and *Cinema Journal*, among other collections, and is also an editor of the journal *Adaptation* and a former editorial board member of *Cinema Journal*. He is a member of graduate groups and an affiliated faculty member in the departments of English, History of Art, German, Women's Studies, Comparative Literature, and Italian. In 2014 he received the Society for Cinema and Media Studies Award for Outstanding Pedagogical Achievement and the Ira H. Abrams Memorial Award for Distinguished Teaching in the School of Arts and Sciences at the University of Pennsylvania.

Lucy Fischer is Distinguished Professor, Emerita Film Studies at the University of Pittsburgh. She is the author of *Jacques Tati*, *Shot/Countershot: Film Tradition* *and Women's Cinema, Imitation of Life, Cinematernity: Film, Motherhood, Genre, Sunrise, Designing Women: Art Deco, Cinema and the Female Form, Stars: The Film Reader, American Cinema of the 1920s: Themes and Variations, Teaching Film, Body Double: The Author Incarnate in the Cinema, Art Direction and Production Design and Cinema by Design: Art Nouveau, Modernism, and Film History*, and *Cinemagritte: René Magritte Within the Frame of Film History, Theory and Practice*. She held a curatorial position at The Museum of Modern Art and received fellowships from the National Endowments for the Arts and for the Humanities. She was President of the Society for Cinema and Media Studies and received its Distinguished Service Award. At Pitt, she received the Provost's Mentorship Award and the Chancellor's Distinguished Research Award.

Angus Fletcher is Professor of Story Science at Ohio State's Project Narrative. His most recent books are *Wonderworks: The 25 Most Powerful Inventions in the History of Literature* (2021) and *Storythinking* (forthcoming).

Patrice Petro is Professor of Film and Media Studies, Dick Wolf Director of the Carsey-Wolf Center, and Presidential Chair in Media Studies. She is the author, editor, and co-editor of thirteen books, including *The Routledge Companion to Cinema and Gender* (with Kristin Hole, Dijana Jelaca, and E. Ann Kaplan, 2017), *After Capitalilsm: Horizons of Finance, Culture, and Citizenship* (with Kennan Ferguson, 2016), *Teaching Film* (with Lucy Fischer, 2012), *Idols of Modernity: Movie Stars of the 1920s* (2010), *Rethinking Global Security: Media, Popular Culture, and the "War on Terror"* (with Andrew Martin, 2006), and *Aftershocks of the New: Feminism and Film History* (2002). She served two terms as President of the Society for Cinema and Media Studies, the largest U.S. professional organization for college and university educators, filmmakers, historians, critics, scholars, and others devoted to the study of the moving image.

Dana Polan is a professor of Cinema Studies in the Tisch School of the Arts at New York University. He is the author of ten books in film and media studies (one, on *The Great Escape*, is in press) and of approximately two hundred essays, reviews, and review-essays. He has done DVD commentaries for close to a dozen films. He is a former president of the Society for Cinema Studies, the primary professional organization for the field, and former editor of its publication, *Cinema Journal*. He has a PhD from Stanford and a Doctorat d'Etat from the Sorbonne Nouvelle. He has been knighted by the Ministry of Culture of the French government for contributions to cross-cultural exchange. In 2002, he was selected as one of the two Academy Scholars for that year by the Academy of Motion Picture Arts and Sciences. A few years back, he served as a juror for non-fiction submissions for the Peabody Awards for Excellence in Broadcasting, and he helped judge the first ever Teheran Silent Film Festival. He currently has two book projects—a co-authored analysis (with music producer Charles L. Granata) on Frank Sinatra's upbeat and downbeat music in the

1950s, and a co-authored study (with film scholar Caryl Flinn) of the TV classic *The Patty Duke Show*.

Ellen C. Scott is Associate Professor of Cinema and Media Studies and Associate Dean of Equity, Diversity and Inclusion at UCLA in the School of Theater, Film, and Television. Her research focuses on the meanings and reverberations of film in African American communities. Her first book, *Cinema Civil Rights* (2015) exposed the Classical Hollywood-era studio system's repression of civil rights issues but also their stuttered appearance through latent, symptomatic signifiers taken up by Black reviewers and activists. She is working on two book projects. *Cinema's Peculiar Institution*, supported by several grants including an Academy Scholars grant, examines the history of slavery on the American screen. *Bitter Ironies, Tender Hopes* explores Black women film critics from the dawn of cinema until the first Black woman made a feature film in 1980.

Murray Smith is Professor of Philosophy, Art, and Film at the University of Kent, Canterbury, UK, where he has taught since 1992. He is a founding member of the Society for Cognitive Studies of the Moving Image, serving president from 2014 to 2017. From 2017 to 2018, he was Laurance S. Rockefeller Fellow at Princeton University's Center for Human Values. He has published widely on film, art, and aesthetics. In addition to *Film, Art, and the Third Culture: A Naturalized Aesthetics of Film* (Oxford, 2017), his publications include *Engaging Characters: Fiction, Emotion, and the Cinema* (revised second edition 2022), *Trainspotting* (revised second edition 2021), *Film Theory and Philosophy* (co-edited with Richard Allen, 1997), *Contemporary Hollywood Cinema* (co-edited with Steve Neale, 1998), and *Thinking through Cinema* (co-edited with Tom Wartenberg, 2006).

Patricia White is Centennial Professor of Film and Media Studies at Swarthmore College. She is the author of *Rebecca* (2021), *Women's Cinema/World Cinema: Projecting Contemporary Feminisms* (2015), and *Uninvited: Classical Hollywood Cinema and Lesbian Representability* (1999). Her work in feminist and queer film studies has been published in *Cinema Journal*, *Film Quarterly*, *GLQ*, *Screen*, and in *Indie Reframed*, *Out in Culture*, and *A Feminist Reader in Early Cinema*, among other collections. She is co-author with Timothy Corrigan of *The Film Experience* (2021) and co-editor, with Corrigan and Meta Mazaj, of *Critical Visions in Film Theory* (2011). White serves on the boards of Women Make Movies and *Film Quarterly.* A member of the editorial collective of *Camera Obscura*, she edited a recent special issue of the journal on the work and legacy of Chantal Akerman.

Introduction to *Cinema, Media, and Human Flourishing*

Timothy Corrigan

For many film audiences, tales of happiness, well-being, and human flourishing might seem only an occasional part of a film and media history characterized by troubled melodramas, violent crime and action films, and tragic historical epics. Yet movie history features numerous films and genres in which cinematic narratives about the pursuit of positive values and human fulfillment stand out as remarkable and defining achievements. Since the 1930s and through the superhero movies of today, social family comedies such as *You Can't Take It with You* (1938), frolicking literary adaptations such as *Midsummer Night's Dream* (1935), musical love stories such as *Singin' in the Rain* (1952), sophisticated animated childhood fantasies such as *Toy Story* (1995), or contemporary global rom-coms such as *Crazy Rich Asians* (2018) have celebrated the personal and social resiliencies and triumphs of people pursuing meaningful social and personal lives, along the way often dramatizing the abilities of individuals and groups to overcome social, psychological, and physical setbacks as they pursue and often achieve different kinds of personal fulfillment. In the majority of these films, various psychological and social crises and impediments both enrich and complicate these pursuits, suggesting that even in films in which the characters' implicit or explicit goals are to achieve certain values, relationships, and achievements, these films often require a narrative drama of conflict out of which the possibility a personal and social well-being might eventually emerge.

Whatever their different narrative trajectories or conclusions, whatever their stake in positive representations, one touchstone for all these movies (and other related media narratives) is value, a broad textual and cultural indicator that aligns questions of well-being and flourishing with a shifting but persistent marker in film and media history. Throughout the global history of film and media, from 1895 to the present, different notions of value

Timothy Corrigan, *Introduction to* Cinema, Media, and Human Flourishing In: *Cinema, Media, and Human Flourishing*. Edited by: Timothy Corrigan, Oxford University Press. © Oxford University Press 2023.
DOI: 10.1093/oso/9780197624180.003.0001

have shaped what matters most in the production of films, their aesthetic forms, and their reception, as way to measure how the movies sustain, encourage, or teach positive ways to thrive as individuals and members of society. These measures of cinematic value have been aligned, at times, with sociological and religious values and morals and, at other times, with economic and political values, as indications of the extent to which film and media practices can or should promote pragmatic, psychological, spiritual, or communal values that lead to human flourishing and happiness. In the first decade of the twentieth century, as part of the *film d'art* movement in France, for example, the uplifting values of canonical literature and classical theater as they were adapted to films offered a way to presumably elevate the cultural tastes of early film audiences not usually exposed to those cultural practices: in 1908, *The Assassination of the Duke of Guise* would become one of many celebrated films within this increasingly global movement that offered classic drama and history lessons to the working-class audiences of early cinema.[1] In the United States, Alice Guy-Blaché's 1911 *The Making of an American Citizen* told a pragmatic moral story for the rapidly growing immigrant audience in New York and elsewhere, describing the successful transformation of those immigrants into mindfully productive citizens. Between 1929 and 1932 the Payne Fund studied how movies could best educate children and adolescents as ethical and civic individuals, paving the way for the many adaptations of classic novels during this period, such as the 1933 *Alice in Wonderland*.[2] Today international film festivals from Cannes and Berlin to Toronto and Sundance provide different platforms for new ideas, visions, and debates about what counts in world politics, contemporary perceptions of beauty, environmental crises, or technological innovation. In all these and other cases, value is not synonymous with flourishing and well-being, but it does frequently indicate the changing but central views and achievements of movies and the touchstones according to which viewers may find models for productive and positive lives and communities. Here, cinematic value, as a foundation for well-being and flourishing, appears as a shifting framework through which a movie offers individuals or social groups a mindful vision of their own past, present, or future life.

This cinematic intersection of well-being, flourishing, and value points directly to the prominent place of movies and media in a cultural space

[1] See William Uricchio and Roberta Pearson's *Reframing Culture*.

[2] See Garth S. Jowett et al., *Children and the Movies: Media Influence and the Payne Fund Controversy*.

between entertainment and art. In this somewhat unique place, the popularity of films and media can also provide an unusually broad platform for both critical observations and emotional elevation. In this place, the widespread psychological and social impact of movies consistently highlights the extent to which movies can reach mass audiences and, in so doing, promote positive assumptions and attitudes which presumably and potentially improve how individuals or groups live and enjoy their lives. Virtually any era in film history can document these critical interactions built upon the balance of popular entertainment and artistic vision. In the first decade of the twentieth century, movies gathered working class audiences (frequently in urban centers and early exhibition sites, such as nickelodeons) as places and forums for social and personal integration. During the Great Depression of the 1930s, movie musicals and comedies often acted almost like therapeutic centers that released audience from their difficult lives on the streets. And in the 1990s and after, the renaissance of documentary films (in theaters and through streaming services) examined pressing issues on the fringes of nature and society and in the political centers of the world to both teach and delight large spectrums of society.

Responding to this cultural status of the movies, scholars and critics have mapped the impact of movies as presumably "the most democratic art." While some critics have railed against the negative effects of films within popular culture (such as their violence, escapist utopias, and stereotyped characters), many others have hailed their positive potentials (such as their democratic values, paths to individual self-awareness, imaginative visions of better lives, and global explorations as part of new understandings and sympathies). Wavering between negative and positive values and views of world images, these historical and cultural tensions underpin many of the essays in this volume, where the attraction of movies can provide a large forum in which to explore how to flourish within a landscape that does not always provide a clear path to that well-being and where finding happiness as communities and individuals may mean overcoming the resistance of the world.

With the arrival of new media culture and the electronic forums of the internet in the last twenty years, the representations of human flourishing and well-being and their ability to address and engage audiences have opened even more opportunities and new challenges. Various older media outlets and practices, from traditional movie theaters to television programming, span much of the twentieth century, but the digital turns of the 1990s and later has massively altered the kinds and spectrum of media that pervade both established and emerging economies around the world. How and where positive values and goals must now intervene is no longer the relatively restricted realm of movies and movie theaters but also includes the internet, social networks, and new forms of electronic creativity and interactivity. This sea change in visual and audio communication has not, however, separated itself from a long history of film; instead, it has made more relevant and urgent the ability to shift the lessons of film history to the new media landscapes of today.

Two of the more notable avenues opened through new media are the significant expansion of the range and kinds of films available to audiences and the increased power and activities offered to those audiences. Numerous streaming sites, from Netflix to the Criterion Channel, now offer viewers an unprecedented variety of genres (from new documentaries about previously unseen cultures to national historical epics outside the US and Europe). At the same time, these new media platforms can often offer viewers more interactivity with the images in their lives than ever before, an interactivity that appears most obviously in the ability of individuals and fans to recreate their own needs, desires, and interests as part of an imaginative dialogue with the films and media they encounter. Both in theory and practice, these new media opportunities can become the grounds for expanding understandings of the world and a mindful confidence in the agencies of self.

The range of topics in this volume covers a multitude of historical periods and topics, which in turn figure in the new media environments of contemporary life. These include discussions of the Aristotelian and classical models of a "good life" that inform animated fairy tales today; 1930s French and Hollywood films which respond to the dire need for productive human relationships in a turbulent decade; the polemical positions of black film criticism through the lens of James Baldwin's work; a discussion of contemporary filmic quests for happiness; the challenges for women filmmakers today in mapping the values of their own world, landscapes of austerity and poverty, in the cinematic homelands today; the scientific, psychological, and philosophical base for human value; and the shifting media frames of modern society and selves.

Although the issues and arguments overlap and engage a broad spectrum of historical periods, theoretical positions, and topics, I have organized them into two broad sections: "Cinematic Quests for Human Value" and "Human Flourishing on the Margins of the Frame." Within this two-part structure appear not only the dynamic historical and intellectual variety that emerges from questions about well-being and flourishing, but also the tension and differences in many films and media products pursuing those questions: in short, where positive values are sometimes vividly foregrounded or where those values must often struggle to find a place in a relatively unaccommodating world.

The essays in the first section focus directly on the motifs of happiness, flourishing, and well-being as films thematically, textually, and culturally address those goals in different ways. Angus Fletcher's "The Lost Optimism of Modern Movie Fairytales" examines the way positive psychology demonstrates how narratives can influence our mental well-being by teaching us to see negative events as products of impersonal, local, and transient causes and positive events as products of personal, pervasive, and enduring causes. For Fletcher, these different narratives for well-being have their historical roots in Aristotle's *Poetics* but return more specifically in Fiovanni Francesco Straparola's 1553 formula for modern fairytales that encouraged the psychologically beneficial beliefs that misfortune can be considered a passing accident while good fortune becomes a long-lasting reality in life. Within this framework, Fletcher locates key movie narratives, from Charlie Chaplin's *Gold Rush* (1925) to Danny Boyle's *Slumdog Millionaire* (2008), and perhaps most prominently in the films of the chief producer of movie fairytales, the Disney studios, where motifs of pessimism, anxiety, and paranoia have recently become more frequent. Pixar's *Up* (2009) becomes important evidence that Straparola's formula can be as commercially successful as Disney's formula, and it indicates that popular Hollywood fairytales can be a "scalable" source of eudaimonia when story choices are informed less by *a priori* moral intuitions and more by the empirical findings of modern historians and psychologists.

In "Media-ting Happiness," Lucy Fischer situates her argument in her classroom experiences, which through the years have tested various interests, strategies, and successes related to flourishing and well-being. Among the many related topics she has taught, film comedy particularly has offered multiple rich possibilities for promoting human flourishing through the regenerative power of laughter. Writers, such as Norman Cousins, provide important perspectives on how laughter and comedy can ameliorate the pain of illness, while others, such as Henri Bergson, help theorize how laughter and comedy provide the potential to promote life-affirming attitudes that counterpoint the mechanical routines that can deaden daily life. As an extension of this framework, Fischer integrates issues related to feminist studies and women and film, and her essay accordingly examines the ways in which wellness and mindfulness emerge as students and readers begin to recognize and free themselves from the constraining and often repressive gender ideologies that restricts their lives. Finally, a third dimension of Fischer's essay touches upon the place of psychoanalysis, mental illness, memory, and hallucination in the movies and the complex issues that they raise in discussing human flourishing, referencing various kinds of "cinema therapy" as practiced by psychologists or psychoanalysts, as well as more recent attempts to use virtual reality to overcome trauma and phobias. With close readings of films such as Michel Gondry's 2004 *The Eternal Sunshine of the Spotless Mind* and Peter Chelsom's 2014 *Hector and the Search for Happiness*, the essay broadly argues for the potential of aesthetics itself to promote human well-being.

In Murray Smith's "Human Flourishing, Film, and the Varieties of Value," the ubiquity and centrality of moving image media in contemporary society raises prominent questions about the role of this media in relation to art, ethics, politics, and the way in which film (in its multifarious guises) acts as a vehicle of various kinds of value. Here, Smith attempts to discusses a variety of historical and contemporary debates concerning the values embodied by film, a foundational discussion that advances his distinctive claim about the powers of film and its place within human polity. For him, film possesses unique representational capacities which account for its rapid growth and diffusion across cultures, and these capacities are best understood in aesthetic terms, where aesthetic value becomes a core member of that family of other values—epistemic, ethical, political, and psychological—collectively essential to human flourishing. In this sense, the aesthetic dimension is not only an essential aspect of film as an art, but a crucial aspect of life well-lived and fully realized. Along the way, and drawing on his previous work in *Film, Art, and the Third Culture*, Smith addresses a related methodological question: what is the relationship between the descriptive and explanatory nature of (positive) psychology and the normative character of claims about human flourishing?

At the core of Dudley Andrew's essay, "Cinema and Creative Community," the arts and the movies specifically not only are the fruit of human flourishing, but they can also be the means by which that flourishing might happen. Indeed, for Andrew, an "un-recognized law of compensation" often brings this benefit to our attention at the worst possible moments in history, and, perhaps especially today, at an alarming moment for world civilization, it is crucial to look back to earlier times that seemed utterly dire to those who lived, or failed to live, through them and discover that powerful ability of the arts to provide havens of well-being. Andrew looks then at those particularly bleak years that begin in 1935 and continue through World War II, when the harshest season of the Great Depression continues through the devastation of the war and ends with the public awareness of the Holocaust camps and the impending threat of nuclear war, an era that W. H. Auden dubbed *The Age of Anxiety*. Within this period, Andrew identifies two cultural and intellectual figures who turned to the cinema as the most promising place to gauge the aspirations and hopes of human beings: Erwin Panofsky and André Malraux. In their distinctive ways, each sees the cinema as the most promising forum for promoting the undying impulse for expression that is the sap of a flourishing civilization. On these two intellectual cornerstones, the essay argues for the singular importance of the cinema as the interplay between popularity and communal aesthetics—not only through a number of inspiring films of the late 1930s and early 1940s, but also through the enterprise of filmmaking itself as a potential for social organization in the drive toward creative community. Charlie Chaplin, Jean Renoir, and John Ford provide the most luminous examples of an attitude toward a massive art that, according to Andrew, we need to measure up to today, if not in the films of our time, then in some other medium that can carry the weight. Who will speak for the continuity of artistic flourishing in our age? Panofsky and Malraux are gone; who will point us to an art in which we can have hope?

The second part of the volume, "Human Flourishing on the Margins of the Frame," explores questions of well-being and flourishing often found outside the mainstreams of film and media culture where individuals and groups often excluded from narratives of happiness and success must overcome social and psychological obstacles in their struggles to formulate alternative mindful visions of life and well-being.

Ellen C. Scott's "Fiendish Devices: Human Flourishing and the Black Watching Subject?" places her essay in the context of the larger tradition of movies as therapeutic value, articulated by both psychologists and film theorists. Some of these positions, according to Scott, provide grounds for pleasurable cognitive alignment; in others, opportunities for secondary or primary identification as a positive vehicle for imagining ourselves; and in still others the movies become simply a welcoming space of relaxation and entertainment. For Scott, however, Black film critics and theorists have commonly constructed the film experience as a far less hospitable space, one of negative reflection and segregation where the screen reflects a caricatured mirror often taking on the dimensions and shape of Kara Walker-esque grotesquerie. James Baldwin's caustic *The Devil Finds Work*, for example, sees cinema not as therapeutic but as quite the opposite—as an escape valve for whites enabling pursuit of insidious neglect of Black subjects—a kind of *false* therapy for white viewers that allows oppression to continue and whiteness to remain ascendant. A profound skeptic about the possibilities of Black flourishing in the US, Baldwin saw in these mainstream Hollywood images a profound lack of hope. Against this background, this essay explores the possibility of Black flourishing through acts of interrogative film criticism, focusing on the work and writing of an under-heralded Black woman film critic, Almena Davis. Davis, editor of the 1940s and 1950s Black newspaper the *L.A. Tribune*, shared Baldwin's acerbic critique of Hollywood's undermining of Black life. But for her, it was through the act of debunking and countering Hollywood's toxic white placidity and plasticity that her own selfhood could flourish and emerge. Her loose play with Hollywood constructions opened a place for the noir, the avant-garde, and the satirical. And in her interpretive writing, which mixed consideration of film, politics, her children, her dogs, and her "premenstrual tension," it was precisely the act of her embodied unmasking of the screen that made her own liminal, gender-porous selfhood legible. Davis becomes a case study of Black feminized, interrogative criticism as a way of life—a recourse for the disappointed, oppressed, and marginalized Black subject to draw therapy, life, and possibility through the aegis of un-abating, avowedly bitter, critique. For Scott, Davis' model of daily, trenchant critique as *self*, one evident in the current cultural criticism and persona of Charles Blow, is as necessary today as ever, as we have as much to fear from fascisms of the screen today as we did in Davis' 1940s and 1950s.

In "Human Relationship as Human Value in Studio Era Hollywood," Dana Polan focuses on the classical Hollywood narrative during the peak of the studio era. These are films which proffered modes and models of humanness and human relationship that are distinguished through a bounded inventiveness. Within this framework, narrative permutations work according to a value system that Polan terms a system of oneness, twoness, and many-ness. Oneness concerns characters who live for or by themselves, eschewing larger bonds of human relationship and ultimately suffering for that isolation. On the one hand, there is the hedonist who thinks only of his or her own pleasure: for example, gangster Rocky Sullivan (James Cagney) in the 1938 *Angels with Dirty Faces* who uses criminality to lead a high life of empty thrills. On the other hand, the cynic, often wounded by human relationship, turns away from pleasures into self-lacerating isolation: for instance, Rick (Humphrey Bogart) in 1942's *Casablanca*. To live solely for one's self, Hollywood films suggest, is to live incompletely. One narrative solution allows the monadic hero to go it alone but only insofar as isolation and separation from society becomes a way to help that society: hence, the fascination for narratives of individualistic sacrifice (maternal melodramas like *Stella Dallas* but also narratives of sacrificial conversion like *Angels with Dirty Faces* itself where Rocky feigns cowardice at his execution so as to turn a gang of boys against the gangster life they had so wanted to emulate). In fact, though, beyond this vague sense that the children are our future, Hollywood films have difficulty imagining collectivity, especially as something that can foster growth and flourishing. Indeed, a converse image of collectivity seems prevalent: the fear people, as a mass, act on under the mark of collective hysteria, the crowd as mob (see, for instance, Fritz Lang's first American film, *Fury*, which suggests how easily everyday American citizens can turn into a lynch mob). Between the stunted individual and the mindless many, Hollywood films hold out the romantic couple as ideal and suggest overwhelmingly that this is where growth occurs: the ideology of romantic love can be so strong that it sets itself up as anti-social and bereft of future benefits, such as in the 1939 adaptation of *Wuthering Heights* which pointedly leaves out the next generation to concentrate on Heathcliff and Cathy turning their back (literally so) to the world of the many (embodied here in polite but conventional British society). Even as films within the system of Hollywood narrative exhibit a wide range of questions (and answers) as to the nature of the good life, it is a system bounded by normative conceptions of human relationship (the heterosexual couple, for instance, as the pinnacle of positive relationship). Nonetheless, many of these films often show the constraints of Hollywood's dominant vision and suggest that the varieties of the Good Life represented in Hollywood film are, even though various, limited in their depiction of human potentiality and, especially, the social constraints that limit such potentiality to privileged sectors in American life.

Patricia White's "Sentimental Miseducation: Women Directors Coming of Age" balances her research and scholarship in psychoanalytic theory with her presiding work in queer and feminist film theory and history. In this essay she anchors those concerns through four related polemics and positions: Sara Ahmed's argument about feminist killjoys, Heather Love's notion of "feeling backward," Ann Cvetkovich's reflections on queer depression, and Lauren Berlant's well-known study of "cruel optimism." Against this background, White nonetheless discovers a utopian element in a perspective on women's genres in cinema and television and the films that appear within those genres. Here, White traces the significant promises of female homosociality, founded in the structures of feeling that sustain viewers even as characters' desires are thwarted. As part of her analysis, she imports central concepts from queer/feminist work on affect and melodrama and applies them to questions of well-being in recent coming-of-age dramas by women directors. Her primary examples include Andrea Arnold's *American Honey* (2016), Desirée Akhavan's *Appropriate Behavior* (2014), Marielle Heller's *Diary of a Teenage Girl* (2015), Anna Rose Holmer's *The Fits* (2015), Greta Gerwig's *Ladybird* (2017), and Desirée Akhavan's *The Miseducation of Cameron Post* (2018). In their different ways, each of these tells stories of a female self at odds with social expectations, and each suggests critical links to the director's own performance of creativity as it elicits the affective participation of the spectator as part of a narrative transformation.

My own essay, "Learning to Adapt, or the Splendors of Infidelity," focuses on the 2003 film *American Splendor*, a film which serves to reframe questions of well-being with an explicitly pedagogical turn. It begins with the assumption that in the twenty-first century (and decades before), to be a truly educated person today you *must* know film history and the important films that describe world film culture, much in the same way that centuries earlier an educated person was expected to know the best of what is known and thought in the world (usually literature and philosophy). A mindfully educated person, in short, needs to know how to understand and to work with moving images and, in many cases, analyze those images as an act of appreciation and understanding. These pedagogical goals mirror the larger significance and value of a personal and social encounter with the cinema today where the intellectual, imaginative, and kinetic ability to engage new worlds and experiences becomes a distinctive and crucial part of individual and social development. For film viewers, these are normally multi-layered or multi-tracked engagements that productively blur the lines between critical analysis and psychological pleasure, and, in the best cases, they integrate the different experiential values of aesthetics, cognition, and ethics as a sustainable activity that invigorates life beyond the film screen. The larger interdisciplinary projects devoted to "human flourishing," "well-being," and "the enhancement of the humanities" typically map and evaluate these goals across the activities of immersion, embeddedness, socialization, and reflectiveness, positions entirely relevant to the cinematic. Here, however, the essay refocuses those broader categories on a particular activity associated with cinematic adaptation, with all its textual and historical layers and with its implicit pedagogical lesson of "learning to adapt." Although this notion of cinematic adaptation commonly refers, for instance, to the textual and creative activity that binds a novel and its reincarnation on a screen of moving images or to the inverse movement that connects a movie with its reiteration as, for instance, an interactive video game, the focus here on adaptive values as a source of individual and social growth concerns a different dimension of cinematic adaptation, namely, the spectatorial dynamics of negotiating these kinds of film adaptations as an emotional, cognitive, social, and even corporeal exercise in changing mobilities. The touchstone for the pedagogy of these adaptive mobilities is then the 2003 film *American Splendor*, a movie ostensibly about the pathologically misfit cartoonist Harvey Pekar, but in fact about the flexibility, delights, and value of shifting representational identities.

In the final essay in the collection, Patrice Petro's "Austerity Media, Impulses to Hope" examines the ideology, economics, and aesthetics of what she calls "austerity media." Here she focuses on texts that tell unconventional stories about marginalized individuals and groups frequently overlooked by mainstream film and media: hoarders, street hustlers, and transgender people, all living on the edge in an age of increasing depravation and austerity. For Petro, an ideology of austerity frequently appears related to the movements that promote self-help and that consequently suggest that individuals rather than social systems of power are responsible for the personal and social crises that describe these lives. With the increasing loss of public resources in the US, popular culture has more and more struggled to make cultural and political sense of these complex and often disturbing situations where affirmative possibilities and directions emerge only with great difficulty. The economics of austerity media and culture moreover become reflected in the proliferation of cheap media productions, which in turn provide compelling examples of austere economic practices in themselves. Reality TV is one of the most prominent and recognizable examples, but so are neo-documentaries, made on extreme micro-budgets, and shot in a neo-neorealist style, including Sean Baker's two remarkable films, *Tangerine* and *Florida Project*, powerful engagements with those austerity cultures and how they are represented. Through an analysis of reality television shows specifically about hoarding and those two recent films, Petro explores the ideology, economics, and aesthetics of austerity, as well as distinct scholarly approaches to understanding austerity's impact and reach. At the heart of her argument, Petro demonstrates how films like Baker's and other media reveal the difficulties and desperations that describe contemporary lives defined by over-consumption, planned obsolescence, and vast mountains of disavowed waste. By showing audiences the often unseen lives and social predicaments that have been shaped by the instabilities of dwelling and dispossession, these works uncover the crucial impulses and desires the seek out and discover prospects for human well-being within the cultural corners on the margins that are often the defining center of our contemporary world.

All the essays included in this volume evolved from a three-day meeting, with presentations and discussions of each chapter in draft form, in September 2018. The meeting was organized by the Humanities and Human Flourishing Project at the University of Pennsylvania and was guided by Project Director James Pawelski. Additional support was provided by Research Director Louis Tay, Postdoctoral Fellow Yerin Shim, Assistant Director Sarah Sidoti, and Research Assistant Michaela Ward.[3] Further support was provided by Eleni Palis (then at the University of Pennsylvania, now in the Department of English, University of Tennessee). The many participants who were part of the development of these meetings and discussions represent a wide range of universities from across the US and the UK, and together they brought a spectrum of backgrounds and interests that articulate multiple personal and professional perspectives that energized and balanced the ambitious goals of the different positions.

The numerous sessions of conversation over these several days produced dynamic debates and conversations which, I believe, not only shaped and developed each individual's topic and arguments, but also identified an important motif that appears in a number of the essays here: how film pedagogy provides a key register and activity for examining and promoting where cinematic well-being, mindfulness, and flourishing become a crucial part of the film experience. The art and industry of movies is obviously a complicated and differentiated business, and watching films can be an equally complicated and differentiated activity. Actively understanding and questioning where cinematic well-being and flourishing can be integrated into our classrooms and into our lives outside the classroom may make film pedagogy a powerful pathway to finding and promoting those values examined in this

[3] To see the full extent and range of this project, see https://www.humanitiesandhumanflourishing.org/.

collection. In a very practical sense, this volume hopes to point in that pedagogical direction.

Works Cited

Auden, W. H. *The Age of Anxiety: A Baroque Ecologue*. Princeton University Press, 2011.

Baldwin, James. *The Devil Finds Work*. Random House, 1976.

Bergson, Henri. *Laughter: An Essay on the Meaning of the Comic*. Martino Fine Books, 2014.

Cousins, Norman. *The Anatomy of an Illness as Perceived by the Patient*. Bantam, 1981.

Jowett, Garth S., et al. *Children and the Movies: Media Influence and the Payne Fund Controversy*. Cambridge UP, 1996.

Smith, Murray. *Film, Art, and the Third Culture*. Oxford UP, 2017.

Uricchio, William, and Roberta Pearson. *Reframing Culture: The Case of the Vitagraph Quality Films*. Princeton UP, 1993.

PART I

CINEMATIC QUESTS FOR HUMAN VALUE

1
The Lost Optimism of Modern Movie Fairytales

Angus Fletcher

Aristotle's *Poetics*

Inked down on a papyrus scroll sometime around 335 BCE, it's the world's oldest surviving attempt to explain how dramatic literature can nurture mental health. Yet for all its dusty age, it still reads like science fiction. It begins by proposing that Greek theater is a technology engineered from narrative inventions. It then suggests that this technology can plug into our psyches to regulate our emotions. And finally, it concludes that such regulation can carry our minds toward eudaimonia, the state of blissful flourishing that constitutes the highest good of mortal life.

If this view of dramatic literature sounds quixotically futuristic today, it was so unprecedented in its era that it bordered on the scandalous. Aristotle's own teacher, Plato, had famously concluded that dramatic literature was the path *away* from eudaimonia. Eudaimonia, Plato was sure, could be achieved only by philosophy, and philosophy was, by definition, the opposite of theater. Philosophy advanced the truth of reason—while theater wallowed in fictions (which is to say, lies) that appealed to the grossest elements of human nature. Yet now here was Aristotle, arguing not only that the stuff of the stage was a source of psychic flourishing, but that the flourishing sprang from the very emotions that true philosophers rejected.

And even this wasn't the most perverse feature of the *Poetics*. Prior to Aristotle, dramatic literature's most fervent defenders had universally concluded that it was a thing of illogic, a sublimely unfathomable gift from the muses. But the *Poetics* averred the opposite. Insisting that dramatic literature was logical in both form and function, it laid out a nuts-and-bolts analysis of the Greek world's most mystical genre: tragedy. Greek tragedy, according to the *Poetics*' analysis, was precisely engineered to improve two

Angus Fletcher, *The Lost Optimism of Modern Movie Fairytales* In: *Cinema, Media, and Human Flourishing*. Edited by: Timothy Corrigan, Oxford University Press. © Oxford University Press 2023.
DOI: 10.1093/oso/9780197624180.003.0002

different aspects of eudaimonia: emotional health (which came from ridding the mind of harmful feelings) and emotional flourishing (which came from the inverse: filling the mind with beneficial feelings). To improve emotional health, Greek tragedy used an *anagnorisis* (a dramatized realization by a character that her fortunes had gone bad) to trigger a catharsis, purging the audience's psyches of unhealthy levels of pity and fear. And to improve emotional flourishing, Greek tragedy deployed another narrative invention: the story twist. If the twist felt both probable and unexpected, then it produced wonder (*thaumasios*), which Aristotle claimed as a psychological good, something that makes life worthwhile.[1]

Because Aristotle's techno-utopian approach to Greek tragedy is so boldly unusual, it has fascinated many readers—and dissatisfied many others—sparking two thousand years of debate over whether or not the *Poetics* gets it right. Does *anagnorisis* really trigger catharsis? Can catharsis purge our brains of fear? Do story twists really generate wonder? Can that wonder contribute to eudaimonia?

These deliberations have been richly interesting. But by trying to pin down the enduring truth-value of Aristotle's claims, they have slowly lost touch with the feature of the *Poetics* with the greatest potential to reshape our here and now: its pragmatic take on dramatic literature as a tool for nurturing public well-being. That instrumentalist approach invites us to inquire broadly into what (and how much) the narrative inventions of dramatic literature can contribute to the greater psychological good. So, to determine what (and how much) the greater psychological good of our modern world might benefit from such an inquiry, this chapter will break from the long debate over the *Poetics*. Instead of trying to ascertain whether Aristotle's ancient work is "right" in some absolute sense, they'll return to it with unabashedly twenty-first-century eyes, exploring whether it might provide a "useful" starting-point for our own consumption of dramatic literature.

This exploration will require us to push beyond the original borders of the *Poetics* into two fresh areas. First, we'll need to venture past the Greek stage to examine newer forms of dramatic literature—like film and television—that are popular today. And second, we'll need to enlarge Aristotle's account of well-being with recent psychological research into topics like emotion and mental flourishing—including the crucial finding that our brains are all a little bit different, so that no two human brains can flourish quite the same.

[1] Aristotle, *Poetics*, 1452a4.

That fresh terrain will pose steep challenges for Aristotle's method. But it will also throw open a new opportunity: the chance to use film and television to experience forms of eudaimonia left unmentioned by the *Poetics*.

Extending Aristotle's Blueprint

There's a simple reason why very little effort has been made, in all the twenty-three centuries since the *Poetics* was writ, to extend its method of analysis onto the many groundbreaking narrative inventions of theater, film, and television that have come to be since the Greeks.

The reason is that Aristotle himself declares in the *Poetics* that Greek tragedy is the ideal form of dramatic literature. Readers who have accepted Aristotle's method have, therefore, also tended to accept his claim about tragedy, giving them small reason to explore more recent forms of dramatic literature. Meanwhile, readers who have critiqued Aristotle's method have had even less reason to extend the *Poetics* onto newer genres of film and television. And so it is that for over two thousand years, the *Poetics* has remained largely what it was at its inception: a document that's either accepted as *the* blueprint for dramatic eudaimonia or rejected as an intellectual misfire.

Yet in our own day and age, a third approach to the *Poetics* has become possible. We now have the option of agreeing with Aristotle—and extending him. That's because we have recently come to appreciate Aristotle as something other than a philosopher. We have come to appreciate him as a psychologist.

Earlier generations knew, of course, that Aristotle had authored a major work on psychology, *On the Psyche*. Yet they understood this work as a description of the eternal workings of the human soul, so they saw it as a contribution to metaphysics (or even theology). Nowadays, our view has widened. As psychology has emerged as a scientific discipline, we have become aware that Aristotle's investigations of the human psyche (particularly those included in his "supplemental" psychology treatises, *On Sense* and *On Memory*) don't rely purely on philosophical deductions. They also make use of the empirical techniques employed by modern psychologists. And like modern psychologists, their goal is often not metaphysical but medicinal, leading to the practical recommendations found in Aristotelian works like *On Sleep* and *On Rhetoric*.

To emphasize these scientific aspects of Aristotle's psychological writings is to discover an author who is less meta-physician than physician. Which is to say, an author who strives to provide his readership with practical handbooks for healthier living. And when the *Poetics* is treated as one such handbook, it ceases to be the necessary summit of dramatic theory and instead becomes the opposite: a useful starting point for further experimental inquiry. Inviting us to continue Aristotle's program of empirical study, it encourages us to search dramatic literature for further narrative inventions that can therapeutically improve our psychological flourishing.

For such a search to qualify as empirical—in both an Aristotelian and a modern scientific sense—it must be inclusive in two key ways. First, it must include all the branching forms that dramatic literature can take upon this earth. It cannot stop with Greek tragedy but must venture into the vast range of cultural traditions and physical technologies that now fill our viewing screens and media libraries. Second, it must embrace the cultural and biological variety of human minds. It must acknowledge that each individual psyche is unique, that there is no universal eudaimonia for all of us, that you and I can desire divergent things from our lives, and that a single work of dramatic literature can play differently for different audiences.

This inclusiveness can feel daunting. Its potential depth and complexity are unbounded, overrunning what any scholar could hope to grasp in a single lifetime. Yet this inclusiveness can also be exciting. It opens up endless vistas of dramatic literature and human experience to explore, and it offers the hope of an immense but precisely indexed anthology of film, television, theatre, and media that can help guide each of us to our own personal versions of eudaimonia.

So, if we want to put together that anthology, how do we get started? How do we forge ahead into the vast diversity of dramatic literature and human psychology?

How do we find the *Poetics*' next page?

The *Poetics*' Next Page

There are endless possible next pages for the *Poetics*. Pages for every inventive script and dramatic production in history. Pages for every one of life's emotional difficulties and opportunities. Pages for every different viewing mind and community. Pages for every form of mental health and flourishing desired by someone on our planet.

To help make the most of the vast opportunity before us, the remainder of this chapter will take its lead from a twenty-first-century analogue of Aristotle's ancient instrumentalism: the pragmatic research calculus of modern psychology. Modern psychology acknowledges that our lives, our minds, and our desires are diverse and divergent, yet it also accepts that certain therapeutic practices are more broadly useful than others. These therapies don't work equally, all the time, for everyone. But because they focus on bigger areas of public concern, or because they work across a wider slice of the general population, they can accomplish more global work.

A focus on this "global" work can seem marginalizing and tacitly normalizing. Doesn't it discount everyone who has an outlying mind or situation or want? Yes, it can—but it can also do the reverse. By efficiently addressing the most common and easily resolved concerns, it can free up the maximum amount of resources for attending to less common and more intractable ones. To use a cinema analogy, it can be like a movie theatre that starts its fiscal quarter by booking a blockbuster film, earning enough upfront revenue to subsidize more local fare over the remainder of its viewing season.

In keeping with this practical approach to diversity, let's seek out the dramatic storytelling technology that would be most beneficial to the greatest number of people in our world today. Let's ask: How would we extend Aristotle's method to get more emotional eudaimonia out of theater, film, and television? How would we take the *Poetics* and increase its *scope* and its *scale*?

First, to increase the scope of the *Poetics*, we would want to look for story devices that nurture optimism, because optimism is a source of psychological flourishing that goes beyond even *thaumasios*—which is to say, beyond even wonder. Wonder is a moment of belief, an instant of possibility. But optimism is ongoing belief, a lifetime of possibility.

And second, to increase the scale of the *Poetics*, we would want to look for these optimism-generating story devices in a corpus of dramatic literature that draws the greatest possible audiences in our here and now. Which is to say, we would want to look at the modern fairytale.

The modern fairytale is an unabashed purveyor of optimism; no matter how dire our straits or wicked our stepmothers, the modern fairytale assures us that things will end in happily-ever-after. And the modern fairytale is also the most dominant genre of twenty-first century cinema. Its ascendance began in nineteenth- and early twentieth-century America, where it was popularized by Horatio Alger novels and by newspaper strips like *Little Orphan Annie*. In the middle years of the twentieth century, its popularity was further expanded by musicals like *The Wizard of Oz* and pulp fictions like *Superman*. And in our own time, it has been exported beyond America by Disney's blockbuster fairytale movies, which now draw a mammoth international audience. In 2019, Disney's global box office exceeded $10 billion, making it the largest distributor of entertainment in the world.

So, do these global modern fairytales contain a narrative invention (or two) for generating mass eudaimonia? Do Disney movies offer a story blueprint for nurturing public well-being?

The answer to these questions will unfold throughout the following discussion. But here it is in summary: Yes and No.

Yes, the original modern fairytales did, once-upon-a-time, contain narrative inventions for nurturing a healthy optimism. But No, most modern movie fairytales no longer do. Instead, Disney and other American fairytale producers have replaced these inventions with storytelling structures that subtly foster anxiety, pessimism, and rage. This creates an opportunity for us to return modern movie fairytales to their roots, making them sources of emotional well-being once more.

The Invention of Fairytale Eudaimonia

The original fairytales are very, very old. We can't be certain of their exact age, because they were passed around by word of mouth and only jotted onto paper in the past few centuries or so. But we think that *Rumpelstiltskin* predates the *Poetics*—and that the basic story of *Beauty and the Beast* might date back as far as six thousand years (da Silva and Tehrani).[2]

Neither *Rumpelstiltskin* nor *Beauty and the Beast* contain fairies—and in fact, most fairytales don't. The name is a modern quirk, coined in 1697 by Madame d'Aulnoy in her folktale collection, *Les Contes des Fées* (*Tales of the Fairies*). But both *Rumpelstiltskin* and *Beauty and the Beast* do contain the one element that audiences now see as essential to any fairytale: a happily-ever-after. In *Rumpelstiltskin*, a miller's daughter outwits a malicious

[2] Da Silva and Tehrani's methods and conclusions have not been universally accepted by folklorists, but the general consensus is that *Beauty and the Beast* and many other folktales that form the basis for modern fairytales have pre-Christian origins.

imp—and ends up a queen with a roomful of gold. In *Beauty and the Beast*, a merchant's daughter is guided by true love to marry a beast—who transforms into a handsome prince with wealth beyond belief.

These fairytale endings have become widely popular with modern audiences because they are perceived as sources of emotional hope. But as it turns out, some fairytale endings encourage more hope than others. Much, much more. The secret to these more hopeful happily-ever-afters was discovered back in 1553 by the obscure Venetian anthologist, Francisco Giovanni Straparola. And the secret is narrative luck.

Long before Straparola, luck had served as a spring of hope in European storytelling. Back in the days of Greek tragedy, Sophocles and Euripides had engineered the notorious *deus ex machina*, a god who intervened in theater plots to divert catastrophe into a happy ending. This device was then adapted by the Greek and Roman architects of New Comedy into the "lucky twist," a narrative invention that exchanged the prudent deity of the tragic *deus ex machina* for a capricious divinity of comic fortune: in Menander's *Aspis* (c. 300 BCE), a goddess of chance transformed a funeral into a wedding; in Plautus' *Aulularia* (c. 200 BCE), a puckish spirit blessed the marriage of a miser's daughter with a pot of gold. These lucky twists had a different psychological effect from the *deus ex machina*; instead of generating awe and faith in the enduring plan of the heavens, they created the experience of an arbitrary miracle, inspiring the feeling that destiny and fate could be randomly broken, that joy could spring from no logical cause at all. And audiences delighted in the feeling. Lucky twists became a near ubiquitous feature of New Comedy—and then tumbled off the stage to inspire optimism in the world beyond. When Julius Caesar crossed the Rubicon in 49 BCE, attempting to twist the whole story of Rome into his own happy ending, he declared: *Alea iacta est*. This is a quote from a now-lost New Comedy by Menander. Roughly translated, it means: "Let's roll the dice." Like a comic character, Caesar was cheerfully trusting to luck.

But as popular as the lucky twist was in Caesar's day, it had largely been pruned out of literature by the time of Straparola, fifteen centuries later. The main source of the pruning was a push among philosophers and theologians for greater metaphysical rigorousness. In the ancient world, a few rogue thinkers (perhaps most notoriously, Epicurus) had allowed for there to be true arbitrariness in life. But most pagan philosophers found the idea of luck to be illogical—and most Christian theologians deemed it sacrilegious. In a universe designed by God, nothing could be random; even the most surprising events had to reflect an eternal design of Justice or Mercy or Providence. So it was that in the Christian Middle Ages, Fortune ceased to be the capricious goddess that the Romans had worshipped as "fickle Fortuna," instead becoming the regularly spinning Wheel depicted in countless medieval manuscripts and stained-glass cathedral windows.

This Christian preference for divine destiny over arbitrary luck became embedded in the narrative structure of European fairytales. The European fairytales that predate Straparola use a range of techniques to encourage a belief in destiny (including overt reference to almighty Providence), but the most common and enduring is to portray the recipient of the happily-ever-after as an individual with noble blood. Sometimes, as in *Sleeping Beauty*, the individual is openly known to be an outcast aristocrat, wrongfully deprived of her throne. But in most cases, the individual is a member of the "hidden" aristocracy. These hidden aristocrats have tumbled so far down Fortune's Wheel that their regal origins have been forgotten by everyone, including themselves. Yet even so, the blood of long-ago kings still flows through their veins. And in the fairytale, their lost ancestry is rediscovered. Their royal blood manifests itself in a noble act of wisdom or virtue—and the once-upon-a-time princess earns back her rightful crown.

Such is the formula for both *Rumpelstiltskin* and *Beauty and the Beast*. In *Rumpelstiltskin*, the miller's daughter reveals her secret nobility by wisely outsmarting a nasty imp. In *Beauty and the Beast*, the merchant's daughter reveals her secret nobility by generously embracing an ugly beast. And afterwards, both women then re-become the wealthy queens that their blood had always destined them to be. Without ever needing to mention Providence, fate, or destiny explicitly, the narrative structure of these fairytales eliminated luck as a source of happily-ever-afters, reserving royal weddings and golden bliss for the chosen. Which meant that if you happened to be one of the great many people whose ancestors were purely ordinary folk, fairytales could dispense no hope to you.

But then in 1553— the year that Straparola published his fairytale anthology *The Playful Nights*—Straparola decided to expand hope's allotment by slipping luck back into the story. And he sprinkled among the anthology's more traditional destiny-fairytales are a small number of fairytales with a revolutionary new storyline: a happily-ever-after that befalls a character who displays no wisdom, kindness, or any other noble virtue (Bottigheimer). The characters in these revolutionary fairytales lack royal blood, secret or otherwise.[3] They are ignoble folk who chance into prosperity.

Here are three examples:

1) In *Costantino's Cat*, a boy inherits a cat—and the cat turns out to be a sorcerous genius who helps the boy become a superrich heir to the throne.
   The boy does nothing to deserve this happy ending. He sulks ungratefully when he learns that his inheritance is a household pet, and after he discovers to his surprise that the cat is magic, he refuses to share his good fortune with his two brothers. The boy's luck may be gold, but his heart is certainly not.

2) In *Adamantina and the Doll*, a girl is dispatched with her family's last savings to purchase food. Instead, the girl squanders the money on a doll—and the doll turns out to be an enchanted minion who brings the girl a wealthy queenship.
   This happy ending is wildly random. The girl doesn't realize that the doll is magic when she buys it. Nor is the girl especially wise or virtuous. She's been sent to the market because her family is starving, so her whimsical purchase of a stuffed toy is deeply illogical—and leaves her older sister horrified.

3) In *Peter the Fool*, a fool catches a fish—and the fish turns out to be a magical wish-granter who helps the fool bumble his way into becoming a prince.
   This happy ending is the most arbitrary of all. The fool not only lacks any noble virtues, but he is actively awful. He torments his mother, is rude to everyone he meets, and uses his magic fish to wish a pregnancy on a ten-year-old girl.

[3] Scholars have debated whether this arc was strictly Straparola's invention. For the debate, see Ziolkowski; Vaz da Silva; Ben-Amos; Bottigheimer, "Fairy Godfather." While Zoilkowski, da Silva, and Ben-Amos raise important qualifiers, Bottingheimer convincingly establishes that Straparola is for practical purposes, the launching point of the modern fairytale. And as I'll suggest below, Straparola adds one crucial narrative element to this fairytale that Bottingheimer doesn't mention: the acquisition of permanent good luck.

The luck in these three fairytales is *so* arbitrary that it can seem like lazy plotting or some other species of authorial hackwork. But there are two strong indications that it's intentional.

The first indication is that *Costantino's Cat*, *Adamantina and the Doll*, and *Peter the Fool* all share an identical narrative formula: a foolish character who, through no merit of his or her own, chances into a fairytale ending.

The second indication is that this narrative formula has been shown by recent scientific research to be a potent source of the psychological benefit most associated with fairytales: optimism.

Straparola's Fairytale Formula as a Source of Optimism

Modern psychologists have discovered that a belief in luck can contribute to optimism (Darke and Freedman; Maltby et al.). And modern psychologists have also discovered that this contribution can be given a narrative boost.

The boost, as the research of Martin Seligman has revealed, comes in the form of two kinds of story (Seligman). The first kind of story increases optimism by establishing a storyworld where good luck is personal, pervasive, and permanent. The second kind of story decreases pessimism by doing the inverse: establishing a storyworld where *bad* luck is *less* personal, *less* pervasive, and *less* permanent. The first kind of story makes us feel like good luck is waiting ahead to smile on our efforts. The second kind makes us feel that the negative things in our life are simply passing spots of bad luck, not reasons to get down on ourselves or fret that a catastrophe is looming.

These two kinds of story can be combined into a single narrative formula that simultaneously increases optimism and decreases pessimism. In theory, this combination of more optimism and less pessimism might seem redundant. Why not just do one or the other? But in practice, the combination is psychologically beneficial. That's because optimism and pessimism operate independently in the human brain, making it possible (and not uncommon) for us to be at once optimistic and pessimistic. When we feel this way, good things produce hope, while bad things produce despair, leading to unhealthy mood swings. To minimize such swings, we therefore need to do more than just tell ourselves stories that just increase our optimism. We need to tell ourselves stories that reduce our pessimism too.

This is what Straparola's new fairytales do. They increase optimism by establishing a storyworld where good luck is personal, pervasive, and permanent. And they decrease pessimism by establishing a storyworld where bad luck is impersonal, local, and transitory. Just as Seligman's research predicts.

Here's how Straparola's fairytales do it.

To increase optimism, the fairytales enrich the New Comic device of the lucky twist with two additional narrative techniques:

- The first technique is to amplify the gains of luck. In New Comedies, the main characters gain wealth and happiness, but they don't start out as indigent or parentless—nor do they go on to become royalty. Such drastic transformations might have been possible in the fantastic worlds of earlier Greek Old Comedies, where homeless wanderers—like the main characters of Aristophanes' *Birds*—could transform themselves into ruling gods. But in the more grounded storyworlds of New Comedy, rags-to-riches ascents were narratively implausible. How could a rustic poorling gain a kingdom? How could a peasant with no royal pedigree acquire noble blood? Yet this is exactly what happens in Straparola's fairytales, where ordinary people become superrich queens and princes, achieving not just good luck but outrageous good fortune.
- The second technique is to make the good fortune into a permanent acquisition. In ancient New Comedies, the main characters benefit from moments of luck, but in Straparola's fairytales, the luck gained by the main characters is more than momentary. It's everlasting, embodied as a material object that, as Straparola goes to great lengths to emphasize, the characters possess for the rest of their lives. In *Peter the Fool*, the fool uses his lucky fish for abominable ends—including wishing a pregnancy on a ten-year-old girl—and yet the fish never deserts him. In *Adamantina and the Doll*, the lucky doll is stolen, tossed out on the street, loaded into a garbage wagon, and dumped out to fertilize a field—yet remains enduringly loyal to the foolish girl who purchased it. So, in the world of Straparola's fairytales, characters are more than momentarily fortunate. They acquire luck for good.

Taken together, these two techniques imbue the ancient device of the lucky twist with Seligman's three optimism-enhancers: personalization, pervasiveness, and permanence. They usher us into a storyworld where good luck is specific to one person whose whole life is transformed in perpetuity.

And at the same time as Straparola's fairytales are narratively constructed to increase optimism, they also make use of a clever story device for decreasing pessimism. The device is to interject short episodes of bad luck that don't occur to the lucky main character. In *Adamantina and the Doll*, there's the goodly king who has the misfortune to be handed the doll as a toiletry wipe—only to have it attach itself with great ferocity to his nether regions. In *Costantino's Cat*, there's the brave lord who has the misfortune to die when he rides off to meet his beloved wife.

These instances of bad luck are all narratively brief, occupying only a small portion of the story's telling. As a result, our experience of reading the fairytale is to focus at length on the personal good luck of the main character; to shift briefly into an instant of impersonal back luck that befalls someone else; and to then return to the ongoing good luck of the main character. Happy events feel personal and endure to the end of the story; unhappy events feel impersonal and quickly moved past.

This narrative elixir may have been invented by Straparola. Although its individual components can be found in earlier comedies and folktales, there's no known fairytale before *The Playful Nights* that uses Straparola's specific recipe: a permanent acquisition of good luck by an ignoble main character, interspersed with brief episodes of bad luck experienced by minor characters. Or the elixir may have been taken by Straparola from a now-lost tradition of oral folktales that was guided by the rough empiricism of experimental storytelling and audience feedback toward narrative structures for boosting hope and lightening despair. But whatever the historical origin of Straparola's fairytales might be, Seligman's research suggests that their ultimate origin extends into the mechanics of human cognition, springing from a psychological drive for emotional hope, shared broadly by different audience members across many generations, that led eventually to the discovery of the story formula: *life can be unlucky, but individual lives are lucky.*

This formula is irrational and philosophically incoherent. But it's empirically tested and psychologically beneficial. It increases optimism by inspiring us to see positive events as a sign of our enduring possession of good luck. And it decreases pessimism by encouraging us to brush off negative events as passing instances of bad luck.

By baffling reason, it nourishes our emotional well-being.

The Lost Fairytale Optimism of Our Present Day

Straparola's fairytales were very popular in their era. In 1699, the French fairytale author, Henriette-Julie de Murat, remarked in the *Avertissement* to her *Histoires sublimes et allégoriques* that *The Pleasant Nights* was republished no less than sixteen times. And in our own time, Straparola's formula has been more successful still. Its fairytale narrative of an impoverished unfortunate who lucks into a happily-ever-after has become a popular subgenre of American cinema that stretches from Charlie Chaplin's *The Gold Rush* (1925) to Danny Boyle's *Slumdog Millionaire* (2008).

Yet as influential as Straparola's formula has been, its effects have been dampened by a countervailing force in the fairytale tradition: an *a priori* moralism that diminishes, and even eliminates, the place of luck in human life. The dampening effects of this moralism began in the European and Islamic Middle Ages with the rise of monotheistic deities who eliminated the possibility of chance, leading influential Renaissance New Comedies like Ludovico Ariosto's *I Suppositi* (1509) to justify their apparently random plot swerves as instances of divine foresight and justice. Straparola was pushing against this moral mainstream when he inked his anthology, and it didn't take long for the mainstream to push back. In 1634, Giambattista Basile revised *Costantino's Cat* into a morality tale that turned the fortunate beggar into an ungrateful villain, concluding with the lament: "God protect us from a tramp who climbs in society!"[4] And in our own here and now, Straparola's fairytale formula has similarly been overwritten by a pair of *a priori* moral principles: poetic justice and innate virtue.

Poetic justice is the rationalist belief that stories are more psychologically beneficial when they celebrate the triumph of virtue and the downfall of vice. This belief was popularized in Renaissance and Enlightenment Europe by moralists like Philip Sidney, Thomas Rymer, and Samuel Johnson. And it was embraced in twentieth-century America by many influential fairytale producers, including all of Hollywood from 1930 to 1968, and by Marvel and DC comics from 1954 to 2001. In the case of Hollywood, the doctrine was institutionalized through The Motion Picture Production Code of 1930, which mandated: "the sympathy of the audience should never be thrown to the side of crime, wrongdoing, evil or sin." In the case of Marvel and DC, the doctrine was institutionalized through the Comics Code of 1954: "In every

[4] *Dio te guarda de ricco 'mpoveruto / e de pezzente quanno è resagliuto.*

instance good shall triumph over evil and the criminal [be] punished for his misdeeds."

Poetic justice seems rational in theory, but in practice, it has operated as a source of fairytales that nourish pessimism and other negative emotions. In the moral cosmos of poetic justice, bad things must (as made explicit by the Comics Code) be "punished," and so unfortunate happenings cannot be passed off as local bits of poor luck. They must instead be traced back to a pervasive and enduring cause: "evil." Unlike in Straparola's fairytales, where villainy is either non-existent or non-consequential, villainy therefore abounds in fairytales of poetic justice. Superman doesn't just rescue children who get accidentally caught on train tracks—he saves Metropolis from mad scientists, Nazis, and other supervillains. The prevalence of such evildoers in fairytales of poetic justice means that their narratives don't prompt us to quickly forget negative events and move on. Quite the opposite: they encourage us to view negative events as evidence of a cosmically persistent malevolence, steering our brains toward anxiety and fear.

The second *a priori* moral belief that has dampened Straparola's formula in modern-day American is the belief that goodness is innate. This belief exists in various degrees and doctrines, from a casual acceptance of American exceptionalism to the rigorous dogmas of Ayn Rand's Objectivism. And it has exerted a monumental influence on modern American fairytales. It inspired Harold Gray to turn his comic strip, *Little Orphan Annie*, into a decades-long screed against the evils of communism. And more recently, it has informed the narratives of America's most influential fairytale teller: the Walt Disney Company.

Walt Disney was himself a strong believer in the innate virtue of select individuals. He was exposed to this belief through his upbringing as a Christian Congregationalist, and he expressed it with increasing explicitness as he aged. There is the Ayn Rand quote inscribed in stone at Walt Disney World's Epcot Center: "Throughout the centuries there were men who took first steps down new roads armed with nothing but their own vision." And there is the "Statement of Principles" of the Motion Picture Alliance for the Preservation of American Ideals (signed by both Disney and Rand): "We believe in, and like, the American way of life . . . the right to succeed or fail as free men, according to the measure of our ability and our strength."

Walt Disney's personal philosophy had a deep influence on Disney's fairytale formula, an influence that continues to this day. And so it is that Disney's movie fairytales are typically parables about individuals with an innate "ability" and "strength" who suffer persecution from mendacious mediocrities. This is the plot of *Snow White*. This is the plot of *Pinocchio*. This is the plot of *Ratatouille*. This is the plot of *Frozen*. A hero who possesses an exceptional skill is tyrannized by a jealous creep who doesn't.

In these Disney fairytales, negative events are produced primarily by unexceptional people who enviously inflict misery on the chosen few. So, to immerse ourselves in these fairytales is to inhabit storyworlds that encourage our brains to feel that there are two likely explanations for the bad things that happen in our lives. One, there are people out there who are maliciously trying to harm us. Two, we are ourselves not one of the chosen, but are doomed to suffer unhappiness because of our innate unworth. The first explanation encourages paranoia and rage. The second explanation induces pessimism and despair.

Neither is particularly good for our mental well-being.

A Happier Fairytale Future

Like Aristotle's *Poetics*, Straparola's fairytale formula has been underused.

Because Aristotle and Straparola encourage us to treat ethics as empirical and emotional, their writings have been overlooked or discounted by theorists and fairytale producers who prefer to ground ethics in reason or other *a priori* sources. But in our scientific day and age, we have come to see the benefits that can come from taking an empirical approach to mental health and well-being. And if we wanted to make more use of Aristotle and Straparola, we could easily do so. As an initial step, we would simply need to enrich our modern movie fairytales with the two main ingredients of Straparola's formula that *a priori* moralities have driven out:

- The first ingredient is storyworlds where permanent good fortune can be gained through a random event, like a lucky doll purchase or a fool's fishing trip. In such storyworlds, happily-ever-after isn't innate in a few special individuals with royal abilities. It's something that we can all come to possess, no matter how ignoble our origins might be.
- The second ingredient is storyworlds where the worst things in life are the result not of evil villains or elaborate conspiracies, but of passing bad luck. In such storyworlds, negative events aren't the sign of a looming

> menace that must be defeated to ward off catastrophe. They are simply the result of blind, localized, and fleeting misfortune.

Both these ingredients are readily compatible with the scientific worldview that underpins twenty-first-century psychology: modern Darwinism. In modern Darwinism, all the good things in our lives are the result of random genetic mutations, chance environments, and other bits of acquired fortune. In modern Darwinism, there is no evil, just painful accident.

And both these ingredients are also readily compatible with the tastes of the same global modern audiences who consume Disney movies. As one recent example, there's Pixar's *Up*.

Up was produced in 2009, three years after Disney purchased Pixar, but before the two studios began merging their storytelling departments in the early 2010s. And *Up*, unlike *Cinderella*, *Snow White*, *The Lion King*, *Frozen*, and other classic Disney fairytales, incorporates Straparola's two main ingredients into its core plot.

The permanent piece of good luck in *Up* is Ellie. Ellie barges into the life of nine-year-old Carl through happenstance and attaches herself to him through no great merit of his own. As she says: "You know, you don't talk very much. I like you!" And like the magical objects of Straparola's fairytales, Ellie remains with Carl always, even after her death. During Carl's grimmest moment of despair, he finds an old note from her, thanking him for the adventure of her life—and encouraging him to take another one. Buoyed by her, he does.

And in *Up*, the most enduring source of negative events is simply bad luck. Although the film contains a villain, he's haplessly ineffective. The main cause of heartache is revealed instead in the film's opening montage, where Ellie suffers an unfortunate miscarriage and then an equally unfortunate death. Tragedy in this storyworld results not from a persistent evil, but from arbitrary circumstance.

Up was a major commercial success, grossing over $700 million worldwide. And *Up* does more than demonstrate that Straparola's formula can be successful today; it also enriches that formula with a narrative innovation of its own. Where Straparola's fairytales imagines happily-ever-after as royal wealth and power, *Up* opts for a more democratic form of enduring good fortune: the lifelong uplift of love.

This is a material good that can be enjoyed equally, by all of us. This is a fairytale gift that really can be everywhere.

Cinematic Eudaimonia After *Up*

Up is a beloved film. But it's not beloved by everyone. And *Up* is a film that encourages optimism. But it hasn't ushered us all into permanent well-being. So, what's next? Where do we go after *Up*?

From the vantage of our instrumental-psychological approach to the *Poetics*, there's no right answer to this question. But to open up some therapeutic paths ahead, let's wrap this chapter by sketching three next steps that continue the pragmatic method that authorized our exploration of movie fairytales.

The first step is toward works of dramatic literature that adapt Straparola's fairytale formula for audiences who don't gravitate (biologically or culturally) to *Up*. Many works of film and television could be included in this category, but to put some meaningful distance between ourselves and *Up*, let's take our lead from someone whose tastes inclined in the opposite direction of big-budget studio animation: French film critic, André Bazin.[5] In the 1940s and 1950s, Bazin's dismay at the unhealthy delusions peddled by Hollywood fantabulism led him to follow the path that Miguel de Cervantes had taken in *Don Quixote* three centuries before: lampooning the romantic fallacies of popular schlock, he encouraged a movement toward "realism." And yet as committed as Bazin was to cinematic realism, he still made room in his viewing repertoire for fairytales of chance. In 1947, at the same time that he was commending Roberto Rossellini's neo-realist films, Bazin praised a fairytale French comedy, *Antoine and Antoinette*, that revolved around a couple whose dreams come true after winning a lottery. The identical plot-device of a lottery win had been used in Hollywood fantasies that Bazin had roundly condemned, but to Bazin, the fairytale of *Antoine and Antoinette* was entirely realistic. Why? Well, because the lottery win was pure luck. It wasn't the result of fate or divine providence or some other imaginary power. It was just the kind of arbitrary accident that somehow happens in life. As Bazin puts it: "Antoine and Antoinette got lucky—unlike the heroes of Hollywood films like Preston Surges' *Christmas in July*, who are fated to be fortunate with a kind of theological grace"[6] (Bazin 14).

[5] For deft elaboration of Bazin's concerns about Hollywood movies, see Dudley Andrew's contribution to this volume: "Cinema and Creative Community."

[6] "Antoine et Antoinette ont eu de la chance, le héros de Preston Sturges: Sa chance. Une chance théologique, à la fois gratuite et méritée, comme la grâce, selon Bossuet."

The second step beyond *Up* would be to look for narrative sources of optimism that don't depend on luck. There are many human cultures and many individual brains that reject luck—or don't find it especially uplifting. And there are also many cultures and many individuals who already embrace luck, but who aren't awash in optimism. As a result, we would want to delve past *Up* and *Antoine and Antoinette* into a wider array of storytelling traditions, searching for other narrative mechanisms that can encourage us to believe that bad events are passing, local, and impersonal—and that good events are permanent, pervasive, and personal.

And finally, a third step beyond *Up* would be to search for sources of eudaimonia besides optimism. Optimism, after all, isn't the only possible building block of a good life.[7] There are many psychological states that artists and psychologists have identified as ingredients of human flourishing: wonder, joy, gratitude, autonomy, meaning, love, self-acceptance, growth, the list goes on.

How could film and television develop narrative technologies for bringing more of those ingredients into our lives?

What would the future chapters of the *Poetics* be?

Works Cited

Bazin, André. "Le film en filigrane: L'art et la manière." *L'Ecran français*, 9 December 1947, p. 14.

Ben-Amos, Dan. "Straparola: The Revolution That Was Not." *The Journal of American Folklore*, vol. 123, 2010, pp. 426–446.

Bottigheimer, Ruth B. "Fairy Godfather, Fairy-Tale History, and Fairy-Tale Scholarship: A Response to Dan Ben-Amos, Jan M. Ziolkowski, and Francisco Vaz da Silva." *The Journal of American Folklore*, vol. 123, 2010, pp. 447–496.

Bottigheimer, Ruth. *Fairy Godfather: Straparola, Venice, and the Fairy Tale Tradition*. University of Pennsylvania Press, 2002.

da Silva, Sara Graça, and Jamshid J. "Comparative Phylogenetic Analyses Uncover the Ancient Roots of Indo-European Folktales." *R. Soc. Open Sci*, vol. 3, article 150645.

Darke, P. R., and J. L. Freedman. "The Belief in Good Luck Scale." *Journal of Research in Personality*, vol. 31, 1997, pp. 486–511.

Maltby, John, et al. "Beliefs Around Luck." *Personality and Individual Differences*, vol. 45, 2008, pp. 655–660.

[7] For an elegant articulation of the limits of equating eudaimonia with optimism, see Dana Polan's contribution to this volume: "Human Relationship as Human Value in Studio Era Hollywood."

Seligman, Martin. *Learned Optimism*. Vintage, 2006.
Vaz da Silva, Francisco. "The Invention of Fairy Tales." *The Journal of American Folklore*, vol. 123, 2010, pp. 398–425.
Ziolkowski, Jan M. "Straparola and the Fairy Tale: Between Literary and Oral Traditions." *The Journal of American Folklore*, vol. 123, 2010, pp. 377–397.

2
Media-ting Happiness

Lucy Fischer

The question of whether or not cinema and media can contribute to human flourishing is an open and complex one. If we consider fiction/narrative cinema (which will be the subject of this chapter) two usual functions are assigned to it (although there are many others): entertainment (generally tied to commercial cinema) and art (generally linked to auteurist or avant-garde film). Of course, ideally, the two purposes will overlap. In arguing for cinema's value to encourage human wellness, however, a paradigm shift is required—imagining the medium (to put it most crassly) as part of the "health care system." Purists (of either camp) will reject this notion.

Certainly, one of the reasons that this topic is now being considered is that the arts and humanities are in crisis in an era in which STEM education and vocation are in ascendancy; and, if the former fields are to survive, a thought revolution is required of them. Whereas in the past the value of cultural transmission was largely assumed, it is now contested, and the disciplines must prove their societal "worth" and "practicality" to endure.

If one chooses to make the case for film's ability to augment human flourishing, the question arises as to how it might do so. In general, discussions of this type focus on film reception—the effect of a movie on its audience. But immediately another query surfaces: What kind of movie will promote this if any, in fact, can?

Here, of course, one is dealing with content. Does one believe that the best texts for augmenting human flourishing will be those that are predominantly joyful, heartening, and inspiring (referencing the most basic and direct conception of media communication—that what one sees on screen is precisely the message that a spectator receives)? If so, this would lead us to privilege narratives with elevated, uplifting stories, or happy endings as well as *dramatis personae* who exude positive emotions and qualities. However, when it comes to art, there is the embarrassing fact that most creators (in film and other media) are not especially cheerful or

Lucy Fischer, *Media-ting Happiness* In: *Cinema, Media, and Human Flourishing.* Edited by: Timothy Corrigan, Oxford University Press. © Oxford University Press 2023. DOI: 10.1093/oso/9780197624180.003.0003 well-adjusted people, and many of their works embrace problems more than solutions, disruption rather than complacency. Similarly, if one turns to commercial cinema, the prevalent conception of drama is one organized by conflict and replete with obstacles—elements seemingly at odds with a hopeful storyline and denouement. Furthermore, there is the point made by Dudley Andrew in Chapter 4 that some of the greatest movies are produced in the most horrific of times.

Darkness Before the Dawn

But there are, perhaps, other more complex means of promoting well-being through cinema that involve the presentation of sometimes disturbing narratives and complicated characters who are not necessarily auspicious "role models" for the well-adjusted person. Here, one thinks of the comic genre which is often considered one whose viewing makes people "feel better." Attesting to this is the host of popular books or articles on the benefits of laughter for allegedly ameliorating the effects of sickness or promoting a sense of psychological welfare.

As for the former, one of the best-known texts is Norman Cousins' book *The Anatomy of an Illness as Perceived by the Patient* (1981) in which he describes his experience of watching comic films to relieve pain from a degenerative disease. More recently, an article states that laughter relaxes the whole body, boosts the immune system, decreases stress hormones, and increases immune cells and infection-fighting antibodies, triggers the release of endorphins, and protects the heart through increased blood flow. As for broader mental health benefits, the same piece also claims that laughter adds joy and zest to life, eases anxiety and tension, relieves stress, improves mood, and strengthens resilience. Finally, it asserts that laughter provides social benefits as well because it strengthens relationships, attracts others to us, enhances teamwork, helps defuse conflict, and promotes group bonding. Summing up, the author's conclusion is that laughter helps people stay mentally healthy by keeping "a positive, optimistic outlook through difficult situations, disappointments, and loss." It assists one in being more spontaneous, letting go of defensiveness, releasing inhibitions, and expressing one's true feelings (Robinson et al.). Some researchers have gone even further, claiming that humor can help manage the agitation of patients with dementia ("The Healing Power").

The interesting thing about comedy is that what causes us to laugh and feel better is *not* necessarily a sanguine or propitious event. Rather, comedy is filled with characters who are unhappy (think of those played by W. C. Fields or Buster Keaton). The form is also full of pratfalls and accidents (think Charlie Chaplin), nasty utterances (think Groucho Marx), gallows humor (think *Dr. Strangelove*, [Stanley Kubrick, 1964]), and politically incorrect stereotypes (think Fatty Arbuckle, Stepin Fetchit or Sasha Baron Cohen). Hence, ironically, it is perhaps the *dark underside of humor* that has the greatest liberatory effect on our consciousness, not its carefree surface. So here we cannot think in terms of naïvely positive content or character type. In fact, the ironic title of Todd Solandz's black comedy *Happiness* (1998), about a pedophile, obscene phone caller, and a murderer is much to the point.

Canonical, here, is Freud's *Jokes and Their Relation to the Unconscious* (1905), which argues that humor helps us release pent up sexual and hostile energies in a safe fashion—leading to a healthier frame of mind. Similarly, Henri Bergson in *Laughter* (1900) sees the act as helping us correct the inhuman mechanical aspects of human conduct, making us more joyful and adaptable social beings. So, if comedy augments our flourishing it does not do so through a direct transmission of constructive content, but through a psychic process by which we reject the behavior of those failed but funny individuals we watch on screen.

But there are some kinds of films in which realistic, multi-faceted characters (neither all bad nor good, neither tragedians nor clowns) must fight to achieve happiness, and the viewer must endure their travails to enjoy their eventual success. In truth, this group would seem to constitute the majority of films potentially able to impact a viewer's sense of well-being, and they do so through difficult life lessons taught.

In this group are feminist films that can educate women about the sometimes-pernicious workings of gender ideology. While such texts may involve a healthy dose of critique ("the hermeneutics of suspicion," as Paul Ricoeur puts it), they are not "negative" texts. Rather, by demonstrating the way life can be constrained by societal assumptions they can lead a viewer to break free of those very constrictions and enjoy her existence even more. If, as J. O. Pawleski observes, what is positive in life entails being able to do what one prefers, women must first confront the centuries when their predilections were suppressed, and they were told what they could *not* do (be lawyers, doctors, professors, scientists, authors, politicians, etc.). Hence, watching such films can potentially free women to overcome their culture's gender limitations and open their lives to their true desires. As Patricia White notes in Chapter 7, often the female "coming of age" film is especially important as a vehicle for dramatizing a young woman's rebellion against traditional gender norms. Here one thinks of early feminist works like Gillian Armstrong's *My Brilliant Career* (1979) which concerns a rural Australian woman's fight to become a writer in the late-nineteenth century. Films can also catalog the battles that women must face in terms of race, as in the recent *Hidden Figures* (Theodore Melfi, 2016) about the difficulties faced by three African American women attempting to work at NASA.

One of the best examples of a film that encourages human flourishing through struggle is *The Eternal Sunshine of the Spotless Mind* directed by Michel Gondry in 2004. Its highly enigmatic narrative tells the story of a rather depressed, aimless, and affectless young man, Joel (Jim Carrey) who meets an artsy and bohemian young woman, Clementine (Kate Winslet), with whom he falls in love. She is impulsive and adventurous and seems to prod him out of his rut. Their relationship, however, soon sours and, as it deteriorates, Joel learns that (through a business named Lacuna), Clementine has had her recollections of him erased—ostensibly because they were too upsetting. Devastated by Clementine's treachery, Joel visits Lacuna and requests the same treatment for his memories of her. For Joel to undergo the erasure procedure, attendants attach a metal helmet to his head while he sleeps and they reprogram his thoughts (see Figure 2.1). As

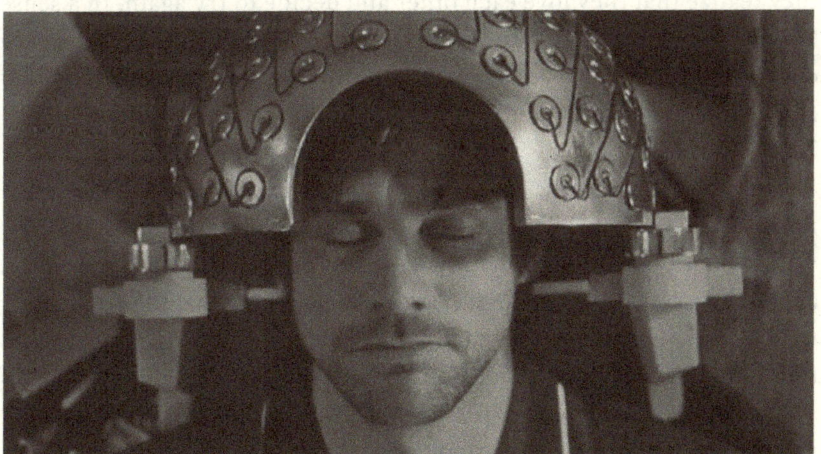

Figure 2.1 Joel undergoes memory erasure in *Eternal Sunshine of the Spotless Mind* (2004).

they do so, we see alternating scenes of technicians performing their tasks and images from Joel's mind. Clearly, the procedure to which Joel submits is meant to decrease his pain and increase his sense of contentment.

The visions that Joel experiences (all presented in a highly experimental and non-realistic fashion) relate to both positive and negative recollections of his relationship with Clementine (the latter including an argument they had over whether or not she would be a good mother), as well as traumatic or embarrassing remembrances of his childhood (when other kids bullied him, when his mother caught him masturbating, when he felt sexually desirous of his female adult neighbor).

His thoughts of Clementine are successfully wiped out (as were hers of him) and the next time the two meet (which the scrambled narrative had convinced us was the first) they think that they are strangers, and a romance begins again. However, it is thwarted when Joel receives an anonymous audiotape and plays it in the car while driving with Clementine. It is a recording of all the terrible things he said about her in the Lacuna office to justify having the procedure done. Listening to it, Clementine is puzzled, shocked, and distressed, leading her to jump out of the car. Upon returning home, however, she finds an anonymous audiotape of her own in the mail and plays it—hearing all the horrible things she told Lacuna about Joel. Despite these dismaying events, the couple reunites and confronts the implications of their insulting recordings but, despite the known limitations of their relationship, they realize that they love each other and decide to try again. In a sense (to draw upon a concept discussed by Tim Corrigan in Chapter 8), the couple has learned to "adapt" to one another as well as to the fact that (as Osgood says at the end *of Some Like it Hot* [Billy Wilder, 1959]) "nobody's perfect."

The title of the film is taken from a quote by Alexander Pope which reads: "How happy is the blameless vestal's lot! / The world forgetting, by the world forgot / Eternal sunshine of the spotless mind! / Each pray'r accepted, and each wish resign'd." To some degree Pope is saying that the only person with a purely happy mind is one who is virginal of all worldly experiences (both good and bad)—not a situation to be envied.

Evidently, medical research is already underway (successfully realized in mice) to find a drug that can erase traumatic memories, for instance, in soldiers that suffer from post-traumatic stress disorder (PTSD). As Dr. Sheena Josselyn states:

> Our findings suggest that one day it could be possible to treat people with PTSD by erasing these traumatic memories. In these people, the memories are intrusive and disrupt their everyday lives. Our goal would be to find a pharmalogical way to target and inactivate just these neurons, sort of like a heat seeking missile-like drug. (Quoted in Knapton)

Whether this will be a salutary development or not is up for debate.

While *Eternal Sunshine of the Spotless Mind* portrays a romance so troubled that the lovers wish to eliminate memories of it from their minds, it also demonstrates the risks of so doing. It argues for the fact that (1) painful memories can promote psychological growth, (2) there is no perfect relationship, and (3) sometimes true love only comes to those who have first faced all their reservations about their partner—even to the point of hate. Here, I also recall a much earlier film with a similar message, F. W. Murnaui's *Sunrise* (1927). It portrays a husband who almost kills his wife (to be with his lover) but stops before doing so. At that moment, he learns that he deeply loves his spouse and will never leave her (see Figure 2.2). While one does not want to recommend attempted murder as a means toward couple-building, the film's melodramatic form teaches us a lesson that we can apply more soberly to real life.

Strangely, even the distressing films can be seen to have value in promoting human well-being. Here the surface content must be ignored in favor of a more subterranean level of the text. For example, although Roman Polanski's *Rosemary's Baby* (1968) is a supremely perverse horror film and would seem to have few elements of positivity, in fact it can be read as helping women by surfacing their secret fears about pregnancy (that the fetus is a parasite, that they are bizarrely "doubled," that their child will be a monster, etc.) (Fischer). Thus, viewing it can give women "permission" to confront and vent the seamy and suppressed side of parturition rather than being forced to spout the Hallmark Card/Pollyanna version of it. If they do, they have a better chance of achieving mental health. Here, again, while the apparent content of the film would rule it out from the perspective of encouraging happiness, its latent message may help do just that.

Clearly, some in the psychiatric community feel that viewing certain films (often with troubling plots or protagonists) can help people deal with their problems. There is a branch of the discipline that uses visual media as part

Figure 2.2 The Man and the Wife are reunited in *Sunrise* (1927).

of psychiatric treatment. It is known as "cinema therapy" and has an entry in J. C. Segen's medical dictionary where it is defined as:

> A form of therapy or self-help that uses movies . . . as therapeutic tools . . . Cinema therapy allows one to use the effect of imagery, plot, music, etc. in films on the psyche for insight, inspiration, emotional release or relief and natural change.

As Denise Mann notes, "An increasing number of therapists prescribe movies to help their patients explore their psyches." There are also some related books, including *The Cinematic Mirror for Psychology and Life Coaching*, edited by Mary Banks Gregerson. As Gregerson remarks, "In cinematherapy . . . healing and *not simple pleasure* is the goal writ large"—a statement that acknowledges that not all films viewed for this purpose will be joyful experiences (2, emphasis added). Furthermore, she notes,

"The reverberations of the staged scenes vibrate into the life of an audience member to create connection, spill over, and paint an enlivening, moving 'ever after' larger than the still portrait moment when crisis becomes health" (4). Even the recent mindfulness movement has taken advantage of film, as is made clear by a *Huffington Post* piece entitled "Mindfulness in Everyday Life: Sitting in a Darkened Theater—Movies and the Mind."

There is also the current use of virtual reality imagery for the treatment of trauma. A 2017 article in the *New York Times* speaks of a car crash victim who was subsequently unable to drive or to cross streets near where the accident occurred. Her psychologist used "exposure therapy" but did not return her to the actual scene of her distress. Rather, he conjured it through a virtual reality product called Daydream View (Metz). Similarly, Robert McLay has written *At War with PTSD: Battling Post Traumatic Stress Disorder with Virtual Reality*, in which he discusses how he uses computer simulations to have returning soldiers face the specter of war.

Was Tolstoy Right?

Tolstoy famously wrote in *Anna Karenina* that all happy families are alike while each unhappy one is different—a maxim that leads us to believe that contented people are boringly similar. But we wonder whether this is entirely true. On one level it appears that, while we may be pleased to hear of people's satisfaction in our daily lives, this is not necessarily what we look for onscreen. Clearly, the producers of cinema have concluded this—given the nature of most art, experimental, and mainstream movies.

Occasionally, there is a film that attempts to portray contentment in an engaging way, and more rarely, one that succeeds. An example of the latter is Mike Leigh's *Happy-Go-Lucky* (2008)—whose title says it all. It concerns a very upbeat thirty-year-old working-class heroine Poppy (Sally Hawkins) and her life as a London primary school teacher. We learn that she has had many travel adventures, voyaging to Java, Malaysia, Thailand, and Australia. She is unrelentingly positive: when her bike is stolen, she barely reacts (joking that she never had a chance to say goodbye to it); when a bookstore proprietor is unfriendly to her, she cheerfully tells him what a gorgeous day it is and wryly encourages him to "stay happy." While there, she notices a book entitled *The Road to Reality* and mumbles to herself, "Didn't want to go there." She goes disco dancing with her flatmate Zoe (Alex Zegerman), takes Flamenco lessons with a fellow teacher, and exercises by jumping on a trampoline (a metaphor, perhaps, for her being an "up" rather than a "down" person). Furthermore, she seems always to be laughing, jesting, or smiling. In scenes of her classroom, she is revealed to be a creative instructor—having her students make bird masks (as they learn about flight migration), encouraging them to wear them, flap their "wings," and make avian sounds. When her younger, more traditional, pregnant sister Helen (Caroline Martin) asks her skeptically whether she is content with having no marital prospects at her age, she responds that she values her freedom.

The main conflict in the narrative arises when she decides to take driving lessons and meets her instructor Scott (Eddie Marsan) who is her complete opposite (see Figure 2.3). He is gruff, pessimistic, authoritarian, and rule-bound—chastising her constantly for not taking her lessons seriously and failing to be "adult." When he complains about her wearing high-heeled boots instead of flats while driving, she quips, "You should see those babies on the dance floor." When he says that "the road to hell is paved with good intensions," she retorts that, "it sounds like fun." He is also racist, telling her to lock her car door the moment he sees two black men on bikes. His world view is entirely negative, advising her to "expect the worst" while driving. On one occasion when she jokes with him, he predicts that she will "die laughing." Given conventional narrative form, we begin to suspect that the film may morph into an off-beat romantic comedy—with two people (who start out hating each other) becoming a couple. Encouraging this view is the

Figure 2.3 Poppy with her gruff driving teacher Scott in *Happy-Go-Lucky* (2008).

fact that, on one occasion, Poppy finds Scott standing on her street (and possibly stalking her) when no appointment is scheduled.

Poppy begins dating a social worker employed by her school. One day, Scott shows up for a lesson and sees her with her beau, and during the session which follows he erupts in anger (seemingly for no reason)—physically abusing her. When she prods him to talk, it becomes clear that he has fallen for her and blames her for allegedly leading him on. She takes his car keys and refuses to let him drive until he calms down (reversing their roles). When he asks about their next lesson, she makes clear that she no longer wants him as an instructor—telling him compassionately to "take care." Zoe thinks that Poppy should call the police (but she declines to do so). She also warns Poppy that she is too nice and cannot make everyone content because people create their own happiness. Poppy is not so sure that everyone has an equal chance to do so.

What is notable about the film is that Poppy is an eccentric, one-of-a-kind individual—and her happiness has its own particularity—giving lie to Tolstoy's pronouncement. While her sunny attitude might, at some points, annoy people—she is certainly not saccharine or Pollyanna—and we see the depth of her feeling in dealing with a school bully (whom she suspects has been maltreated) and Scott's breakdown. At those moments she is appropriately serious and thoughtful. While the film nods at conventionality by making sure to depict Poppy with a promising boyfriend, it rejects the standard rom-com "battle of the sexes."

Pursuits of Happiness

While the films we have discussed do not overtly set out to explore issues of well-being, there are some that do. In these plot lines, protagonists do not necessarily begin miserable or disturbed, needing to wrestle with their demons to achieve stability (as in *Eternal Sunshine* and so many other films). Neither do they begin entirely satisfied (as in *Happy-Go-Lucky*). Rather, they are simply curious to learn the secret to a good life. But several questions arise about these dramas. First, what do they imagine as answers to that question? Second, are those answers satisfactory?

One of the most literal works in this category (given its title) is the dramedy *Hector and the Search for Happiness*, directed by Peter Chelsom in 2014 and based on a François Lelord novel. Its hero (the namesake of the movie, played by Simon Pegg) is an awkwardly comical but successful London psychiatrist with a beautiful live-in girlfriend Clara (Rosamund Pike); seemingly, he faces no major challenges in his life. Rather, he is simply a bit bored with his well-ordered existence (we are told, for instance, that he "hadn't changed in years"), and his narcissistic bourgeois patients who face no serious dilemmas. One, for instance, complains of having to cut down employing her nanny from seven days a week to five. Another, who is a fortune teller, tells him that he will soon take a journey and reminds him of a lost love named Agnes (whom she inexplicably knows about).

Following this, Hector tells Clara that he needs to get away alone to research what makes people gratified, ostensibly to help his patients (but, clearly, also himself). Seemingly, he has no planned itinerary but simply flies from place to place around the world—all the while keeping a journal in which he writes down the maxims that he learns from his various encounters along the way. They are printed on-screen as though offering advice to the audience as well. In Hector's quest, we are reminded of a point that Dana Polan makes in Chapter 6—that only socially and economically privileged people have the luxury to contemplate, no less pursue, their sense of "human flourishing."

His first flight is to China and on the airplane, he meets a wealthy businessman who takes him under his wing (see Figure 2.4). He tells Hector that money can, in fact, buy happiness and, upon arrival, treats him to an

Figure 2.4 Hector touring China in *Hector and the Search for Happiness* (2014).

enjoyable evening on the town and introduces him to a beautiful young woman with whom he spends the night (although he falls asleep before they have sex). He writes in his journal that happiness can mean "the freedom to love more than one woman at the same time"—but soon learns that his date is a prostitute who has been paid to entertain him by his newfound friend. Clearly, that lesson goes down the drain as he learns another: "Sometimes happiness is not knowing the whole story." He next visits a monk in the mountains of China and the man tells him that he is happy precisely because he has been through so much (including prison). As he says, "avoiding unhappiness is not the road to happiness."

Hector then goes to Africa to visit an old doctor friend. On the plane, he asks a woman what makes her happy and she responds, "family and children." After partying with some villagers in a rural locale, he leaves by taxi but is kidnapped by some outlaws who imprison him. He thinks to himself, "Fear is an impediment to happiness," but is terrified nonetheless. While captured, he asks the gang leader what constitutes contentment for him, and the outlaw replies: "If you want it, you take it." The thugs eventually release Hector in the middle of nowhere and, running down the road, he thinks to himself, "Happiness is feeling completely alive."

The last stop on his trip is Los Angeles, where he has arranged to meet his old flame Agnes (Toni Collette); she is now happily married with two children and another one on the way. She is upset with Hector for conceiving her a fantasy woman over the years, always wondering "what might have been" between them. Cautioned about this, Hector thinks to himself, "Nostalgia is not what it used to be." Agnes has arranged for him to meet a famous professor (Christopher Plummer) whose field of study is human flourishing; the man inverts the usual phrasing by saying that happiness is the pursuit, not the goal. In his lab, he attaches electrodes to Hector's head and studies images of his brain as he thinks of things that make him alternately sad, scared, or happy. We see images of what Hector imagines—including the sight of Clara marrying someone else—which sends him into a panic. Conveniently, Clara telephones him at this precise moment and he confesses to her that he has achieved wisdom: happiness is being with her and unhappiness losing her. While still in the lab, Hector thinks of all the places he has traveled, and the viewer sees a montage of retrospective imagery. Considering the life lessons people have offered him, he thinks to himself, "It's all of them." He returns to London and weds Clara, having "learned to love like never before."

Periodically, throughout the narrative, Hector recalls himself as a young boy and the film seems to imply that happiness resides in recouping one's childhood. Furthermore, there is a focus on having children in the storyline. We are told that Clara does not want to be a mother (which is portrayed as a drawback) and later Hector accuses her of "smothering" him (adding that "smother" is the word "mother" with an additional "s"). Furthermore, the African woman he meets on the airplane tells him that the good life involves having a family, and his contented former girlfriend will soon be the mother of three.

All in all, the film offers a bundle of clichés. We know from the beginning that Hector will find happiness in what he already has but does not yet value—his relationship with Clara. The only chestnut that the narrative does not entirely deliver is the sight of the two with a baby—but we suspect that children will soon follow their union. The drama also hints (through flashbacks) that satisfaction involves recapturing one's youth, another hackneyed notion—this, despite the fact that many people's early years are anything but happy. In one of the last shots of the film, in fact, we see a fantasy of Hector as an adult holding his childhood dog in the same position that we have earlier seen him portrayed as a boy. In keeping with traditional morality, Hector never sleeps with the Chinese woman he meets and momentarily thinks he loves. She turns out to be a prostitute—so romancing her in addition to Clara is off the table in terms of providing a predictable happy ending. While Hector is told by the monk that avoiding unhappiness is not the route to human flourishing, he is ecstatic when freed by the kidnappers and able to return to his comfortable life. In thinking that *all* the guidance he has been given is equally valid (despite its many contradictions), the film cops out again, refusing to hierarchize any advice as superior. In the end, Hector is a bourgeois gentleman once more—although married and marginally more at peace with his profession. When the narrator informs us that "everything" in his life is now "up for change," we remain unconvinced.

Furthermore, there is an additional problem with the film. It portrays the universe (especially the second and third worlds) as a place that white privileged individuals can use to solve their problems—ones that pale in comparison to those of the people that they meet. The Chinese prostitute, for example, who is ostensibly "studying tourism," has chosen this profession and endured her abusive primp only because she cannot survive any other way. Similarly, during his visit to a remote African clinic, he dances with the poverty-stricken natives and his *joie de vivre* is energized. Beyond this,

Africa is portrayed as a nightmare, plagued by horrific air travel and rampant criminals.

Conclusion

In exploring how fiction dramatic cinema may potentially encourage human flourishing, we have investigated various kinds of films. In discussing comedies, we have found works that often produce laughter and well-being by portraying characters who are not necessarily happy themselves nor positive role models. In discussing the horror film, we have seen how a grim onscreen experience may advance well-being by allowing (at least momentarily) a spectator to confront her worst fears. In these cases, such readings are encouraged by notions that narratives can productively release pent-up worries or correct negative human tendencies.

We have also examined a more common type of film in which characters start out troubled but achieve some level of contentment along the way (as in *Eternal Sunshine of the Spotless Mind*). Furthermore, we have discussed the uncommon instance of a film that announces its intent to explore the good life: *Hector and the Search for Happiness*. Finally, we have considered a movie that presents a fully satisfied individual who changes not at all (Poppy in *Happy-Go-Lucky*). The character has no need to discover happiness because she is already thriving when the story begins.

While, one could argue, that all these diverse plot types have the possibility of encouraging well-being on the part of the viewer, it is not clear that they do so. Learning a film's alleged "life lesson" is not synonymous with absorbing it (any more than the behavior of a patient in psychoanalysis alters at the moment she understands how or why her conduct is destructive.) As reception studies have taught us, what one gleans from a film is not uniform and neither is the impact of that which is gleaned.

To use a trope from one of the films we have analyzed, in *Happy-Go-Lucky*, Poppy's optimistic frame of mind does not "convert" the glum bookstore salesman, her grumpy sister, or the cynical Scott. All remain as mired in their gloom as they were before encountering her. So, why, we might ask, is there any reason to think that the film in which she appears (or any other we have mentioned) has a greater chance of converting the spectator?

While Mary Banks Gregerson entitles her book *The Cinematic Mirror for Psychology and Life Coaching*, it is unclear that viewers routinely see themselves reflected in the characters onscreen or recognize the characters in themselves. Clearly, it is possible that they do and that their behavior can be transformed accordingly, but it is certainly not a given.

Works Cited

Banks, Mary, ed. *The Cinematic Mirror for Psychology and Life Coaching*. Springer, 2010.

Bergson, Henri. *Laughter: An Essay on the Meaning of the Comic*. Translated by Cloudesley Brereton and Fred Rothwell, Martino Fine Books, 2014.

Cousins, Norman. *The Anatomy of an Illness as Perceived by the Patient*. Bantam, 1981.

Fischer, Lucy. "Birth Traumas: Parturition and Horror in *Rosemary's Baby*." *Cinema Journal*, vol. 31, no. 3, spring 1992, pp. 3–18.

Freud, Sigmund. *The Joke and Its Relation to the Unconscious*. Edited by Joyce Crick, translated by John Carey, Penguin Classics, 2003.

Gregerson, Mary Banks, ed. *The Cinematic Mirror for Psychology and Life Coaching*. Springer-Verlag, 2010.

Knapton, Sarah. "Memories Could be Erased to Cure Soldiers of PTSD, Say Scientists." *The Telegraph*, 18 February 2017, www.telegraph.co.uk/news/2017/02/18/memories-could-erased-cure-soldiers-ptsd-say-scientists/.

Mann, Denise. "Movie Therapy: Using Movies for Mental Health." WebMD, www.webmd.com/mental-health/features/movie-therapy-using-movies-for-mental-health#1. Accessed January 2019.

McLay, Robert N. *At War with PTSD: Battling Post Traumatic Stress Disorder with Virtual Reality*. Johns Hopkins University Press, 2012.

Metz, Cade. "Therapy in a Dose of Illusion." *New York Times*, 31 July, 2017, B1.

Niemiec, Ryan N., and Danny Wedding. *Positive Psychology at the Movies: Using Films to Build Virtues and Character Strengths*. Hogrefe, 2008.

Pawelski, J. O. "Defining the 'Positive' in Positive Psychology: Part II. A Normative Analysis." *Journal of Positive Psychology*, vol. 11, 2016, pp. 357–365. https://doi.org/10.1080/17439760.2015.1137628.

Ricoeur, Paul. *Freud and Philosophy: An Essay on Interpretation*. Yale University Press, 1970.

Robinson, Lawrence, Melinda Smith, and Jeanne Segal. "Laughter is the Best Medicine." *Helpguide.org*, www.helpguide.org/articles/mental-health/laughter-is-the- best-medicine.htm. Accessed January 2019.

Rockwell, Donna. "Mindfulness in Everyday Life: Sitting in a Darkened Theater—Movies and the Mind." *Huffington Post*, 30 April 2014, www.huffpost.com/entry/mindfulness-movies_b_4827320.

Segen, J. C. *The Dictionary of Modern Medicine*. CRC Press, 1992.

"The Healing Power of Humor." AARP Bulletin, June 2018.

3

Human Flourishing, Philosophical Naturalism, and Aesthetic Value

Murray Smith

Philosophical problems are characteristically rather abstract—consider the rather dry, not to say exceedingly boring, title of this chapter—and with reason. It is in the nature of philosophy to generalize away from the particular. (A philosopher colleague of mine says—only partly in jest—that he dreams in free variables.) Nonetheless, the abstraction of philosophy presents a special difficulty in the field of aesthetics because the core subject matter of aesthetics is the highly concrete business of engaging with—acquainting ourselves with and appreciating—particular aesthetic objects: the sunset we savor, the milk that's gone off, the novel we immerse ourselves in, the movie that thrills, the music that sends a shiver down our spine. So, I want to get a specific example in front of us, right off the bat. That example is the Talking Heads' hit "Once in a Lifetime." Written by Talking Heads and producer Brian Eno—effectively a fifth member of the band at this point in its history—the song was released as a single in 1981 following its appearance as the opening track on side 2 of the album *Remain in Light* in 1980, receiving extensive airtime on MTV through its memorable music video incarnation.[1]

Take a listen to the song. I imagine you will fall into three groups: those who already know and value this music; those of you who are rock fans, but not very familiar either with "Once in a Lifetime" or with Talking Heads, and who will think this music is worth checking out; and those of you with no interest in or knowledge of rock, and for whom the song will be not much more than noise.[2] I'll come back to this thought toward the end of my discussion.

[1] The credits for the song, as they appear on the single, are somewhat intricate: "Initial Music by David Byrne, Chris Franz, Jerry Harrison, Tina Weymouth, & Brian Eno. Additional Music by David Byrne & Brian Eno."

[2] As will be evident, I use the term "rock" here in a very broad sense, as a kind of supergenre encompassing a large family of styles of recorded popular music tracing their origins to the American vernacular traditions of blues, gospel, and country music. For a related but different view, see Gracyk.

Murray Smith, *Human Flourishing, Philosophical Naturalism, and Aesthetic Value* In: *Cinema, Media, and Human Flourishing*. Edited by: Timothy Corrigan, Oxford University Press. © Oxford University Press 2023. DOI: 10.1093/oso/9780197624180.003.0004

Figure 3.1 Frames from the music video for "Once in a Lifetime" (1981), choreographed by Toni Basil, and co-directed by Basil and David Byrne.

Now, let me confess, when this example first occurred to me, it was for idiosyncratic reasons—the kind of reason that, we say, shouldn't figure in properly aesthetic judgments. It was the song's famous lyrical refrain that came to mind: "and you may ask yourself . . . how did I get here?" Let me also note that *Remain in Light* was given to me by my closest circle of high-school friends, as an eighteenth birthday gift. They presented it to me in the local pub, and at the end of the evening, having been ritually filled with many pints of English bitter, wheeled me home in a shopping trolley. (That was the *anaesthetic* experience!) And so I asked myself: How did I get from there to being invited to deliver the Beardsley Lecture at the Barnes Foundation?[3]

So, I have a personal attachment to "Once in a Lifetime;" it figures in *my* history in a way that gives it a unique significance for me. But I don't believe it is completely contingent on these very personal reasons that, thirty-seven years later—at the time of writing—this music still resonates with me. Of the many aesthetic encounters I must have had around the time of my eighteenth birthday, or even on the very day, most of them are long forgotten. *Remain in Light*, by contrast, hit my turntable the day after my delivery from the pub, and commanded my attention and interest then and for years to come. It still does. It has survived the test of time. And of course, although I have cast this story in highly-personal terms, it is not just my enduring, fascinated attention that the record has secured—my appreciation takes place in a community of appreciators (that of the "art rock world"). As is often, perhaps even typically, the case, our purely personal reasons for esteeming a work are entangled with those shared, intersubjective reasons available to anyone willing to engage with the work—perceptually, cognitively, contextually—as the proper target of aesthetic deliberation.

To take a step toward such reasons, let's turn our attention to a critical assessment of "Once in a Lifetime," in which journalist and music critic Malcolm Jack offers the following "verdictive judgment"[4] on the song (note that Jack's piece was written quite recently, in 2016): "'Once in a Lifetime' is a thing of dizzying power, beauty and mystery . . . it sounds like nothing

[3] This chapter was originally presented as the Beardsley Lecture, under the title "Philosophical Naturalism, Aesthetic Experience, and Aesthetic Value," sponsored by the Philosophy department at Temple University as part of the American Society for Aesthetics Eastern Division 2018 annual conference, at the Barnes Foundation, Philadelphia, April 20, 2018. I have tried to preserve the original character of the lecture even while amending certain passages and adding material to bring out the connections with the question of human flourishing.

[4] By "verdictive judgment" I mean a final and overall judgment—a verdict—on the aesthetic value of a work. See Zangwill, chapter 1.

else in the history of pop." I choose this as a representative piece of ordinary criticism. Several things are striking about it. The first is Jack's recourse to two canonical aesthetic categories: beauty (named directly), and the sublime (evoked by the phrase "dizzying power"). But it is Jack's claim that the song "sounds like nothing else in the history of pop" that I will, in due course, focus upon. This, too, I take to be a typical critical claim, characteristic of a particular type of aesthetic praise. To cite one further example, in support of this typicality claim: we can see both motifs—the invocation of beauty and the sublime, and the claim that the music offers a powerfully novel experience—in this comment on *Remain in Light* posted on the *bandbyweek* website: "The music, like the cover, is breathtakingly beautiful, revolutionary, and offers a completely new experience every time you encounter it."[5]

Note also Jack's invocation of the "mystery" of the work. The idea that great artworks are somehow beyond explanation is familiar as well; but this is where I get off the bus. You might think of this gesture as an innocuous bit of rhetoric, consolidating the claim that the song has a sublime character—that which exceeds our understanding is bound to have an air of mystery about it. Part of the naturalistic approach that I want to defend here, however, involves the thought that we can explain the wonders of artworks—the experiences they can afford us, and the value they thereby embody—without explaining those experiences and evaluations *away*. We shouldn't confuse the experience and the explanation; nor should we expect an explanation of a sublime experience to itself exhibit sublimity. The explanation doesn't threaten the experience. Moreover, while talk of the "mystery" of the power of an artwork may be harmless enough as "mere" rhetoric, it is quite misleading if we take at face value the metaphysical implications of such language. The power of artworks is not to be "explained" by invocations of some supernatural realm beyond human comprehension—think Roger Scruton—and in that sense intrinsically mysterious.

Through this example, I hope to have introduced most of the major themes of this discussion: the nature of aesthetic experience, the value we ascribe to such experience, its place in the world and our capacity to explain it. But let me add to these another theme, which will in the end serve to enrich and amplify the primary concerns I have sketched. That theme is the (supposed) elitism of aesthetics as a field of study. I'm not sure this charge quite hits the mark; after all, popular filmmaking, comic books, and video games are all

[5] https://bandbyweek.wordpress.com/2014/05/13/remain-in-light-cover-art/.

thriving areas of debate in aesthetics. Perhaps it would be fairer to say that the diet of examples is limited and (small "c") conservative.

But immediately adjacent to the charge of elitism (right or wrong) is an important fact about the aesthetic domain: its diversity. The world is filled with a superabundance of aesthetic objects, practices, and sources of value. And as Samuel Scheffler argues, because we are finite beings, there are many more valuable things in the world than can be valued by any individual: "I may, for example, go to the opera from time to time, and I may regard operagoing as a valuable activity, and yet I may still not value it myself. Even though I participate in the activity and believe that it is a valuable activity, operagoing may leave me cold" (27). We can recognize that some things are valuable even though we don't actively value them ourselves. But, I would add, it is only when we become active valuers of a given practice—connoisseurs, aficionados, fans—that we develop an expert sensitivity to the nuances of that practice. (I remember listening to Beethoven's 5th around the time of my eighteenth birthday, in an effort to "get into" a tradition that I recognized had value. But it didn't stick, and so I lack that kind of perceptual and appreciative expertise in relation to classical music.) And as active valuers with such expert sensitivity, we also exercise discrimination: we judge some instances to be better or worse than others, and we debate these judgments with others who share such expertise. Discrimination within a practice seems to be intrinsic to aesthetic appreciation, at least in the context of the arts, applying as readily to the rap fan as to the opera fan.

Naturalism, Valuing, and Flourishing

The naturalistic stance informing this essay, to which I have already alluded, is most directly traceable to a generation of mid-twentieth philosophers and other intellectuals committed to understanding the nature and implications of the success of the sciences (paradigmatically, the natural sciences).[6] But naturalism is an older and broader tradition, and in the current context, it will be helpful to consider the theme in relation to the Godfather of naturalism, Aristotle. The Greek philosopher's writings ranged widely across

[6] In *Film, Art, and the Third Culture: A Naturalized Aesthetics of Film* (2017), I defend a form of "co-operative naturalism," which seeks to complement (rather than supplant) traditional humanistic methods with those drawn from the (natural *and* social) sciences.

topics within and beyond what we now consider philosophical ones, including many—like biology—that we consider scientific rather than philosophical. That is because Aristotle was an example of a "natural philosopher," that is, a philosopher with a deep curiosity about the material world and an appetite for empirical evidence—in marked contrast to his mentor Plato; effectively the precursor to a scientist before the scientific revolution of the seventeenth century (Leroi).

Aristotle's perspective on humanity wasn't detached from this broader naturalism. Aristotle called humans the *zoon politikon*, the political animal, by which he meant, among other things, to emphasize the idea that humans are naturally social creatures, who realize themselves not in isolation but in communities and political structures. "[T]he state is by nature clearly prior to the family and the individual," says Aristotle (*Politics* Book I, 2). Individual human agents may flourish and achieve *eudaimonia* by pursuing and realizing themselves within social structures, a form of agency giving rise to a sense of purpose and meaningfulness. The things pursued by humans in such settings are determined by what matters to them—by what they *value*. But what in the world is a value, and what sense can we make of values and valuing in the context of a naturalistic worldview?

On one view, a value is a kind of desire. Thinking of values as a type of desire, or at least as emerging from desires, is an important first move in giving a naturalistic account of (aesthetic) value, since desires are a kind of impulse basic to the animal world. Desire enters the world with living entities for whom sustenance and shelter are essential, and thus for whom some conditions are more desirable—better than—others. It is worth dwelling on this point a moment longer, as it will help to give shape to the naturalism I want to defend, and thereby to distinguish it from other established positions, naturalistic or otherwise. On my view, intentional states—like desires, but also beliefs and emotions—are part of the natural world. Human intentional states are doubtless more complex, conceptually and in other ways, than their non-human analogues, but they are continuous with them. When Paul Grice distinguished between "natural" meaning and "non-natural," intentional meaning, then, he used an unhappy but telling choice of wording (Grice; see also Smith, *Film, Art, and the Third Culture* 34). The distinction is real and important enough, but it is not a distinction between the natural world on the one hand, and a transcendent world of human meaning and intention, or a world "beyond being" (in the Platonic formulation), on the other. On my view, intentions are as natural as smoke from a fire or the dark hue of rain clouds. In other words, what I'm aiming for is an inclusive, non-reductive naturalism—one that recognizes the distinctiveness of human beings while insisting that they are nonetheless part of the natural world, broadly conceived.

It is probably clear enough how desires might be accommodated within such a picture. But what about values? What's the relationship between the primitive desires of simple organisms and the complex values, aesthetic and otherwise, embodied by artworks? How do we get—in the words of Daniel Dennett (2017)—from bacteria to Bach? A value is no ordinary desire, but rather an "idealized" desire, one refined through reflection. Moreover, values have an intrinsically intersubjective character, in two senses. First, the reflective spotlight that we train on our desires is by no means wholly private, but rather has a social character in the sense that we often arrive at insights about ourselves and our desires through dialogue with others. Second, as a consequence, at least some of the norms that we arrive at through this (interpersonal) reflective process will constitute shared standards. Reserving the term "value" for those desires which have undergone this process of social reflection is to carve nature at an important joint (which is not to deny that there may be other joints). The intersubjective character of aesthetic evaluation is, of course, very much to the fore in Kant's account—along with a claim regarding the foundation of that intersubjectivity: "The judgement of taste exacts agreement from every one; and a person who describes something as beautiful insists that every one ought to give the object in question his approval and follow suit in describing it as beautiful . . . We are suitors for agreement from every one else, because we are fortified with a ground common to all" (§19).

Our understanding of the distinctive character of aesthetic value is sharpened by putting it in the context of the array of other core human values. We value of our own well-being (prudential value), the well-being of (some) others (moral value), the nature and quality of the polity we inhabit (political value), and having an accurate grasp of the world (epistemic value). And sometimes we value things for their own sake, or for the self-rewarding experience that they afford; we value them, that is, *aesthetically*. What does that amount to? Consider the following passage from Roger Fry's well-known analysis of aesthetic experience:

> If, in a cinematograph, we see a runaway horse and cart, we do not have to think either of getting out of the way or heroically interposing ourselves.

> The result is that in the first place we *see* the event much more clearly; see a number of quite interesting but irrelevant things, which in real life could not struggle into our consciousness, bent, as it would be, entirely upon the problem of our appropriate reaction. I remember seeing in a cinematograph the arrival of a train at a foreign station and the people descending from the carriages; there was no platform, and to my intense surprise I saw several people turn right round after reaching the ground, as though to orientate themselves; an almost ridiculous performance, which I had never noticed in all the many hundred occasions on which such a scene had passed before my eyes in real life. The fact being that at a station one is never really a spectator of events, but an actor engaged in the drama of luggage or prospective seats, and one actually sees only so much as may help to the appropriate action.[7]

In attending to an object or event in this aesthetic fashion—at a remove from our practical interests, although not without knowledge of those ordinary interests—we are able notice aspects of it to which we would otherwise be blind. As Fry puts it elsewhere in the essay, "[i]t is only when an object exists in our lives for no other purpose than to be seen that we really look at it" (16). In a more formal contemporary statement, Robert Stecker writes that an aesthetic experience is aesthetic if and only if it is "the experience of attending in a discriminating manner to forms, qualities or meaningful features of things, attending to these for their own sake or for the sake of this very experience" (4).

This is an orthodox definition, in the context of contemporary debate, but it is worth stressing a couple of implications of it. The first is that, on this definition, there is little to separate "aesthetic value" from "entertainment." (The connection is clear in the centrality of the idea of "pleasure" in both philosophical aesthetics and cultural theory.) The class connotations differ, but can aesthetic value and entertainment be distinguished at the denotative level? The second implication is that, according to this characterization of aesthetic value, such value is, on the one hand, one type of value among others, and on the other, a kind of "framing" value allowing us to find "autotelic" (self-sufficient) satisfaction in other kinds of value. This is an important element in Stecker's characterization, which states that the content of aesthetic experience may range across the "forms, qualities, and meanings" of objects,

[7] Fry 12–13; quoted in Nanay 33–34.

and a point exquisitely made many decades earlier by Jan Mukařovský, who argued that "[t]he influence of aesthetic value is not that it swallows up and represses all remaining values, but that it releases every one of them from direct contact with a corresponding life-value" (89).

This feature of aesthetic value is an important part of its distinctive contribution to human flourishing. All the basic forms of value canvassed above are important to human well-being. The good life is bound to involve sustained engagement with moral and political matters, as well as a measure of self-interest. Knowledge—epistemic value—is vital too; as Aristotle puts it, "All men by nature desire to know."[8] The pursuit of these values, singly or in combination, is very evident in the other chapters comprising the volume in your hands, although not always bearing the labels I use here. Many of the essays exemplify the tradition of ideological critique in film and media studies, exploring the extent to which films limit or distort our understanding of the world in general or of human potentiality in particular, or alternatively challenge such distortions and help to deepen and expand our understanding. Several of the case studies explored by my co-contributors focus on cases of what Miranda Fricker (2007) famously dubbed "epistemic injustice," where the harm or injustice at stake specifically bears on questions of knowledge—as in Ellen Scott's case study of black spectatorship of classical Hollywood cinema, where the work of film critic Almena Davis acts as a corrective and redress to the false, pernicious, and thus unjust images of black life in such cinema.

On Mukařovský's view, however, aesthetic experience possesses a special capacity to integrate, and afford us a reflective perspective on, other forms of value. Echoes of this perspective on the special value of art and the aesthetic can be heard in Dana Polan's recognition of the "inventiveness" of Hollywood, the accent on creativity (especially under conditions of adversity) in the chapters by Dudley Andrew, Timothy Corrigan, and Patrice Petro, and most directly in Lucy Fischer's plea that we acknowledge "the regenerative power of laughter," and the general "potential of aesthetics . . . to promote human well-being' (Corrigan, "Introduction to Cinema, Media, and Human Flourishing" 5 and 6).

[8] Intriguingly, in the same passage in the *Metaphysics* in which this sentence appears, Aristotle also recognizes aesthetic value: writing of the "delight we take in our senses," Aristotle notes that "even apart from their usefulness they are loved for themselves" (quoted in Lear 1).

The breadth of aesthetic value also explains why an essay like the one you are reading, centered on a musical case study, finds its place in a collection on cinema and media. On the view advanced here, aesthetic value is central to human well-being, and such value can be instantiated by works and practices in an indefinitely wide range of media. From this perspective, novels, films, and songs are more alike in virtue of the kind of aesthetic value they bring into being than they are unalike in virtue of contrasts in the media through which they are realized. And this point is only underlined when we think about the extent to which popular music is closely bound up with (kino-) audio-visual media, through fashion, the art world, graphic design, music video, and feature filmmaking. Like a great many rock musicians, Eno and Talking Heads all attended art school, and the significance of the visual and performative framing of their music is evident from their music videos, including the video for "Once in a Lifetime," as well as the two features showcasing their music, the live performance film *Stop Making Sense* (1984) and David Byrne's *True Stories* (1986).[9]

What we establish through characterizations of aesthetic experience and value along the lines sketched above is the *capacity* for such experience and value—a capacity that any creature with sufficient cognitive power might possess. But what about the *content* of such experience? Here we return to what I described earlier as the problem of aesthetic diversity—the sheer range of aesthetic forms and practices that we witness as we survey distinct periods and places. But why exactly is this fact a *problem*—and what is it?

I think we can tease out two questions here. First, how is such diversity to be explained? Why do we not see more stability and regularity in our aesthetic practices? And second, given that we do have such a superabundance of aesthetic objects, practices, and sources of value, how do we navigate within such a world of such extreme aesthetic diversity? How, in particular, does evaluation figure in such navigation?

Kant, as we have seen, thought he had an answer to this: "we are fortified by a ground common to all." These days, we are rather more skeptical about this; the problem of aesthetic diversity, as I am calling it, is one way of recognizing one of the intellectual leitmotifs of our age—the emphasis on cultural difference. Such difference is often held to make the Kantian ambition of universal assent to any given aesthetic judgment to be no more than a philosophical fantasy. And perhaps a malign fantasy: Alexander Nehamas

[9] On the art school connection, see Frith and Horne.

argues that Kantian universality is not only unachievable, but quite undesirable, when we think about the role of aesthetics in human flourishing, and especially the important relationship between taste and individuality (*Only a Promise of Happiness* 83). Is it possible to reconcile Kant's universalistic ambitions with the contemporary stress on both the fact and the value of diversity, cultural and individual?

I believe it is—up to a point. The route to such reconciliation lies through the notion of "bioculturalism." Bioculturalism describes a perspective on human nature which regards the nature–nurture dyad as a false dichotomy. An emphatically naturalistic idea, it has an Aristotelian pedigree: Armand Marie Leroi describes Aristotle's conception of the *polis* as "an organic–artefactual hybrid" (315). Kim Sterelny gives contemporary expression to the perspective when he argues that there is no "culture/biology divide, either in human phenotypes or in human environments. The environment does not segment into biological and cultural aspects. Food, for example, does not divide into items eaten solely for social or ritual reasons (communion wafers are the exception, not the rule) and mere metabolic servicing, when we shovel anything digestible down our throats. Finding, preparing, and eating food typically serves social as well as metabolic ends, and answers to cultural as well as ecological constraints" (739). How does such bioculturalism bear on aesthetic value?

What humans find engaging and self-rewarding is, in the first instance, a matter of how they are built, physiologically and mentally, which is to say, how they have been constituted by evolution. But, more or less uniquely among species, humans have evolved as, or into, "enculturated" animals. Whatever basic capacities are (to use Kant's phrase) "common to all," the maturing of a human being involves the tuning and calibration of our biological endowments to the frequencies of the culture into which we are born, or into which we have later assimilated. That is why aesthetic value is, and indeed must be, "multiply realized in diverse populations," as Peter Railton (89) puts it. And that, in turn, is why—I hope to demonstrate—the aesthetic domain is characterized, not by universal assent to the same judgments, but *at once* by diversity, disagreement, and a degree of convergence.

Note that a biocultural perspective on the aesthetic is consistent with the "contextualism" advocated by, among others, Jerry Levinson (17–27) and Greg Currie (116–118)—with the view, that is, that aesthetic experience, at least in the context of art, necessarily takes place in an art-historical, and more generally, cultural context. Artworks cannot be properly or fully appreciated when displaced from the specific "world" in which and for which they were made, as I noted at the outset in relation to *Remain in Light* and the "art rock world." Dominic Lopes points to another pertinent case: "In *Our Films, Their Films* . . . Satyajit Ray remarks that movies get 'colour from all manner of indigenous factors such as habits of speech and behaviour, deep-seated social practices, past traditions, present influences,' going on to wonder whether these 'minute local variations' will only 'puzzle and perturb—and consequently warp the judgement of—the uninitiated foreigner'" (Lopes, "On the Question" 6). Bioculturalism comfortably accommodates, then, and indeed helps us make sense of, the contemporary emphasis on cultural difference and cultural specificity.

But my claim is that bioculturalism can reconcile that emphasis on difference with the Kantian stress on universality—or at least recognizes a complementary pressure toward convergence in aesthetic judgment. How can bioculturalism square this circle? Recall again the phrase with which Kant concludes the passage from §19 of *The Critique of Judgement*: he writes of "a ground common to all." Unlike many variants of contemporary cultural theory, bioculturalism does not deny the existence of such a common ground: our biology is incomplete without cultural realization, but—and this is the important complementary point—our cultural competencies depend on our biological capacities.

We must be careful, however, not to caricature either biology or culture and cultural experience. On the one hand, the biological dimension of our being itself admits of a great deal of variation—from genetic variation to phenotypical differences in build, hair and eye colour, left/right-handedness and laterality, and so on, to the profound differences in cognitive style captured by the concept of neurodiversity. On the other hand, cultures are not wholly separate spheres sealed off from one another, but interpenetrating traditions of practice, existing at many scales.[10] So we cannot rest content with a version of bioculturalism conjoining biology, conceived as an engine of uniformity, with culture, conceived as the only source of variation. Uniformity *and* variability are evident in *both* domains—that is one motivation for positing the composite concept of the "biocultural." Bioculturalism points to the idea that, whatever differences exist between individuals and groups, there will also be many shared capacities, beliefs, and values.

[10] This is one of the themes of "What Difference Does it Make?", chapter 6 of my *Film, Art, and the Third Culture* (2017). See also Smith, "*The Battle of Algiers*" 106.

This, in turn, allows us to recognize what Currie has dubbed the "openness" of (the aesthetic dimension of) art: the availability of artefacts with an aesthetic dimension to some degree of appreciation *prior to* an understanding of the context of the artefact. "Someone who knows nothing of the culture of a contemporary society very different from our own is not thereby precluded from beginning a journey of aesthetic discovery," Currie writes. "We accept that there is a pathway to the appreciation of artworks that moves gently uphill from wholly untutored looking through to curatorial levels of expertise . . . [t]he doctrine of Openness says that such pathways exist, connecting any culture with any other" (109, 111). In a similar spirit, Lopes underlines that, for all their cultural difference, Ray's films are not beyond our comprehension or appreciation: "I'm not saying you can't get Ray's movies. I'm saying that getting them requires initiation into [their] world, where initiation means acquiring [a particular kind of] competence" (6). The openness of art plays a significant role in its social and socializing functions, by affording "new ways of relating across different cultural environments" (4), in the words of Tay, Pawelski, and Keith. As Currie notes, we must all begin as novices in the world(s) of art, and anyone who ventures beyond the cultural and aesthetic practices with which they are familiar will immediately find themselves returned to "Go" on the journey to full appreciation. In this way, aesthetic experience may act as a gateway to the appreciation of other—less transparent—kinds of meaning and value embodied in artworks and other artefacts. This, then, is the sense in which there is, in human experience in general and aesthetic experience in particular, a "ground common to all."

How might all this apply to the case of *Remain in Light*? Here we need to go into a little more detail about the project. One of the most prominent features of *Remain in Light* was its engagement with various kinds of African music, and in particular the music of Nigerian composer and bandleader Fela Kuti. The result of that engagement is very evident on many of the tracks on *Remain in Light*—an early example of what would come to be dubbed "worldbeat." Compare the opening cut of Kuti's *Afrodisiac* (1973), "Alu Jon Jonki Jon," for example, with "The Great Curve" from *Remain in Light*. Both feature a large, percussion-driven ensemble—at this point Talking Heads were a nine-piece band in their live incarnation; previously they were a four-piece outfit—laying down a sustained, propulsive polyrhythm, supporting a dynamic interplay among vocals, brass, keyboards, and guitar. (Kuti's influence on *Remain in Light* is explicitly acknowledged by an outtake called

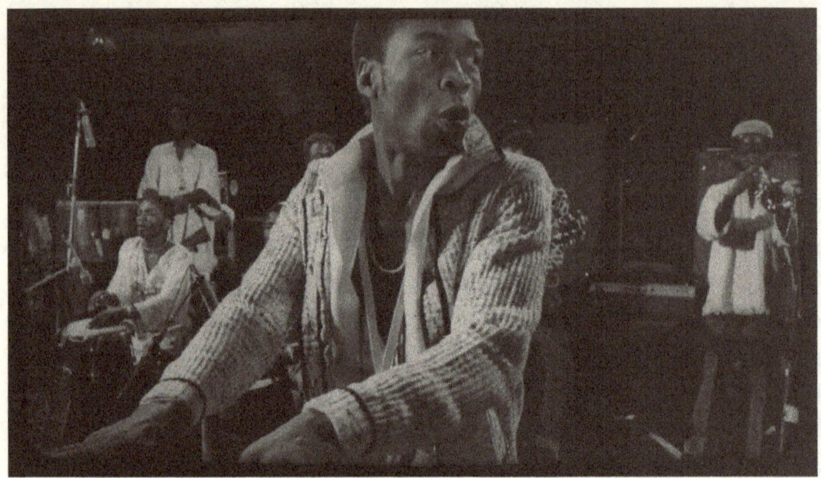

Figure 3.2 Fela Kuti with his band Africa 70, Berlin, 1978.

"Fela's Riff," included as an extra on the expanded 2006 CD reissue; the riff in question closely resembles the "Alu Jon Jonki Jon" riff.)

Across the 1980s, David Byrne became increasingly involved with the promotion of "world music"—that is, the distribution of an array of popular, non-Western musical traditions to a Western audience. At a certain point in the course of his activities as both musician and musical entrepreneur, however, Byrne became frustrated and skeptical about the legitimacy of the category "world music," penning an essay in the late 1990s titled "I Hate World Music." Reflecting on that essay many years later, Byrne stated: "the term 'world music' was becoming common, and I felt like this term was becoming a catch-all phrase for basically exotic-sounding restaurant music. Background music that you could put on and ignore, and you didn't have to take the artist very seriously. It didn't really affect your life, it just provided a pleasant, exotic background. And I was kind of saying: let's get rid of *that* idea."[11]

I think we can see at work here what I would like to call *the dialectic between the open and the closed, the universal and the cultural, the convergent and divergent, aspects of aesthetic experience*. On the one hand, we have Byrne's concern that "world music" had turned into a form of superficial—and morally and politically dubious—exoticism, reducing the music to the level of "a woman dancing with bananas on her head."[12]

[11] See the interview with Byrne at https://www.youtube.com/watch?v=Wu_d9_VW6Qo.
[12] See the interview with Byrne at https://www.youtube.com/watch?v=Wu_d9_VW6Qo.

Figure 3.3 The expanded live line-up of Talking Heads, Dortmund, 1980 (from left to right): Steve Scales, Chris Frantz, Busta Jones, Dolette McDonald, Adrian Belew, David Byrne, Tina Weymouth, Bernie Worrell, and Jerry Harrison.

But against that, we need to remember that, with Talking Heads, Byrne had helped create a new genre—"worldbeat"—of depth and complexity. And the creative agency of Talking Heads in this regard was in fact an echo of what Fela Kuti had achieved in the preceding decade, for Kuti was regarded as one of the architects of "AfroBeat"—the blending of West African musical practices such as juju and highlife with American funk, jazz, and rock (a perfect example of the conception of culture as a field of multi-layered, interpenetrating traditions of practice, sketched above). So, it would be wrong to think of the interactions among different musical traditions as being *inevitably* superficial, or politically problematic, appropriations. And the possibility—indeed the *reality*—of blending musical traditions depends on the openness of the aesthetic dimension of art.

Expanding and Inhabiting Musical Idioms

In the space left to me, I want to use the case of *Remain in Light* to develop one more substantial proposal concerning aesthetic experience, aesthetic value, and the ability of naturalism to provide a robust and satisfying account of them. To introduce this last idea, let me begin by conjoining Jack's euphoric claim that "Once in a Lifetime" "sounds like nothing else in the history of pop," with my own proposal (in *Film, Art, and the Third Culture*) "that aesthetic experience arises when our perceptual, affective, and cognitive capacities are engaged in a way that goes beyond their normal functioning, and that such engagement prompts us to savour and reflect upon the resultant experiences . . . the vocation of art is to offer us an adventure in perception and cognition" (7). This hypothesis, which I label (following Lopes) "expansionism" (645–646), has dual sources of inspiration. On the one hand, it owes its origin to Romantic theories of art, with their emphasis on the artist as an aesthetic adventurer, at work on the frontiers of experience. Indeed, my formulation of the expansionist thesis borrows from a well-known "manifesto" by Stan Brakhage, a filmmaker very much in this tradition. In a famous passage, Brakhage invites us to:

> Imagine an eye unruled by man-made laws of perspective, an eye unprejudiced by compositional logic, an eye which does not respond to the name of everything but which must know each object encountered in life through an adventure of perception. How many colors are there in a field of grass to the crawling baby unaware of "Green"? How many rainbows can light create for the untutored eye? (25)

But expansionism also takes its cue from a proposal in naturalized, cognitive aesthetics: that we not only depend on our ordinary cognitive capacities to create and appreciate aesthetic works, but that those very capacities may be stimulated, stretched, and pulled in unique ways in aesthetic experience.

I should immediately note three caveats. The first is that although my examples are principally perceptual—concerning audition and vision—aesthetic expansion ranges across all stages and layers of human psychology. This accords with the definition of the aesthetic, drawing on Mukařovský and Stecker, that I offered earlier. But to the extent that this broad, encompassing approach to the aesthetic is on the right tracks, we should break the narrow or preferential link between aesthetic experience and the perceptual. It is not only conceptual art that is shut out or marginalized by such a definition; much of literature is excluded from a conception of the aesthetic (too) tightly connected with perception, because perception plays only an instrumental role in the appreciation of many kinds of literature (as we can see from the fact that we can acquaint ourselves with such works through sight or touch—that is, via conventional visual uptake, or braille).[13]

The second caveat is that the "expansive" dimension of aesthetic experience is but *one* axis of aesthetic value; the third, that its realization is a matter of degree. Not every work in every aesthetic tradition will seek to maximize this dimension of experience; and it may be that "expansion" with respect to one parameter of perception, cognition, or emotion will necessitate that other parameters remain familiar. Two contrasting cases bring out this point. David Bordwell argues that Christopher Nolan's *Memento* (2001) features just such a tradeoff between its innovative, backwards-staggered temporal structure and other, much more familiar features, such as various crime film tropes and storytelling devices ensuring clarity and redundancy. "Seldom has an American film," writes Bordwell, "been so daring and so obvious at the same time" (79). Diana Raffman, meanwhile, argues that twelve-tone composition is not "perceptually real" (86)—that is, listeners cannot experience such musical structures *in perception*—because too many familiar musical signposts and handholds are removed. What many would regard as the more authentic experimentalism of dodecaphony—relative to Nolan's dance with crime thriller conventions—comes at a price.

Perhaps it is also worth adding that the locus of aesthetic expansion resides in the *type* of experience created, not (or not merely or principally) in particular tokens of experience. It is important to take this observation on board in order to fend off the objection that, at a certain level of analysis, *all* experiences offer us something new, just to the extent that they are numerically and (to some extent) qualitatively distinct experiences. Each time I eat a bag of Marks & Spencer Belgian chocolate-coated peanuts, it is a new experience in this very rudimentary sense, even though it is a totally generic food item I have consumed dozens of times before. If this is all the claim of

[13] The close tie between perception and aesthetics extends back to the promotion of aesthetics as a distinctive area of philosophy in the eighteenth century—the word "aesthetic" deriving from the Greek for "sense perception"—and persists in current debate. Levinson, for example, writes of aesthetic experience taking "any aspect of the perceivable world" as its object (14); see Nanay, *Aesthetics as Philosophy of Perception*, for an overt and sustained contemporary example. Zangwill, chapter 8, specifically defends the "weak dependence thesis": "Aesthetic properties depend in part on sensory properties, such as colors and sounds . . . without sensory properties, there would be no aesthetic properties" (127). Unsurprisingly, Zangwill's conception of the aesthetic is much narrower, and more narrowly formalist, than the accounts of the aesthetic advanced by Mukařovský and Stecker. In a footnote Zangwill confesses that he himself is "not sure of the weak dependence thesis as regards literature" (137). This is not the place to pursue the point, but a plausible way forward on this issue is to place the imagination, rather than perception, at the center of aesthetic experience. Zangwill explores this possibility briefly (29–30, 204).

aesthetic expansion comes to, then it wouldn't be identifying anything distinctive or interesting. No two experiences of washing the dishes are exactly alike, when we conceive of them as (precisely) particular experiences. The same goes for particular aesthetic experiences; listening to a piece of music many times over will generate as many unique experiences of it, insofar as the specific features of the work we focus upon on each occasion are bound to vary. It is also the case that the degree to which we find a particular experience expansive varies both across individuals, and for individuals across time: at different points in my listening history, I may be entirely unfamiliar or highly conversant with the conventions of AfroBeat; and I may have much greater listening experience and expertise with contemporary African music than (say) my brother possesses.

All of this is true, but beside the point. Where expansive aesthetic experience is successfully created, the relevant framework for that experience is not each token experience, but the type of experience that a work (or group of works) makes possible. When Jack states that "Once in a Lifetime" "sounds like nothing else in the history of pop," he's not making a point about specific (token, particular) experiences of the song, but about the originality and expansiveness of the song as a work composed at a specific historical moment, in principle available to anyone with the right expertise to experience it as such. Or alternatively, sufficient openness of mind to embrace the openness of art to begin the journey toward acquiring such expertise, and the experience available through its exercise. This allows us to see how the expansionist thesis fits with the contextualist perspective previously discussed.

Such expansion can be realized at various levels, from that of the framing technology of representation, to the level of genre, to that of the individual artist. Perhaps expansion is easiest to understand in relation to the first of these levels. Think of the way in which each successive major development in the technology of the moving image—from "silent" cinema to the talkies, colour, widescreen, to 3D, 4D, and CGI—creates a new, distinctive kind of visual experience irrespective of the specific content of any specific movie. In the case of music, a parallel form of expansion occurs through the emergence of electric and electronic instrumentation, and the use of recording technologies as creative tools—through the rise, that is, of the record producer as a creative artist and the recording studio as an instrument. (The emergence of the *sound designer* in filmmaking as a creative role forms an exact parallel.)

This returns us directly to *Remain in Light*, an album for which Eno, one of the most accomplished of all record producers, played a critical role. Eno's mastery of electronic treatments is evident across the entire record, but one might consider the bleeping, burbling synthesizer passage midway through "Born Under Punches (The Heat Goes On)" (2.45–3.20), and the sped up, slowed down, reversed and layered guitar solo bisecting "Crosseyed and Painless" (1.55–2.53), as exemplary. And my use of the word "mastery" here points us to another complexity pertaining to the "expansive" aspect of aesthetic experience. For there are many familiar—as opposed to innovative or expansive—aspects of the style of *Remain in Light* to which aficionados of Talking Heads and/or Eno and/or new wave music more generally will be attuned. These stylistic elements arise from the ability of the band members to *inhabit* fully the musical tradition in which they are active (and which sometimes, as in this case, they helped to create); such "inhabitation" is one of the other key dimensions or axes of aesthetic experience we need to recognize alongside aesthetic expansion. A particular example of such musical inhabitation involves the ability of a group of musicians to (inter)lock into a *groove*, as analyzed by Tiger Roholt—a subtle but distinctive inflection of a composition's basic rhythm, an inflection which requires performance expertise to create, and appreciative expertise to discern and feel. We rightly associate such groove with funk, but rockers can master groove in their own way: this is the secret, for example, of AC/DC's apparently simple riffing.[14]

Appreciation of such familiar dimensions of music works in an interplay with attention to and appreciation of a musical act's ability to *expand* the tradition—often through cross-pollination with other musical idioms. The importing of elements from one practice into another is a common catalyst of expansion (thereby embodying one of those "new ways of relating across different cultural environments" that contribute so much to the social value of art).[15] Consider, in this connection, the striking guitar break falling at 1.56–2.35 in "The Great Curve," the closing track of side one of *Remain in Light*. Here Adrian Belew's angular, discordant guitar-synth solo rides on the underlying AfroBeat groove, building up to syncopated brass stabs and culminating with Byrne's refrain, "The world moves on a woman's hips." The solo itself a cunning blend of old- and new-wave sensibilities, mixing distortion and tremolo-arm "dive bombing" with idiosyncratic phrasing and

[14] Roholt characterizes groove as "the *feel* of a rhythm" (1). His examples range from Frank Sinatra to Gene Vincent, The Beatles, Sly and the Family Stone, Led Zeppelin, Dr Dre, Brandy, Amy Winehouse, and Tame Impala.

[15] See the discussion of the "openness" of art, previously discussed. The quotation is from Tay et al. 4.

harmonic dissonance. Set against the AfroBeat backdrop, the thrilling, expansive strangeness of the solo is even more marked.

I have cast this example, like my earlier examples, in terms of expansion at the level of musical content. But expansion also manifests itself, at least as importantly, in terms of appreciative skills and sensitivities: that is, in terms of learning how to hear something as a purposeful aesthetic gesture (rather than as an accident or as mere "noise"). In this respect it is notable that at least many of the innovations in aesthetic *creation* discussed in this essay seem to depend on *appreciation*, for presumably Kuti and Talking Heads only thought to blend their "native" musical traditions (that is, those musical traditions which they inhabited—with which they were intimately familiar—and which were thus "native" *to them*) with other traditions because they had first come to appreciate these latter forms as listeners. One might think of this an "appreciation-first" view of art and the aesthetic—where appreciation is a precondition of creation, and thus creation involves or is a kind of appreciation.

Let me conclude by drawing together some of the threads of this chapter. I have argued:

- first, that different aesthetic practices and traditions develop our capacity for aesthetic experience and value in different ways, but on the basis of a shared biocultural foundation—a "species-typical" ground common to all, consistent with the idea that there are substantial variations across cultures and individuals;
- second, active valuing—appreciation—within a given aesthetic tradition involves a continuous refinement and expansion of appreciative (and for the practitioner, performance) skills; and
- third, that such refinement and expansion takes us away from the common ground, limiting and complicating, but by no means eliminating, the possibility of appreciation across aesthetic practices—which remains possible due to the openness of the aesthetic dimension of art.

So, we may be suitors to agreement, but the agreement we can hope to achieve will at once be enabled *and* constrained by the biocultural nature of human beings.

A last thought on naturalism. Naturalism is not new in aesthetics: if one thinks not only of Aristotle, but of Hume, Dewey, and Santayana as naturalists, then it becomes clear that naturalism is a perennial perspective in aesthetics. It was prominent at the time the American Society for Aesthetics was founded in the 1940s, and it is highly visible today. And yet there is a reluctance to embrace it wholeheartedly. Why?

In a nutshell—the fear of reduction. If the natural world is for us—after Darwin—a "disenchanted" world, then the domain of aesthetics might be (and has been) seized upon as a space of re-enchantment. Think again of the language in which Jack describes "Once in a Lifetime." A naturalized perspective on aesthetic experience might seem to threaten that restoration. But I hope to have shown here that the perceived threat and the fear arising from it are misplaced. Naturalism gives us the tools to understand the distinctive place of art and aesthetics in human affairs, and their significance for human flourishing. We can locate and explain aesthetic activity, experience, and value in us and in the world even as we retain that sense of wonder—or as I have put it, the adventure in perception and cognition—that the aesthetic dimension affords us, and that brought us all here today in the first place.

Works Cited

Andrew, Dudley. "Cinema and Creative Community." *Cinema, Media, and Human Flourishing*, edited by Timothy Corrigan. Oxford University Press, 2023, 74–88.

Aristotle. *Aristotle's Politics: Writings from the Complete Works*, edited by Jonathan Barnes, Princeton University Press, 2016.

bandbyweek. "Remain in Light Cover Art." *bandbyweek*, 13 May 2014. https://bandbyweek.wordpress.com/2014/05/13/remain-in-light-cover-art/.

Bordwell, David. *The Way Hollywood Tells It: Story and Style in Modern Movies*. University of California Press, 2006.

Brakhage, Stan. "Metaphors on Vision." *Film Culture*, vol. 30, special issue, fall 1963.

Byrne, David. "Crossing Music's Borders In Search of Identity; 'I Hate World Music.'" *New York Times*, 3 October 1999, Section 2, 1. https://www.nytimes.com/1999/10/03/arts/music-crossing-musics-borders-in-search-of-identity-i-hate-world-music.html

Byrne, David. "Talking Heads David Byrne Hates World Music . . . Or Does He?" THNKR YouTube channel, 6 September 2012. https://www.youtube.com/watch?v=Wu_d9_VW6Qo.

Corrigan, Timothy. "Introduction to Cinema, Media, and Human Flourishing." *Cinema, Media, and Human Flourishing*, edited by Timothy Corrigan, Oxford University Press, 2023, 1–13.

Corrigan, Timothy. "Learning to Adapt: From Pathology to Splendor." *Cinema, Media, and Human Flourishing*, edited by Timothy Corrigan, Oxford University Press, 2023, 134–49.

Currie, Gregory. "Art and the Anthropologists." *Aesthetic Science: Connecting Minds, Brains, and Experience*, edited by Arthur P. Shimamura and Stephen E. Palmer, Oxford University Press, 2012, 107–128.

Dennett, Daniel C. *From Bacteria to Bach and Back: The Evolution of Minds*. W. W. Norton and Co., 2017.

Fischer, Lucy. "Media-ting Happiness." *Cinema, Media, and Human Flourishing*, edited by Timothy Corrigan, Oxford University Press, 2023, 36–50.

Fricker, Miranda. *Epistemic Injustice: Power and the Ethics of Knowing*. Oxford University Press, 2007.

Frith, Simon, and Howard Horne. *Art into Pop*. Methuen, 1987.

Fry, Roger. "An Essay in Aesthetics." *Vision and Design*. Chatto and Windus, 1920. Original published in the *New Quarterly* (1909), pp. 11–25.

Gracyk, Theodore. *Rhythm and Noise: An Aesthetics of Rock*. Duke University Press, 1996.

Grice, Paul. "Meaning." *Studies in the Way of Words*. Harvard University Press, 1989, pp. 213–223.

Jack, Malcolm. "Talking Heads—10 of the Best." *The Guardian*, 21 September 2016. https://www.theguardian.com/music/musicblog/2016/sep/21/talking-heads-10-of-the-best.

Kant, Immanuel. *The Critique of Judgement*. Translated by James Creed Meredith, Clarendon Press, 1952.

Lear, Jonathan. *Aristotle: The Desire to Understand*. Cambridge University Press, 1988.

Leroi, Armand Marie. *The Lagoon: How Aristotle Invented Science*. Bloomsbury Circus, 2014.

Levinson, Jerrold. *Aesthetic Pursuits: Essays in Philosophy of Art*. Oxford University Press, 2016.

Lopes, Dominic McIver. "Pictures and the Representational Mind." *The Monist*, vol. 86, no. 4, January 2003, pp. 632–652. https://doi.org/10.5840/monist200386432.

Lopes, Dominic McIver. "On the Question, How Should I Live, Aesthetically?" Paper delivered at the British Society of Aesthetics annual conference, St Anne's College, Oxford, 8 September 2019.

Mukařovský, Jan. *Aesthetic Function, Norm and Value as Social Facts*. Translated by Mark E. Suino, Michigan Slavic Contributions, 1979.

Nanay, Bence. *Aesthetics as Philosophy of Perception*. Oxford University Press, 2016.

Nehamas, Alexander. *Only a Promise of Happiness: The Place of Beauty in a World of Art*. Princeton University Press, 2007.

Petro, Patrice. "Austerity Media, Impulses to Hope." *Cinema, Media, and Human Flourishing*, edited by Timothy Corrigan, Oxford University Press, 2023, 150–60.

Polan, Dana. "Human Relationship as Human Value in Studio-Era Hollywood." *Cinema, Media, and Human Flourishing*, edited by Timothy Corrigan, Oxford University Press, 2023, 103–17.

Raffman, Diana. "Is Twelve-Tone Music Artistically Defective?" *Midwest Studies in Philosophy*, vol. XXVII, 2003, pp. 69–87.

Railton, Peter. "Aesthetic Value, Moral Value, and the Ambitions of Naturalism." *Aesthetics and Ethics*, edited by Jerrold Levinson, Cambridge University Press, 1998, 59–105.

Ray, Satyajit. *Our Films, Their Films*. Orient Longman, 1976.

Roholt, Tiger C. *Groove: A Phenomenology of Rhythmic Nuance*. Bloomsbury, 2014.

Scheffler, Samuel. "Valuing." *Reasons and Recognition: Essays on the Philosophy of T. M. Scanlon*. Oxford University Press, 2011, 15–40.

Scott, Ellen C. "Fiendish Devices: Human Flourishing and the Black Watching Subject." *Cinema, Media, and Human Flourishing*, edited by Timothy Corrigan, Oxford University Press, 2023, 89–102.

Smith, Murray. "*The Battle of Algiers*: Colonial Struggle and Collective Allegiance." *Iris*, vol. 24, autumn 1997, pp. 105–124.

Smith, Murray. *Film, Art, and the Third Culture: A Naturalized Aesthetics of Film*. Oxford University Press, 2017.

Sterelny, Kim. "Po-Bo Man?" *Studies in History and Philosophy of Biological and Biomedical Sciences*, vol. 35, 2004, pp. 729–741.

Tay, Louis, et al. "The role of the arts and humanities in human flourishing: A conceptual model." *The Journal of Positive Psychology*, vol. 13, no. 3, 2018, pp. 1–11. https://doi.org/10.1080/17439760.2017.1279207.

Zangwill, Nick. *The Metaphysics of Beauty*. Cornell University Press, 2001.

4
Cinema and Creative Community

Dudley Andrew

Allergic to polls and particularly to assessments of my internal states, I don't respond well to questions that ask one to rank pain, frustration, pleasure, or particularly happiness on a scale of one to ten. Nor am I ready to say that happiness is the goal of that which flourishes. Certain things may flourish best when one is least content.

So let me put aside the vocabulary and tools of the social sciences and rely instead on the twin engines of the humanities: history and interpretation. How better to grasp human flourishing than to look lovingly, critically, but above all historically, on the arts, for this is where our species has most freely exhibited its aspirations and its fears. I take the cinema to be the commanding art of the last century, the arena within which those aspirations and fears staged their appearance if not most vividly, then certainly with the most consequence. And for two reasons. A collaborative art involving huge financial and cultural resources, cinema demands that those who make it share a vision and come to cooperate. Once made, the work pleads for sympathy, wanting a mass public (theoretically, everyone in the world) to cooperate in responding to it. While literature, painting, and the theater may let individuals flourish, the cinema will flourish as a vast human enterprise or not at all. So, looking back over the last one hundred years, what stands out so memorably are not just the films that continue to glow on our screens today, but the way they came into being, the way these images, whether documentary or fantasy, shimmering before us today were "realized" in their day.

Some of those days, far too many of them, were terrible, yet movies flowed onto screens at a fairly constant annual rate. Yes, both world wars forced a slowdown, even a shutdown in certain places, but there seems little correlation between the production of great films and periods of relative social progress and economic growth. In fact, let me venture a dangerous hypothesis: striking cinema has often been produced in periods of repression and social anguish. Look at the Brazilian movies of the 1970s, when the country

Dudley Andrew, *Cinema and Creative Community* In: *Cinema, Media, and Human Flourishing.* Edited by: Timothy Corrigan, Oxford University Press. © Oxford University Press 2023. DOI: 10.1093/oso/9780197624180.003.0005 was in the grip of the Generals, or at the remarkable Polish films leading up to the labor strikes of 1980. From the point of view of cinephilia, the success of the Polish Solidarity movement and then of liberal democracy was paradoxically a letdown. Polish films grew soft and uninteresting in the 1990s as the country rejoiced in its freedom. Then there is the remarkable Iranian cinema that for the past three decades has flourished—there is no better word for it—under a regime that stamps out so many expressions of freedom and happiness. International festivals are annually uplifted by the brilliant Iranian films that somehow get made. Although seldom directly political in theme, they grab us with their sense of urgency.

By contrast over the same period, American cinema, although often spectacular and entertaining, has not seemed particularly urgent. Not until the past two years, anyway. Today, the repression and constriction that is suddenly so alarming in this country (tightened borders, a heavier and hotter environment) could, in compensation, bring us a spate of significant films to look forward to. This certainly happened in the dozen years, 1936–1948, that I take to be the worst period of the worst of centuries, when nevertheless (or consequently) "The Classic Hollywood Cinema" grew to its greatest strength in terms of audience and influence. While an unprecedented economic depression dissolved into the most terrible of wars accompanied by the horror of genocide that gradually came to light, films frequently gave audiences a reason to believe in a future in which their society might soon flourish and perhaps do so amongst, and with, other societies, thus projecting a universal liberal future.

The ideals of universalism had to vie with, and wait out, the inflammatory nationalisms of the 1930s; due to the coming of sound, cinema could stoke patriotic fervor just through the foregrounding of a nation's language and music. In response, several key public intellectuals supported a general (rather than a national) film aesthetic, taking cinema to be the Esperanto of the twentieth century. In the mid-1930s, Erwin Panofsky, recently in the United States after fleeing Hitler, took time out to write a talk that would become a canonical essay, "Style and Medium in the Motion Pictures." Why, particularly at this moment, would a lionized art historian trouble himself with the movies? Here's why:

> Whether we like it or not, it is the movies that mold, more than any other single force, the opinions, the taste, the language, the dress, the behavior, and even the physical appearance of a public comprising more than

> 60 per cent of the population of the earth. If all the serious lyrical poets, composers, painters and sculptors were forced by law to stop their activities, a rather small fraction of the general public would become aware of the fact and a still smaller fraction would seriously regret it. If the same thing were to happen with the movies, the social consequences would be catastrophic.

Panofsky spoke these words in the nadir of the depression, which was also the zenith of Nazi control over the country he had just fled and the highpoint of a brand of atavistic national chauvinism that was in place in nearly every part of the world. Yet the optimism of Panofsky's "Style and Medium in the Motion Pictures," an address and then a publication celebrating the prestige accorded cinema at the newly established Museum of Modern Art, was not fatuous. The movies did provide a "medium," a climate that is, within which humans could (and can) be seen to develop and thrive.

Panofsky polished his talk in 1947, publishing it just before the onset of the Cold War. Times may have appeared marginally more hopeful, yet the specter of mass annihilation loomed in recent images of the Nazi death camps and of the Japanese cities of Hiroshima and Nagasaki. Undoubtedly, the privilege of the long view of the art historian contributed to his humanist serenity. This privilege certainly had that effect on the equally famous André Malraux during precisely the same dozen turbulent years. In 1936, Malraux outlined the overarching history of art that he would begin to publish in 1947 as *Les Voix du silence*. He would take up cinema as crucial to the most recent chapter in the book of civilization, because it exhibits for the twentieth century humankind's perpetual struggle for spiritual liberation over the shackles of history and death. Malraux, it must be noted, was hardly writing from a disengaged and lofty perspective. He knew the struggle for liberation firsthand, for his ideas on cinema came out in 1940, a year after he had produced one of the most magnificent of all French films, giving a precise title to that struggle, *Espoir*. While the film came out too late to help staunch the historical disaster of the Spanish Civil War (he wanted its international distribution to recruit financial, military, and political support for the Republicans), it wound up commemorating the deaths of those who were being killed even while the film was in production. Malraux found tragic hope in the courage of the people standing up to their fate. He stamped on enduring celluloid the images of their faces, at once common and noble, using templates that

Goya and El Greco had long ago forged for the Spanish people . . . and for all humankind.

As the Spanish War faded out like a grim short subject before the devastating feature of World War Two, Malraux published his "Sketch for a Psychology of Cinema," the final installment of a five-part preview to *Les Voix du silence* written between 1937 and 1940 in *Verve*. Opening and closing on the theme of cinema's international mass appeal, Malraux ascribed to cinema a fundamentally new phase of the arts of representation, one that provides a strikingly different social function for art. In this, his "Sketch" resembles the views of Walter Benjamin who had courted his favor and whom he had already cited in 1936 (see Andrew, "Malraux, Bazin, Benjamin"). Malraux realized the extent of cinema's distinct and enormous potential when, on a memorable occasion, he had seen a Charlie Chaplin film projected on an outdoor stucco wall mesmerize a crowd of mainly illiterate Persians. He became convinced that cinema was uniquely able in our era to deliver the myths by which humans conceive of their lives and deaths; Chaplin showed ordinary people that they were capable of standing up to the dehumanizing forces bearing down on everyone in the machine age.

Malraux's "Sketch" came out in *Verve* 8 (June 1940), published simultaneously in French and English. Had he waited until summer's end he would surely have alluded to the irruption of myth in two momentous examples. First was Chaplin's *The Great Dictator*. Drawing on Charlot, an already mythical being—indeed the most recognizable one in the world—Chaplin turned the horror story of current politics and particularly the threat of genocide into a universal allegory, expecting comedy to devastate the German war machine. The other example also comes from late 1940 but involves not the birth of a new film but the discovery of the most ancient images then known, the cave paintings in Lescaux, France. What a shock to realize that 17,000 years back, human beings were already representing features of their world, expressing, or so it seems, its power and their awe. Among the staggering Lascaux discoveries are 350 proto-cinematic pictures of horses; looked at with imagination, these seem to race across the history of civilization to meet Eadweard Muybridge in 1886 when he fixed the majestic movement of a horse's gallop in the first chronophotograph.

Can we today recover the faith in art that Malraux and Panofsky somehow shared during the most difficult period of a terrible century? The current century finds us in a panic over the prospects of the extinction of civilization, whether through an environment we are making unlivable, or through the nuclear Armageddon we had thought to have skirted, or through the advances of artificial intelligence that may stamp us with an expiration date? Can we, like those profound scholars eighty years ago, reach toward hope by recognizing a continuity that keeps current developments in the visual arts attached to, and sustained by, a story of human art-making so long it feels timeless? What forms exist today that are comparable to the promise those men found in the motion pictures?

Rather than speculating on the social state of the arts today and tomorrow, on the nourishment or the toxins they may be carrying through the cultural circulation system, let me survey more thoroughly the situation within which Malraux and Panofsky lived and wrote. Understanding what encouraged their confident view of cinema might in turn encourage us as we look at the past and the future of the images around us.

Without question both men were thinking of Hollywood. How could they not measure the scale of its biggest successes? At its best, American films reached innumerable minds and souls everywhere, broadening those minds, exhilarating them, and sometimes even bringing them into a feeling of unity. Attic sculpture, Tang dynasty poetry, and Italian frescoes had exalted particular places and peoples, but films like *City Lights*, *Sleeping Beauty*, and *The Grapes of Wrath* were screened not just in America but around the globe, and nearly simultaneously. Hollywood genres were constellations recognized by anyone anywhere who paid attention to the cultural heavens; so too were its most luminous stars.

This period was named "Classical Hollywood," not just because of the pleasing balance in plot, lighting, and rhythm that many of its products seemed so effortlessly to have struck, but because of the tangible rapport that had developed between producers and viewers. Feedback through box-office and criticism helped push producers forward and upward in a spiral. For the studios aimed to please and to challenge the best instincts and tastes of the audience with new ways—call them styles—of acknowledging the natural and social world.

Despite the nationalism of the time, Hollywood's art and the international audience it entertained (in the fullest sense of that term) matured in tandem. For Eric Rohmer and André Bazin this made it sociologically analogous to Elizabethan theater or to German symphonic music of the late eighteenth and early nineteenth centuries. Analogous but not comparable, for the scale of Hollywood's public and its consequently heterogeneous nature, is unprecedented. Shakespeare and Mozart entertained large, moderately homogenous audiences, enough of whose member were sufficiently discerning to demand and deserve increasingly sophisticated works of art. By contrast, Hollywood's public has been indefinite in size and constitution. At whom are its films targeted? Producers aim, we imagine, for the largest box office, while the most artistically ambitious screenwriters and directors want to impress their peers and to win over the class of critics who speak on behalf of the public and in the interests of the art they are especially attuned to.

Up to 1947, the studios were vertically integrated, with each of "the majors" turning out a movie per week to play in the theaters it owned. Talent being under contract, actors, writers, directors, and technical personnel could be counted on to work together on genres that grew increasingly refined and varied, able to feed a consistent audience at home and shape tastes around the world. Such regularity meant that most productions were perforce unremarkable; still, producers and viewers pooled their best instincts frequently enough to uplift even jaded critics. Listen to Otis Ferguson in *The New Republic* in February 1940, when war had been declared but had yet to heat up or directly involve the United States. (Three years later this, our best critic, would die in that war.) Ferguson, emerging ecstatic from *The Grapes of Wrath*, wrote:

> This is everybody's picture—everybody working with one of the world's ace movie directors, which is as it should be . . . The public is *going* to this picture; the non-political awarding groups will put it top of the list for 1940; and the film books of 1950 will put it down as a milestone in the art of the motion picture . . .
>
> It ends as they move on down the road again in the cab of the truck, toward twenty days' picking, and Ma snorts at the idea of her being scared. *Her?* She's been scared before, she says, but she's had it knocked out of her. We'll go on, she says. We may get kicked but they can't get rid of us, rich men or not; sometime they won't scare so many of us any more, because we go on, because they can't kill us; we're the people.
>
> And so the people will go to see and hear, and I hope they'll listen to it. Because this is their show, for and by; it is more their show than any show on the face of the earth (Ferguson).

Though credited to Darryl Zanuck, John Ford, Henry Fonda, Nunnally Johnson, Greg Toland and of course John Steinbeck, this film did feel like "everybody's picture" because it addressed the depression and spoke for the audience to whom it was displayed. The New York critics and the National Board of Review named it Best Picture of 1940, perhaps because they felt involved in a shared expression, a cooperative experience in a dangerous historical moment.

In the chapter he devotes to *The Grapes of Wrath* in *The Cultural Front*, Michael Denning rightly questions the myth of its populism. The film went into production in the Twentieth Century Fox lineup just a few months after the book's sensational release. Its populist sentiment was a commodity bought from Viking Press and adapted to be intelligible to a mass movie audience, while being sufficiently softened to be digestible to the middle class, too. In Hollywood's most flourishing era, a wealthy studio grew plumper by purveying a social situation and a hope in social solidarity that all audiences, domestic and foreign, could acknowledge. As Malraux proclaimed at the end of his "Sketch," the cinema may be a phenomenon of untold value in being capable of uniting the human race through the myths it recounts, but at the same time it is also an industry.

Malraux could believe in cinema as both art and industry because French cinema was a cottage industry. He had worked close enough to it to realize that, unlike Hollywood, it was weak, uncoordinated, and seemingly manageable if you approached it shrewdly. In the most fortuitous circumstances, it could shelter a production as a site of solidarity and congenial coordination. With no studio system to deal with or rely on, *Espoir*, like nearly all French films made after 1934, was put together as an ad hoc venture. No studio CEO dictated the conditions; instead of assembly-line production, the French took an artisanal attitude toward the fashioning of their more ambitious films, allowing each the chance to establish its own look and style. This system, although constitutionally fragile, allowed space for a project to magnetize a group of individuals into a coordinated body, a team or *équipe*.

French cinema flourished in just such a weak industrial climate, and it did so most memorably from 1936–1938 during the brief tenure of the Popular Front government. Despite bitter debates, I can think of no moment in the twentieth century that better represents what I take to be human and artistic flourishing. Grass roots cooperation led to a socialist government that instituted prescient social programs (the forty-hour workweek, paid vacations, adult education, houses of culture). A cultural front that fostered the participation of all classes had blown across the country after the fascist riots of February 1934, and had even put a socialist government in place. Intellectuals came down into the streets to help make this happen, and the street, as Marcel Carné famously remarked, is where the camera needed to be.

In 1936, French films captivated audiences in Japan, Argentina, and throughout Europe; a score of them played in New York that year. Among these stands *La Belle Équipe*. An ingratiating melodrama starring Jean Gabin and Vivian Romance, it was in production in June when the socialist Léon Blum was installed as head of government, and it premiered in September after things had already started to go downhill for his fledgling leftist coalition. Actually, the film's own ambivalence matches perfectly that of its moment. For *La Belle Équipe's* first half follows five working-class buddies as they rise from near destitution to the celebration of a utopia they think they have constructed. Having pooled their meager resources, they won the lottery and are able to abandon their tenement lodgings to build a dancehall on the Marne where they can spread the joy of their camaraderie. Then, on account of a woman, jealousy poisons friendship, followed quickly by dispersal and death. This dispiriting conclusion so threatened the box office that a second, happy ending was commissioned. Theater owners could elect to screen whichever they thought would please their clientele. In this way, audiences actually helped complete this ambivalent movie.

La Belle Équipe's importance begins with the significance of its title. Today "équipe" is a sports brand, with a media franchise and an apparel outlet. The term covers the camaraderie of rugby, cycling, and principally football. In the 1930s the term was also the common designation of the basic film production unit in France; this sets it against the studio systems at work in Hollywood, Japan, the UK, and Germany. French films were put together by small teams consisting of director, writer, and star who snagged a friendly moneyman, the producer. Once the production was underway, the *équipe* would grow to include set designer, composer, and cameraman. The memorable films of the 1930s consisted of rather stable *équipes* that moved from one project to the next. Their films might be made in any facility whatever and under extremely different circumstances, but the *équipe* provided a singularly unified tone to each film and across the several films any given group turned out.

And so *La Belle Équipe* refers both to the fictional story of those five men who pool their lottery winnings, and to the creative team made up of director Julien Duvivier, writer Charles Spaak, and star Jean Gabin, who managed to pool their resources to quickly bring a film called *La Belle Équipe* to life on the banks of the Marne in late Spring 1936. You might say that Duvivier's *équipe* had already won the lottery when their previous effort, *La Bandera*, took in a fortune; its phenomenal earnings were enough to get *La Belle Équipe* off the ground. Gabin and Duvivier had also teamed up on *Golgotha*, *L'Homme du Jour*, and *Maria Chapdelaine*, and soon would make the blockbuster *Pépé le Moko*. Just after *La Belle Équipe* was beginning to screen in theaters, Gabin and Spaak joined Jean Renoir's group to adapt Maxim Gorky's *Lower Depths*. Once together, this new trio then embarked on the most famous film of the decade, *La Grande Illusion*.

I am not alone in finding Renoir's string of masterpieces from the 1930s to be unequalled in film history, or in ascribing their consistency to the esprit and inventiveness of his team. This included Eugene Lourié, a Russian émigré artist who became his constant set designer, enabling his tracking shots and location sound. In interviews and in his autobiography, Lourié gushes with stories about their "teamwork." The team was made up of composer Joseph Kosma, Renoir's editor (and mistress) Marguerite Houlé, and Jacques Becker, his very close friend and later a premier filmmaker in his own right, alongside whom could be found co-writer Karl Koch and Renoir's nephew Claude, a cameraman and Major actors were more fickle and moved temporarily or permanently from one team to another. The truth is that only a few teams remained intact for long. I would be exaggerating to suggest that such a lovely idea of artistic collaboration was the norm, rather than the exception, in a business like cinema, but you can see the idea of the *équipe* at work more often than not in the twenty-five films of export quality France produced each year (about one-fifth of their annual output). And you can't miss it in Renoir.

Despite a kernel of truth about the force of a director's personality spelled out in "la politique des auteurs," creativity in cinema is a function of teamwork. The director's governing sensibility needs to monitor all artistic decisions if a film is to live and breathe; still, even unrivalled talent depends on the inventiveness of those who cluster around a director. Unquestionably one of the artistic geniuses of the twentieth century, Renoir was something more: a social genius who attracted creative people and got them to produce not only their best work but to produce it in harmony with a worthy project. Alain Bergala recently spelled this out eloquently (115).

No film better exemplifies the social joys of creativity and cooperation in what it looks like and says, as well as in the way it was made, than *Le Crime de Monsieur Lange*, distributed just a few months before the 1936 election, in time to boost the Popular Front to its narrow victory. Two *équipes* joined forces (Renoir's and that of surrealist poet Jacques Prévert) like two cyclones meeting to form an unpredictable yet devastating comedy all along the cultural and political weather front. The production of *Le Crime de Monsieur Lange* dismayed reporters who were incredulous at the pranks and high spirits on the set. The spontaneity of the acting and the inventiveness of style are tangible in this ideal example of Popular Front filmmaking. Surely its contagion brought many spectators to the polls a few months later to vote left.

An unambiguous political allegory, *Le Crime de Monsieur Lange* plays out almost entirely in a large Parisian courtyard that houses a laundry, a publishing house, various workers, and a concierge. The idea of figuring the nation in the microcosm of a courtyard came naturally enough from Renoir's set designer, Jacques Castanier. He and Jacques Becker started to organize a production team, using some actors from the radical improv "Groupe Octobre," led by Jacques Prévert, with whom they had just collaborated as designer and actor respectively. When Renoir took over as director, Castanier introduced him to Prévert to refashion the script. In Prévert's version, the timid Amedée Lange, a publisher's assistant by day, scribbles romantic stories all night about Arizona Jim, a cowboy who rights social injustice. Lange's nefarious boss, Batala, promises to serialize his stories but does so only when his own mystery series, "Javert," falls flat. Renoir's film turns into a contemporary urban western itself, when Lange becomes the hero who kills the capitalist Batala and saves the socialist "cooperative" that the people in the courtyard have created after Batala had temporarily fled to avoid his creditors.

Just as the cobblestones of Castanier's courtyard studio set form a pattern of interlocking yet individual stones (Conley), so the cooperative flourishes through the shared labor that turns Lange's inspirations into the collective imagination visible in the graphic novels and then the films all the building's inhabitants work so enthusiastically and joyously to turn out. By contagion of cultural distribution (magazine kiosks, movie theaters), this courtyard spirit fans out to inspire Paris and to allow us, the audience, to foresee a future society as a pattern of interlocking courtyards, all thriving in largely chaotic, sometimes feisty, but fundamentally exuberant collaboration.

Happy or not—and usually not—Renoir's subsequent eight films right up to WWII are nothing if not the definition of human flourishing. However, not all of them spread out so contagiously to the public. *La Marseillaise*, an historical pageant made less to commemorate the 150th anniversary of the Revolution, than to reignite fervor for the expiring Popular Front, found favor only in the USSR. French audiences wanted to see the stars they idolized incorporating the legends of 1793; Renoir gave them unknown actors taking on the roles of anonymous citizens who learn to build a nation by working in solidarity. As a ritual of this collective effort, the recruits marching toward Paris learn to sing a new and catchy anthem and to sing it together. To make the nation or the world flourish, Renoir implies, it will not do just to passively admire heroes and leaders. Everyone must play a part; everyone must sing, even if off-key. The genuine revolution is that of ordinary citizens who must bring fervor and imagination to the details of their life, contributing to shared projects that promote the uplift of the human spirit.

Renoir realized that the new historiography his film exemplified had yet to take hold.[1] It was a film made before its time. Almost thirty years later in 1967, floating in on the final wash of the New Wave, he thought *La Marseillaise* would find its audience. Again, he was mistaken but his rationale seems faultless. Cinema in 1967 believed in its prowess and felt connected to a growing revolutionary spirit in youth cultures across the globe. These in turn were putting pressure on traditions that held back desire and community. The New Waves of Japan, Latin America, Czechoslovakia, and France became increasingly political as the 1960s marched toward the culminating moment of Spring 1968. That was the moment when hopes were dashed for a cinema free of the ideology of stars and spectacle, free of the oversight of banks and of cultural commissions.

The vision of a society thriving on spontaneity within cooperation that seemed within reach in Paris in 1936 and then out of reach in 1968, was beautifully evoked in the wisest film I know about the conditions of human flourishing, *Jonah Will Be 25 in the Year 2000*. Written by novelist and art critic John Berger and directed by Switzerland's foremost cineaste, Alain Tanner, in 1975, it follows a ragtag group of renegades from May 1968 who keep alive its memory to pass on to a child born during the making of the film. A high school teacher fired for radicalizing his class, a farm laborer who loses his job for creating a counter-cultural pre-school in a greenhouse, and a labor organizer who flaunts and disrupts urban development at every turn are among the free, but disappointed, spirits living communally on a farm outside Geneva that developers have their eye on. In its sublime, culminating moment—a grand dinner to which everyone has contributed—each individual offers a name and a wish for the baby about to emerge into the world,

[1] The historian Georges Lefebvre was a consultant on *La Marseillaise*, and Renoir availed himself of the methods of the incipient annales of school historians in salting details of food, clothing, and practical life into episodes that promote history from below rather than a tale of namable dramatic figures (see Andrew and Ungar 166–174).

Jonah, whom the whale of history will spit onto the shores of the new century when he is 25.

Berger and Tanner's nostalgia for the social exuberance of Popular Front cinema[2] and for the effervescence of the 1960s, does not keep them from demanding that we imagine the possibilities of a society to come, a society that will make room for, indeed be formed by, the creativity and cooperation that is more inherently part of cinema than of any other art I know.

Jonah came out the year that Hollywood recovered its stranglehold on the world, beginning with *Jaws*, which was then followed by *Star Wars* and *Close Encounters of the Third Kind*. Spectacle has again flourished. Has *Jonah*'s title character participated in the "turn toward myth" that critics have noted in the cinema after the year 2000? What would those who named him in 1975 think of the myths which capture the imagination of our time: *Avatar*, *Iron Man*, *Harry Potter*, and the Marvel franchise? These blockbusters provide our human community with the characters and stories that we think with. Their scale and their technology come from a world beyond those for whom they are made. We citizens have become spectators of a world made by others for themselves, although we think it has been made for us.

How do we reclaim a chance for a community of creativity and cooperation? "Seek this in New Media," some whisper or shout. Perhaps they are right. Perhaps the cinema's potential as a force for imagining a creative community has migrated from the movies to other sites. Even if this be so, to whom should today's culture turn for the long view that Malraux and Panofsky provided in their day? Who can we trust to direct us to the arts in which we should put both our faith and our efforts? For without collective belief in the possibilities that art holds out—for vision, for critique, and for community—humankind will not just be diminished, it will wither.

Works Cited

Andrew, Dudley. "*Casque d'Or*, Casquettes, and a Cask of Aging Wine." *French Film: Texts and Contexts*, edited by Susan Hayward and Ginette Vincendeau, Routledge, 1990.

Andrew, Dudley. "Malraux, Bazin, Benjamin: A Triangle of Hope." *Art, Film, New Media: Museum Without Walls*, edited by Angela Dalle Vacche, Palgrave, 2012.

[2] Tanner makes sure to affiliate his film to the Popular Front by using the actor Raymond Bussières to evoke that earlier period. Bussières had performed in Jacques Prévert's Popular Front films (Andrew, "*Casque d'Or*").

Andrew, Dudley, and Ungar, Steven. *Popular Front Paris and the Poetics of Culture.* Harvard, 2005.

Bergala, Alain. *The Cinema Hypothesis.* Translated by Madeline Whittle, Vienna: SYNEMA, 2016.

Conley, Tom. "A Pan of Bricks." *Enclitic*, vol. 1, spring 1977, pp. 27–33.

Denning, Michael. *Cultural Front: the Laboring* of *American Culture in the Twentieth Century.* Verso, 2010.

Ferguson, Otis. *New Republic.* 12 February 1940, vol. 103, no. 7. Reprinted in *The Film Criticism of Otis Ferguson*, edited by Robert Wilson, Temple University Press, 1971.

Malraux, André. "Sketch for a Psychology of Cinema." *Verve* 8, 1940.

Malraux, André. *La Psychologie de l'art.* Skira, 3 volumes, 1947–1950. Reprinted as *Les Voix du silence*, Gallimard, 1952.

Panofsky, Erwin. "Style and Medium in the Motion Pictures." *Critique* vol. 1, no. 3 (January–February 1947). Reprinted in *Film Theory and Criticism: Introductory Readings,* edited by Leo Braudy and Marshall Cohen, Oxford University Press, 2004.

PART II

HUMAN FLOURISHING ON THE MARGINS OF THE FRAME

5
Fiendish Devices
Human Flourishing and the Black Watching Subject

Ellen C. Scott

Throughout cinema history, ad men, psychologists, and film theorists alike have conceived of movies as having therapeutic value. In some formulations, films provide grounds for pleasurable cognitive alignment; in others, opportunities for secondary or primary identification replicating the Lacanian mirror phase, and in still others simply a cool, welcoming space of relaxation and entertainment. Black film critics and theorists, however, construct "the movies" as a far less hospitable space—one of negative reflection and segregation—the screen reflecting a caricatured mirror with the dimensions and shape of Kara Walker-esque grotesquerie. James Baldwin's caustic *The Devil Finds Work*, for example, sees cinema not as therapeutic but quite the opposite—as an escape valve for whites pursuing insidious neglect of Black citizens—a kind of *false* therapy that allows oppression to continue and whiteness to remain ascendant. For Baldwin, a profound skeptic about the possibilities of Black flourishing in the United States, Hollywood's saccharine, imagineered images represented among the deepest signifiers of irony and hopelessness.

This paper will explore the possibility of Black flourishing through acts of interrogative film criticism, focusing on the work and writing of an underheralded Black woman film critic, Almena Davis (later Lomax).[1] Davis, editor of the 1940s and 1950s Black newspaper the *Los Angeles Tribune*, predicted Baldwin's acerbic critique of Hollywood's undermining of Black life. In a review that seems to foretell Baldwin's "On Being White . . . and other lies," she found *Imitation of Life* (1959) a "fiendish device to injure the pride of colored people in being themselves . . . and an equally fiendish plot to curse every white child with a complex of innate color superiority, as if the racial superiority

[1] The term "interrogative" associated with film spectatorship hails from bell hooks (115–132).

Ellen C. Scott, *Fiendish Devices* In: *Cinema, Media, and Human Flourishing.* Edited by: Timothy Corrigan, Oxford University Press. © Oxford University Press 2023. DOI: 10.1093/oso/9780197624180.003.0006

complex many of them have were not already devilish enough" (Baldwin). She was a consistent attender of the movies—one of Hollywood's most regular Black critics and among the most avid Black writers about film of her era. But for Davis, ironically it was through the act of debunking and countering Hollywood's toxic white placidity and plasticity that her own selfhood could flourish and emerge. Her loose play with Hollywood constructions opened a place for the noir, the avant-garde, and the satirical. And in her interpretive writing, which mixed consideration of film, politics, her children, her dogs, and her "premenstrual tension," it was precisely her embodied unmasking of the screen that made her own liminal, gender-porous self-hood legible. In this chapter, I will take Davis as a case study of Black feminized, interrogative criticism as a way of life—a recourse for the disappointed, oppressed, and marginalized Black subject watching "America" to draw therapy, life, and possibility through the aegis of unabating, avowedly bitter, borderline hysterical critique. Davis' model of daily, trenchant critique as *self*, one also evident in the current cultural criticism and persona of Charles Blow, is as necessary today as ever, as we have as much to fear from fascisms of the screen today as we did in Davis' 1940s and 1950s.

The Lady Editor Who Refused to Edit Herself:

Almena had nine lives. Like so many Black women, she had multiple careers, multiple self-motivated reiterations. She was born in Galveston, Texas but raised in Los Angeles. She was a reporter for the *California Eagle* but moved on to publishing her own newspaper after conflict with *Eagle* publisher Charlotta Bass. Almena began editing the *Los Angeles Tribune* in 1941 and would edit the paper for nearly twenty years. She claimed to have won the printing press for the paper in a bet. While this claim is improvable, the paper did indeed go from being *The Interfaith Churchman* to becoming the *Los Angeles Tribune*, edited by Almena and published by Lucius Lomax, a lawyer and the son of notorious "Old Man Lomax," who, according to Donald Bogle, was one of the West Coast's biggest numbers runners, gambling house owners and procurers, "a murderer and a criminal" in the words of his grandchildren but also a godfather of Black Hollywood.[2] Although clean

[2] According to his granddaughter, Melanie (who was Almena's daughter), he rode with Pancho Villa during the Mexican Revolution and then moved back to Texas and eventually to Los Angeles,

cut by contrast with his father, Lucius Lomax, Jr. fathered two of Almena's children—and in 1948, his wife, Carmelita Lomax, named Almena (and her co-worker Alice Key) in a sensational divorce suit that made headlines in nearly every paper in the Black press (Cook; Briggs; Lamar, "Almena Davis Named"; Lamar, "Editor Named Co-respondent"). This would have silenced most respectability-minded Black women. But for Almena this defamed public-ness was only the beginning of a more free-form existence outside of the bounds of Black normalcy. After the divorce scandal, Lucius married Almena and they went on to have four more children. All the while, Almena kept writing and editing the paper. The *Los Angeles Tribune*, a paper which made calculated show of impropriety in spite of the substantial education of its literarily-inclined, upwardly mobile, fiscally-middle-class agents (Almena and Lucius), reveals the American middle class for what it is: a people only one generation removed from the "street." Through writing that is grim, wry, and at once literary and vernacular, the paper showcases a penchant for finding itself in what others considered sinful and an adolescent willingness to wrangle the tabloidesque as the exciting pinnacle of Black middle-class existence. And through it, Almena and Lucius at once profoundly challenged Black respectability politics with a rhetoric borrowed from the very real gangsters they knew and made it possible to see and "read" the middle class (Black *and* white) as a witty, literate, mooching, semi-criminal band of nouveau riche pretenders.

Davis' nine lives included several formative relationships, including one with LA's first Black mayor, Tom Bradley, a pilgrimage to the Birmingham Civil Rights movement in 1960 where she published a magazine (more like a linotype "zine") with her children,[3] and an appearance on *You Bet Your Life* where she outshined Joe Louis in her boxing and sports knowledge.[4] She often attempted to be a "Serious" writer—of mainstream journalism (for *The Los Angeles Times*, UPI, The Associated Press, and Copley News Service, all of whom she, upon rejection, attempted to sue for racial discrimination),[5]

purposing "shady endeavors" all the way. "He established a series of bootleg operations and whorehouses up and down the West Coast starting in Yakima, Washington. His operations were gambling, whorehouses, and bootleg liquor which he ran with his sister" (Bogle 77–78).

[3] For issues of the *Tribune* magazine, see Almena Lomax collection Box 28, folders 17–23, Emory University Special Collections. (Img_8821).

[4] *You Bet Your Life*, March 3, 1955.

[5] Almena Lomax to Richard Nixon, May 14, 1974. Box 1, Folder 4, Almena Lomax collection; Emory University Special Collections. [Image 9046])

of criticism (for *The New Yorker*), of short stories (for *Harper's* and *McCall's* who said "this is well-written but just too fragile for us,"[6]) and of a novel and a memoir, all of which met with rejection that must have been as painful as her attempts were bold and fearless. Her rejections file, found among her personal papers, showcases her battles with "becoming"—and a life of aspirations that never fully blossomed in segregated America. She did not respond to failure with defeat, embarrassment, or increasing fervor for "success." She responded to it with resistance, with criticism, with the sardonic: she reformed the standard she had failed into something more human. In the areas of dignity, respectability, and success, rather than conforming, she reformed the canons through her radical practices of writing and selfhood. She was brutally honest—and the ways she "made it" tell us something about how to survive now.

I experience Davis like a voice from the present commenting derisively and with crystalline clarity on the past. So exacting was her critique in terms of what it required of American racial and gendered vision that it seems to transcend its moment and offer a stinging critique for our own time and its half-stepping notions of racial "diversity." I frequently return to Almena—and usually when I do I am not sure whether to wince or to wink at her. The reason I return is that she teaches me always and again, through sputtered nuggets and poetic shards, how to live rather than survive. She reminds me of what Black brilliance is—and it is not whitelikeness; it is fast and there—and seeing in the dead of night.

Almena on the Scene of the Movies

I am trying to count how many of Davis' reviews begin with something like: "the film was a whole lot of bosh from beginning to end;" (Davis, "The New Movies" 3 Aug. 1946) or "maybe resignation is the proper mood for approaching movies. Then anything more entertaining than a prayer meeting will be positively dazzling" (Davis, "The New Movies" 7 Sept. 1946). Or "Something happened to me the other night. My husband and I went to the preview . . . and I was shocked to find myself enjoying it!" (Davis, "The New Movies" 10 Dec. 1949). She often attended previews and shock and surprise

[6] Robert Hemenway to Almena Lomax, June 12, 1967. Box 1 Folder 3. "The Editors" at McCall's to Almena Lomax, n.d. Box 1 Folder 4. [Rotated Image 9380]

often guide her reviews and reveal to the reader Hollywood's often laughable strangeness and misplaced, unintended pleasures. Her writing does not engage with the spectacle in the movies but rather confronts the movies as failed illusion—as an ideological Manhattan project—one that with each self-proclaimed success brought American society to the brink. Foreign films like *Rome Open City* (1945), *Dedee* (1948), *Paisan* (1946), and *The Baker's Wife* (1938) fared better in her judgment, and she campaigned with local theater managers to bring more of them in (Davis, "The New Movies" 8 June 1946; Davis, "The New Movies, 12 Nov. 1949; Davis, "For Adults Only"). Often her own desire overrode the film's narrative as the center of the review. As with the rest of the writing in the paper, Almena's voice is grim, wry, and equally unafraid of an elaborate vocabulary that exceeded the journalistic (exemplified terms like contumely, lorgnette, asceticism, "pendulous belly" and "acrid stench") and Black vernacular. Despite being loose and unprincipled, the writing has a code, both ethical and stylistic, although sometimes the code is so thick, localized, and personal that we have no idea what she is talking about.

When Hollywood did succeed, in Almena's estimation, it was normally through the unpredictable, uncanny, or pure evil. For instance, Hollywood's ghostly output repeatedly impressed her. Like Richard Dyer in *White*, Davis read Hollywood's whiteness as most effective and evocative when it was projecting death or devilish evils. "Ray Milland is superb as Nick Beale, one of the devil's emissaries who goes around trying to break good men; but I suspect that half of his Oscar should go to whoever made him up. They're making magic out in Hollywood these days, a magic that can make a man's eyes actually dilate with evil and unearthliness, a magic that makes his skin look like something that was just dug up from somewhere cold and clammy; and I'm scared of them. They come as close, those Hollywood boys, to constructing a devil as I am willing to admit he exists" (Lomax, "The New Movies" 2 Apr. 1949). Lest we think that Davis' reaction was only to the cosmetics, she had a similar reaction to Elvis Presley on *The Ed Sullivan Show*: "And we never did see the pelvis of Elvis, even when he was standing still: only his bust. The reason his face is phenomenal is that we have never seen evil so triumphant and rampant in our lives as the face of this 21-year old. If he isn't the 'strange and bitter fruit' of the South, we don't know what is" (Lomax, "Notes on Ed Sullivan).

She used the brunt of the tabloid style—with its naked eye and rumored knowledge, against the studios, whose dangerous mediocrity she discussed not only in film reviews but in her more general Hollywood coverage. Her account of Nikita Khrushchev's visit to Hollywood was particularly powerful in this regard. Almena quipped: "He saw emptiness, and self-aggrandizement, and 'adult children' playing with gigantic toys which adds up to nothing" (Lomax, "Anti-Flies"). Almena also used Khrushchev's visit as an opportunity to "read" oversold Hollywood star Marilyn Monroe as an aspect of Hollywood's failed ideological project. "She looked three parts mermaid, one part beatnik . . . Her celebrated bosom was crammed up into her chest so that it looked liable to pop loose from its moorings at any minute and go flopping around like perch. Her waist nipped in unbelievably, like a hair-pin curve on the road and then ballooned out monstrously into her bottom. Screen stars all look slightly unkempt off the set, like children whose mommas left them to dress alone; and Marilyn hadn't bothered to match her pallid arms to the chalk-whiteness of her face . . . In our own eyes, accustomed to this 'decadent American culture' she looked like a gargoyle" (Lomax, "Don't Imitate Americans"). If her sizing down of the Hollywood ego was evident in her descriptions of actors, it was also evident in her descriptions of the studio heads. In anticipating disgust for *Porgy and Bess*, she took aim at Samuel Goldwyn after visiting the studio: "The whole atmosphere at the Goldwyn Studio is calculated to impress you that you are in the presence of a 'Great I Am,' the High Lama of Celluloid . . . The place is dotted with the private preserves of Mr. Goldwyn. Mr. Goldwyn Parks Here. Mr. Goldwyn Drinks Here . . . Mr. Goldwyn Goes to the Potty Here . . . When finally you are ushered into the presence of this Napoleon, you find him an ordinary mortal with a face like a plumber's wrench, a few grey hairs spiraling up on his dome and an expression which is partly that of Leo 'Sunshine' Fonarow [first owner of LA's Victor's department store] . . . and partly that of a man who knows what to do with a plumber's wrench, plus a little oil. The air is heavy with sycophancy, although even it has to battle for a place in the sun with Goldwyn's own worship of himself" (Lomax, "Notes for Showfolks" 15 Aug. 1958). With a style of critique sharpened through the dozens (and borrowing from its flow), Almena cuts Goldwyn down to size as nearly no other Hollywood critic dared.

As her critical voice reached its mature vintage, she discussed the narrative insides of "the movies" even less and concerned herself more with the actors and how they were sold. For example, she dedicated multiple columns to the advertising of *Anna Lucasta*; and she accused Black press Hollywood writers of selling out to studio interests—becoming mere "publicity agents" rather than critics (Lomax, "Notes for Showfolks" 6 Feb. 1959). She sensed Hollywood was designing publicity events with "the hard sell" to have a "dizzying effect so that you didn't know whether the film was any good or not" (Lomax, "The Business of Sex"). Even Eartha Kitt, she felt was dangerously close to succumbing like so many stars to being "bought" by Hollywood and advertisers. Eartha, Almena claimed, "did a regular turn out in Hollywood the day 'Anna' opened, giving out autographs. The way Hollywood's mind operates, and the way she's typecast, she's lucky it was just autographs she was asked to pass out at Hollywood and Vine. After all, judging by the advertising of the picture, they might have built her a crib, like in the old days that at Fort Huachuca, and installed her inside on a chaise lounge, with Rex Ingram on the outside barking, 'Next!'" (Lomax, "The Business of Sex"). Whether it was critiquing Hollywood's poor plots or "reading" the bodies of Hollywood stars or Black performers, Almena's distinctive interpretive style moved beyond the narrative to unearth what was at the radical core of America's visual, racial project. Accordingly, she uncovered the ideology of these films but with a blunt candor, wittiness, and breeziness not typically associated with Hollywood writing.

Almena Davis/Lomax, Hollywood, and the Triumph of Racial Hysteria

Against this background of Hollywood mediocrity, the movie capital's racial failures provided a singular clarity on the problem with American race relations. And Almena dealt quite differently—less smirkingly—with Hollywood's racial failures than with its failures in storytelling. The screen had a social import—and because of its local proximity and the fact that so many of her friends were caught up with striving toward it or watching it, she could look at it with appropriate side-eye. But she wrote about Hollywood not only because it was local but because she knew the screen's impact on Black well-being in America. And thus, it caused her not only to produce caustic critique but also on-the-ground protest.

One might rightfully ask: why do critics such as Baldwin and Davis return to the oppressive object, especially when it is film, rather than say, a president, and can be avoided? In part it is because critique enables refined vision that cannot be achieved without it. But it is also because through the destruction of lies—against their current—the truth ascends. And when these lies obstruct from view a whole race's selfhood, the destruction of untruths has all the more power to unleash being. Thus, on the foundation of a steady stream of reviews flippantly and casually revealing Hollywood's ordinariness, came a fierce challenge reserved for the institution's work around race. Almena protested films more fervently and consistently than any other single Black activist during the Classical Hollywood era. She did so with a style that combined intimacy (her own children were picketers) with clever direct-action tactics. These protests were desperate, acid, aching, personal, sometimes sad, but always pulsing with articulate urgency. My first encounter with Almena came through the papers of the NAACP where I discovered a letter she wrote to Walter White, the organization's leader and Executive Secretary. Even his supporters viewed White's Hollywood campaign as nebulous at best, troublesome and fruitless at worst. But Almena completely understood it as a vital part of the broader civil rights project, suggesting ways to extend it through her proximity to Hollywood. She asked White to join her protest of *Tales of Manhattan* (1942). "Our procedure" she wrote of the *Los Angeles Tribune's* campaign against Hollywood's racial bias, is "to print a detailed criticism and then picket the first theater where the film was shown. In addition, copies of the criticism and of the picket story were sent to writers of the film, actors in it, the director and the producer." In the case of the *Tales of Manhattan* campaign, she told White, "the review and the story, or parts of it were carried in *PM*, also the *Pittsburgh Courier*, in addition to our own paper."[7] White, however, was wary of Davis, whose tactics were more direct and who printed Black actors' skepticism regarding his Hollywood campaign in her column.[8] Nevertheless, Almena had a plan that worked not through mass but direct action in the sightlines of the Hollywood elite responsible for the films and concerned about racial backlash. She used this strategy with *Tales of Manhattan* effectively, she claimed, scaring the studio out of even more troubling scenes in *Cabin in the Sky*. In 1942 alone, Almena used the paper to orchestrate highly visible protests against *Tales of Manhattan* and *Tennessee Johnson*. During the war years, having heard of Disney's Uncle Remus project, which would become *Song of the South*, she would announce her in paper a protest of all animated films "betraying an alarming tendency to caricature Negroes in a vicious manner," beginning with *Angel Puss*, a

[7] Almena Davis to Walter White, Sept 14, 1942. General Office Files; Films—General; Papers of the NAACP, Library of Congress, Washington DC.

[8] Walter White to Almena Davis, April 28, 1942. General Office Files; Films—General; Papers of the NAACP, Library of Congress, Washington DC.

little Black Sambo cartoon released in 1944. She would also protest MGM's projected production of *Uncle Tom's Cabin* in 1944. When *Green Pastures* came to TV in 1959, she also lambasted it: "Nobody has ever suggested that *Green Pastures* is a lot of stereotyped crud because it is supposed to deal with the Negro's religion. But we suggest it" (Davis, "Channel-time").

It may be that the only appropriate, human response to fascism is constant, hysterical, creative resistance. And, as a Black Angeleno, Almena saw fascism most clearly, not in Hitler but in Hollywood. She had an apocalyptic, apoplectic reaction to the anti-blackness of cinema. At her picketing in 1942 she held a sign saying: "*Tales of Manhattan* is the Bitter End" (Davis, "Newspapers picket"). And when it came to *Imitation of Life*, which she previewed in 1959, her response was equally totalizing, despite the fact that the film was generally liked by Black critics: "This picture the Negro cannot take. This picture the Negro will not take. This picture the Negro should not take. This is the bitter end . . . the straw that broke the camel's back . . . also the razor's edge separating the races emotionally in this country, between love and hatred" (Lomax, "'Imitation of Life'"). She published successive articles lambasting the film and picketed the theater with the *Los Angeles Tribune* staff and her family:

> Our theory is that the financially rocky, shaky, tottering Universal International Studios had its coattails pulled . . . by the old and dastardly architects of "Massive Resistance" by the bright lads who planted the bug in the ear of . . . Orval Faubus and got him to call out the National Guard to oppose the Federal Government . . . What is worrying the *Tribune* is that the Universal-International has libeled, slandered . . . "tended to exposed the public contempt or ridicule," an international institution known as the "fine brown frame." . . . Lousy, hackneyed, contrived, poorly acted, even unwholesome pictures which find middle-aged female stars making love to men young enough to be their sons are everyday with Hollywood. Pictures which reveal the people who make them as little used to ideas of adulthood, genuine emotion, and motherhood on celluloid as they are in real life are ground out by Hollywood as regularly as Lana Turner gets a new boyfriend or Dick Haymes a new wife . . . So what if this picture bears no resemblance to reality—not even counting the fantastic hearse drawn by four white horses in a day of Capri pants, trapeze dresses and 1959 convertibles . . . ? This is Hollywood. Everybody knows it is crazy-man-crazy and get the loot! (Lomax, "Some Afterthoughts")

The central Black storyline of 1959 for the news editor Davis was not an anachronistic hearse drawn by four white horses nor a Black mother who apologizes to her white mistress for dying nor a fair-skinned Black child who simply wants to be white because "color's" ugliness induces hysteria. The story of 1959 for Davis was the story of herself and her daughters full of race pride, that of Elizabeth Eckford as visible leader of the Little Rock 9 (whom Almena directly invoked as counter-image in her review of *Imitation of Life*), that of Black Pearl Bailey and white Louis Bellson and their newly adopted Black child; it was the story of Black "girls" knowing their beauty and value. And it was hysteria-inducing that the Black mood she experienced as an Angeleno, one that Hollywood executives clearly knew about but narratively denied, was so far removed from the screen's rendering—and worse that their screen, in the stilted *Imitation of Life*, seemed fit to undermine Black progress. *Imitation of Life* was offensive and "should be banned" because of its distance from the Black "now" of 1959. Before the phrase "black is beautiful" became Black power axiom, Davis intuited *Imitation of Life* as an assault not only on Black citizenship but an aesthetic assault on the *beauty* of blackness—"the fine brown frame." "*Imitation of Life* sets the concept of democracy not to mention race relations back 100 years, to the day when we were held in slavery out of some massive misconception, some propaganda, some theory that because their skins were darker, they were inferior and only of 'slave caliber'" (Lomax, "'Imitation of Life'"). In one of her many review/commentaries on *Imitation of Life* and before *Loving v. Virginia*, Davis insisted that white people were marrying Black people and that even young Sandra Dee was liable to fall for a Black man. Although *Imitation of Life* flirted with an interracial storyline, the narrative of happy, Black–white intermarriage was an emerging chapter of American interracial history that it decisively avoided: "There are innumerable white people whom the color line has not stopped from 'marrying Negro' . . . Sandra is young but she'd be surprised at how incidental it is if he is blue, green, yellow or a green-eyed monster if he's got 'that certain something'" (Lomax, "'Imitation of Life'"). Sex, she boldly suggested, here and elsewhere, was the great equalizer. And perhaps most importantly, Davis centered her critique of the film through the eye of the Black-girl spectator, whose spectatorship she saw not as exception or marginalia but as so axiomatic that she was ready to take down the movie—bodily—for violating it: "We feel [*Imitation of Life*] will cause a traumatic shock to every brown child who has ever smiled a shy smile of gratification in the mirror because she knew she looked nice . . . . I have six children, two or three of whom are as fair as 'Sarah Jane' or 'Peola'; my mother with blue-gray eyes and auburn hair made her living as a white woman because of the foolishness of white people in denying Negroes jobs as 'expert alterers' in women's dress shops—but she chose a brown-skinned man to wed and spent her Sundays in her home with her brown-skinned children" (Lomax, "'Imitation of Life'"). Based on her experience with her children and her mother, Almena alters the narrative of passing that *Imitation of Life* offers, suggesting that Black people don't pass to avoid other Black folks or because of a fear of "color" but rather because of the perverse boundaries imposed by white prejudice. Like Black woman critic Fay Jackson, who, on the release of the 1934 version of *Imitation of Life*, had identified the studio's pathological avoidance of the ascendant "militant mulatto" demanding overdue Black rights, Almena saw herself and her children in this off-white light (Jackson). What the racially motivated films of 1959 needed to show, according to Davis, was the pride and militancy of Black people, one that Davis knew and that the (white) nation would learn of soon with the ascendancy of Malcolm X and Black Power—but for Davis this was a militancy that was female and trenchantly witty. If Hollywood dared not to know this in 1959, it deserved, in Almena's opinion, to face not only pickets but also riots. However, Almena was one of the only Black critics to oppose the film, a fact that she explained by suggesting that other Black press critics had become press agents for Hollywood and sold the race down the river. Nevertheless, her many columns over the course of months lambasting *Imitation of Life* took the film as the center of a complex of civil rights failures of the 1950s and showcases how her film reviewing became the eye of a broader social problematic she was reading—the core of an ideological web much larger than the film itself—one that she aimed to bring down and which was central to addressing the nation's pressing "race" and civil rights problems.

Raising the Alarm

Almena Davis, through her incisive critique of American culture through film analysis, bridges the gap between the idealism of the war years and the trenchant politics of the Black 1960s; between the strident 1940s and the cynical, sophisticated, outspoken Black 1960s, between the reserved politesse of Lena Horne's onscreen image and James Baldwin's liquidly acerbic prose. Her embodied writing stands apart from the film text, spinning itself strangely outside of cinema's narrative power, flush with its own poetry, enmeshed spectatorial phenomenology, and her own fleshy substance.

In the same way that Baldwin's and Charles Blow's New York is the foil against which vision is possible, for Davis proximity to the Hollywood factory and its half-baked products became the prism that made seeing both Hollywood and *sick*, white America possible. She reveals a version of 1950s Black America as forged in struggle—not just a struggle to survive or overcome but a struggle to *see* clearly—a struggle with possessing vision itself in the midst of various trippy ideological ruptures endemic to the World War II, post-war, "civil rights" and soul eras—and indeed, to the whiteness of America itself. She said, remarkably, what she thought. In an era where even documentary newsreels at best showcased a Black subject imbued with a practiced varnish of gentility and humility as the preferred mode for white consumption and Black race pride, Almena, through writing, got down and dirty. Almena was an icon for an alternative version of the Black 1940s and 1950s, a version of these decades that repression hid. Even before King, she rankled at the humility that was the price of Black public respectability, choosing instead something less than respectability—but with an untrammeled voice. What King gave America was a performance designed to undo racist stereotypes about Black masculinity—and particularly Black criminality and unfitness for citizenship. What Almena gave was a raw, unvarnished truth of observation—and a resulting political militancy that she felt, embodied, and believed.

What does Almena teach us about the prospect of the flourishing of the American human? For Almena, it was impossible for the American to flourish as long as inequality compromised complete justice. Almena's radical sensibility about what constituted equality stretched from the courthouse to the movie screen. In the screen's curious symptoms, perhaps more than anywhere else, she read America's reality—and its fate. What Almena sought from Hollywood and America was recognition of the power, citizenship, and beauty of the "fine, brown frame," an unapologetically black and distinctively femme frame. This was a striving for not only Black equality, but for truly intersectional equality along lines of gender, class, and race—and a category that the respectability-minded had more trouble with but which was utterly determinative of American race relations: sexuality. While the American promise went unfulfilled for Almena and so many other Black Americans in her lifetime, what gave her life was the fire in her belly, the many-angled critique that strengthened her resolve and the writing that was her outlet in expressing that resolve. Through critique, she was able to forge a place in a country that denied Black people voice and equal opportunity for flourishing. And through that critique was she able to find—and to give—the Black power to do more than imitate life.

Works Cited

Baldwin, James. "On Being White . . . and Other Lies." *Essence*, April 1984.

Bogle, Donald. *Bright Boulevards, Bold Dreams: The Story of Black Hollywood*. One World Press, 2006.

Briggs, Cyril. "Wife Says Lomax Sired Almena Davis' Babies." *California Eagle*, 5 February 1948, p. 1.

Cook, Jane. "Who's a Lousy Lover?" *Afro-American*, 31 Juli 1948, p. A12.

Davis, Almena. "Channel-time." *Los Angeles Tribune*, 20 February 1959, p. 22.

Davis, Almena. "Newspapers Picket Movie House Showing Offensive Film." *Los Angeles Tribune*, 17 August 1942.

Davis, Almena. "The New Movies." *Los Angeles Tribune*, 8 June 1946, p. 19.

Davis, Almena. "The New Movies." *Los Angeles Tribune*, 3 August 1946, p. 18.

Davis, Almena. "The New Movies." *Los Angeles Tribune*, 7 September 1946, p. 18.

Davis, Almena. "The New Movies." *Los Angeles Tribune*, 10 December 1949, p. 11.

Dyer, Richard. *White*. Routledge, 2013.

hooks, bell. "The Oppositional Gaze." *Black Looks: Race and Representation*. South End Press, 1992, pp. 115–132.

Jackson, Fay M. "Fredi Washington Strikes New Note in Hollywood Film." *The Pittsburgh Courier*, 15 December 1934, p. A8.

Lamar, Lawrence F. "Almena Davis Named in Sensational Divorce Suit." *Atlanta Daily World*, 10 February 1948, p. 2

Lamar, Lawrence F. "Editor Named Co-respondent." *New York Amsterdam News*, 7 February 1948, p. 1.

Lomax, Almena. "Anti-Flies . . . and the Christian Science Monitor Dug Our Khrushchev Coverage." 16 October 1959, p. 11.

Lomax, Almena. "'Don't Imitate the Americans.' Khrushchev Will Doubtlessly Tell People." *Los Angeles Tribune*, 25 September 1959, p. 3.

Lomax, Almena. "For Adults Only: Being Some Reflections on the Pukka Sahib After seeing Raimu and *The Baker's Wife*." *Los Angeles Tribune*, 22 January 1949, p. 10.

Lomax, Almena "'Imitation of Life' Libel on the Negro Says Tribune Reviewer. Should be Banned in the Interest of National Unity, Picketed if Shown." *Los Angeles Tribune*, 30 January 1959, p. 20.

Lomax, Almena. "Notes for Showfolks." *Los Angeles Tribune*, 15 August 1958.

Lomax, Almena. "Notes for Showfolks." *Los Angeles Tribune*, 6 February 1959.

Lomax, Almena. "Notes on Ed Sullivan, Elvis Presley." *Los Angeles Tribune*, 9 January 1957, p. 17.

Lomax, Almena. "Some Afterthoughts on Why Imitation of Life is a Libel on the Negro Race." *Los Angeles Tribune*, 30 March 1959, p. 3.
Lomax, Almena. "'The Business of Sex' . . . Ed Murrow Program Shows How It's All Become A Part Of The 'Hard Sell.'" *Los Angeles Tribune*, 23 January 1959, p. 9.
Lomax, Almena. "The New Movies." *Los Angeles Tribune*, 2 April 1949, p. 11.
Lomax, Almena. "The New Movies." *Los Angeles Tribune*, 12 November 1949, p. 11.

6

Human Relationship as Human Value in Studio-Era Hollywood

Dana Polan

As a scholar within cinema studies, I define my work primarily as that of cultural history with an emphasis on studio-era Hollywood and its place in American life. So when I began to prepare to think about how our discipline might be impacted by a discourse of flourishing (and perhaps, in turn, influence it—not perhaps an improbable sentiment with regards to the study of a popular art that has been so consequential for so many citizens across our modernity), I turned to the film historical past only to discover that one movie of interest to me had sort of beaten me to the punch.

In the very first moments of the 1939 MGM B-movie, *Bridal Suite*, the successful capitalist father (Gene Lockhart) is berating his wastrel scion (Robert Young) for a life of dissolute irresponsibility (he has just once again missed his own wedding to a seeming rich woman because of a several-day alcoholic bender). The dad threatens to cut off his allowance and let him live on the pittances of family allotment his doting mother can provide. Responds the offspring, "But I don't want to just live, dad. I want to *flourish*" to which the father replies, "Marry that Bragdon girl if it can still be arranged. *Flourish* on her millions if she has any. You won't *flourish* on mine."

I had other reasons—ones I'll come back to—for returning to this film within the context of Hollywood's dramatizations of what might be the Good Life. But I hadn't seen it in a long time (way before joining the dialogue on human flourishing from which this chapter serves as one outcome) and predictably I hadn't remembered the details of this specific interchange of father and son. They now strike me as so germane, within the context of the collective project of investigation on film studies' pertinence to human flourishing, to the reflection I want to offer here. (For useful introduction to the human flourishing project, which spreads outwards from psychology to become a veritable philosophy of life and a call indeed to rethink guiding attitudes in

Dana Polan, *Human Relationship as Human Value in Studio-Era Hollywood* In: *Cinema, Media, and Human Flourishing*. Edited by: Timothy Corrigan, Oxford University Press. © Oxford University Press 2023.
DOI: 10.1093/oso/9780197624180.003.0007

disciplines across the sciences, humanities, and social sciences, see Pawelski; Pawelski and Tay.)

It matters, no doubt, that the two rich people of *Bridal Suite*—one not worried about the life of irresponsibility and one so adamantly against it—mean veritably the opposite of what is intended, as I understand it, by the human flourishing project. For father and son, even though they come at it from opposite systems of estimation, "flourishing" is a mark of idle richness, a luxuriating in the cultivation of pleasures of the moment that commits to nothing deeper. It is the province of the rich to have the money and time that could permit them to just follow whims in this way if they so choose (predictably, in so many films from Depression-era Hollywood it is the older capitalist, the father figure, who uses privilege wisely—to lead an unwasteful, productive life—while the offspring are dissolute). The sort of flourishing that *Bridal Suite* takes umbrage at is based on privilege and is all about doing nothing meaningful. This is something I want to return to later in this chapter and raise as a caution: while the human flourishing project admirably intends something very different, I sense from the outside that the very idea that some of us are abundant in things that offer us the potential to flourish can sometimes appear indeed as privilege, as province of an elite who are afforded margins of freedom not always available to others.

At the end of *Bridal Suite*, the young wastrel converts to a life of responsibility and meaningfulness—and doubly so. Falling in love, while away for a rest cure, with a hard-working innkeeper (Annabella) who inherited the venue when her father died (it is at this inn that the wastrel has come to hide out), the young man learns the value of true love (rather than superficial flirtation or marriage only for purposes of financial gain) and realizes a great deal of his respect for the innkeeper is based precisely on her pluck and fortitude in the world of work. He asks his dad for the lowliest job in the company and the film ends with the declaration that true love and hard work go hand-in-hand to define the good life.

Over the last years, I have regularly taught a course, varying between undergraduate and graduate levels, on "Hollywood 1939," centering on a year that many writers deem the highpoint of the studio system but where I am more concerned with the broad range of film productions, A and B (such as *Bridal* Suite) alike which, taken as a whole, hew to no one stylistic or ideological norm. There are many levels at which we could direct an inquiry as to well-being in the context of the studio system—its operations (film-making practices—for which I would include administrative practices) and its output (the films themselves). To inquire into the possibilities and potentials of human flourishing within the industrial process that is the making of mainstream movies could perhaps entail that we pinpoint where the human itself intervenes into that often machinic and technical activity. For instance, we could interrogate the production process itself to question where and when it can foster individual or collective well-being: we might examine when and how the labor of film-making fosters positive values (we could cite the virtue of artistic creativity, the pride in craft accomplishment, financial reward, and so on) or blocks it (as when the labor process is hampered by injustices from economic to racial [uneven access to the Hollywood labor pool] to sexual [as in recent issues around workplace harassment from the lowest to highest ranks of the Hollywood hierarchy]). Conversely, we could move from production to reception and wonder how and when the experience of film (its narratives, its stylistics) can entail inspiration and uplift (or, quite the contrary, block those): here, film studies has had recourse to a variety of models of response, from the psychoanalytic to cognitive psychology to objects-relation theory and so on (the positive psychology that underlies the investigation into human flourishing has perhaps had less hold in the field). I want to return to questions of reception—and of the possible effects and impacts of movie-watching—later in this chapter.

Yet while my course fully examines the production process especially to pinpoint philosophies of craft accomplishment among film-makers both above-the-line and below-the-line (and maybe hints also at reception through journalistic writings at time along with secondary studies of the response that comes in the form of things like fan mail), I also look centrally at the films themselves as another level in which the human intervenes (insofar as with rare exception Hollywood gives us stories of humans [and even when it deals with the non-human as in animal films, the latter are generally anthropomorphized to the emotions of people]).

Increasingly, I have come to feel that the narratives from studio-era Hollywood dramatize—put into performance—modes and models of humanness and human relationship in a manner that I would qualify as "bounded inventiveness." I'll return to the bounded side of this in a bit, but first I want to offer recognition—and even appreciation—of the inventiveness.

Hollywood, quite simply, tells many kinds of story. This inventiveness at the level of narrative *content* bears comparison to—and may well be complementary with—the important, recent argument about an inventiveness to Hollywood cinema, in this key period of its history, at the level of narrative *form*. In *Reinventing Hollywood: How 1940s Filmmakers Changed Movie Storytelling*, David Bordwell outlines the myriad devices by which filmmakers worked to add distinctiveness to their creations, often in friendly competition with each other. No doubt the very title of Bordwell's massive investigation inspired me in my own thoughts on Hollywood *inventiveness*: as I say, I take an approach that looks at the creativity of stylistic traits as complementary with one that examines, as I do, the stories told (and may describe them, as I do, as comparable to real-life happenings). For instance, just as Bordwell pointedly wants to challenge reflectionist arguments that take works of popular art to somehow embody the *zeitgeist* of a time, an interest in the diversity of the kinds of human stories Hollywood films offer up requires no assumption of deep cultural reflection. As with the competitive engagement with devices that Bordwell outlines, it could well be the case that there are proximate, directly industrial causes for story diversity: for instance, as we'll see in a moment with the case of 1930s screwball comedy, it is likely the case that the plethora of narrative possibilities that are worked out in the genre derive from the challenge to vary foundational formula (such as the narrative of remarriage that, famously, philosopher Stanley Cavell found in a number of instances of screwball).

In terms of diversity of narrative content, I'm struck, for instance, that even if *Bridal Suite* ends in encomium to an intertwining of love and work as the things that make us most worthy, it first stages the question of life's worth *as question precisely*—as something to be argued out, to be investigated, to be dramatized, to be narrativized. Like so many films of the time, it seems to be engaged in a working out of narrative possibility and of narrative options. And I'm struck also—and this relates to why I wanted originally for this project to return to *Bridal Suite*—how this film that ends so firmly on the side of monogamy can do so only at the very ending. Despite its title, *Bridal Suite* almost has *no* bridal suite in it (indeed, as noted, it begins with a missed wedding) and is only bit by bit about the steps that lead up to romance and then, in this case, culminate in marriage (in the very last moments of the film, the hero and heroine are discovered by his father in bed in his compartment on an ocean liner bringing him back home, and at first, the dad thinks the young ones have had illicit, irresponsible pre-marital sex only to then be apprised of their married status). "Bridal suite" indeed could work as a title for so many films of the studio system but perhaps ironically insofar as marriage often seems a mere afterthought, not really what deep and passionate commitment to another person necessarily has to be about. To take a fanciful example, no doubt *Gone with the Wind* is too big, too prestigious, a film to ever be imagined with another title, but just think what the title "Bridal Suite" would do for it: it would, for instance, add emphasis and further irony to Scarlett's unromantic and pecuniary approach to the institution of marriage where she plows through a series of eligible men, some already engaged to other Southern belles, and works to employ them to her own, self-aggrandizing needs. Above, I have suggested that Hollywood's inventiveness is a *bounded* one—and we would indeed need to recognize that the inventiveness I outline is not the same as an unbridled, anything-goes proliferation in which all narrative options are equally open: there certainly are the pressures of what we might term "dominant ideology" that mean that some options are more proffered and preferred than others. Yet a film like *Gone With the Wind* (and of course, there is in a way no other film like *Gone With the Wind*) may be an example of what I will later term limit-cases, cases at the fringe of boundedness, insofar as its reprobate heroine refuses normativity—refuses, in particular, to honor institution and rule and regularity. (Importantly, she is not unambiguously punished for this: yes, she's terribly sad that Rhett's walked out on her but she's resilient enough to see that "tomorrow's another day" and that further-adventures-of-Scarlett-O'Hara may well be in store.)

To return to the film that actually, officially, is titled *Bridal* Suite, it is significant that, as with so many Hollywood films from the studio era, marriage is desired throughout the film but, once achieved, brings narrative to a screeching halt. The dominant ideology is that marriage is forever but the reality for the world of storytelling is that it cuts off stories and breaks the flow that is Hollywood's dream logic. The famed writer Elmer Rice captured this in his strange 1930 novel, *Voyage to Purilia*, a blunt allegory which imagines another planet as if it corresponded to life as lived within the conventions of a Hollywood film (i.e., according to puerile codes, hence the name). Thus, on Purilia, all young women want is to marry but the minute they do so they disappear. Marriage is a goal and an ending (Rice).

In this respect, I'm less interested in the values that *Bridal Suite* comes to espouse in its last moments than that, in offering these as an answer to a question (what makes life meaningful), it first must set the situation up *as a question*. And this for me is much of the narrative inventiveness of Hollywood cinema: it stages possibilities, puts them into play, works through options, investigates alternatives, and so on. For instance, while *Bridal Suite* may finally, emphatically come down (but only in its very last moments) on the side of certain, specific values of monogamy and responsibility, values we might even term "ideological," other screwball comedies remain as resolutely on the side of irresponsibility. Think, for example, of 1938's *Bringing Up Baby* where the goal of a man and a woman is to have as much madcap fun as possible and eschew the world of work for as long as possible. Marriage is pointedly what isn't wanted (because it will inevitably be to the wrong person). At this film's very end, Susan and David affirm their love and the world collapses around them, leaving him clutching at her from scaffolding: no need even to allude to a "bridal suite" here as the madcap fun to be had has nothing to do with marriage—or sex even.

Pointedly, the couple in *Bringing Up Baby* sows a lot of destruction in their path through pleasure, and the two bring hurt to a lot of people, some of whom seem guilty only of stuffiness or even bland normality. Screwball comedies are often simultaneously affirmative of a world of fun but intolerant of anyone who doesn't get along with the program (which can often mean the mass of society)—and in this respect, as Adorno and Horkheimer (in the 1944 *Dialectic of Enlightenment*) argued of mass-produced odes to pleasure and fun, they are conformist and coercive even as they argue for freedom.

The ideology of exclusive and asocial romantic love can be so strong that it starts to set itself up as anti-social and independent of any future benefits (in a screwball comedy like *Bringing Up Baby*, you live only for the moment and improvise in relation to it to derive maximum madcapness from it). Living in the present and deriving from it as much pleasure as possible is considered to be living the good life.

It is significant in this respect that many genres of the studio system in Hollywood show couples for whom having children is not a consideration, neither in the present (they are childless) nor in the future. This goes along with that delaying or deferring of marriage that I noted before: marriage—and what conventionally comes from it—is only a late thought in such narratives and creates little legacy; in *Bringing Up* Baby, there is almost the implication that the destructive, energetic fun the couple has together, which often leads from escapade to escapade with a rare capturing of breath, is itself the substitute for, or sublimation of, sexual relationship.

Here, an extreme example of lack of concern for progeny and future generations that might benefit from the flourishing of the couple here and now, especially within the institutionally sanctioned bonds of matrimony, would be the 1939 adaptation of *Wuthering Heights*, which pointedly leaves out the next generation so central to the novel and concentrates on Heathcliff and Cathy turning their back (literally so in the last scene where she, dying, is carried by him to the window to look out on their beloved moors) on the world of the many (embodied here in polite but conventional British society). Like the screwball comedy, *Wuthering Heights* sublimates sexual encounter and turns it into something joyous and celebratory in other ways—most pointedly in a scene where Catherine returns from a party at the Lintons; she starts to admire her society dress in the mirror; then, seeming to feel guilt at this dress-up betrayal of her association, tears it off and runs in peasant outfit to meet Heathcliff in the moors where she passionately tells him to fill her arms with heather (the scene then culminating in a montage of the two wildly gathering stalks only to fall into an embrace as the scene fades out). No doubt, there is some of the discretion of the Hays Code at work here, but the strictures against sexual encounter almost seem beside the point: passion is an end in itself and not needing sexual release and certainly not requiring procreation as its purpose. (Later, when Cathy does marry Linton, a peasant girl offers her a stalk of heather as symbol of the union, and the irony is clear—and the critique of marriage is clear: for the euphoria Cathy experienced with Heathcliff and sacrificed for conventionality, she has gained nothing from marriage but a mockery of real relationship.)

At the end of *Wuthering* Heights, both Cathy and Heathcliff have died as material beings, but they live on as a ghostly couple and they are given virtual existence by a dreamy superimposition that inserts them over the landscape of the moors: they remain cinematically present. In other words, the film (as we see in the sterility of Cathy's marriage with Linton) may reject matrimony, but it is no less invested in celebrating the heterosexual couple as a special force, an energy that transcends physical limits (just as Susan and David at the end of *Bringing Up Baby* can float above the wreckage of a joyless world). Conversely, as James Baldwin reminds us, in an essay recommended by another contributor (Ellen Scott) to the film and media studies component of the human flourishing project, there is the rare film like the bitter *You Only Live Once* (1937) that no doubt *does*, like *Bridal Suite* or *Wuthering Heights*, acknowledge the power of the romantic couple and *does*, like *Bridal Suite* specifically, suggest, in the moment of the Depression, that having gainful employment is better for the couple's survival than not, *but* also then chronicles all the real conditions that, in the moment of the Depression, can make it difficult, if not possible, for the couple to survive (their entrance through the portals of heaven has little of the eternal glory of *Wuthering Heights*). As Baldwin suggests, the rareness of *You Only Live Once* within Hollywood production lies in its very bitterness and bleakness: buoyant optimism tends more to be the norm of studio cinema (in *Wuthering Heights* love can live on after death) and constitutes much of that boundedness that I alluded to earlier as setting general limits around the inventiveness of Hollywood narratives.

Strikingly, Baldwin finds that another film of Henry Fonda's also pushes at the boundedness of dominant ideology, *The Grapes of Wrath* (1940), and it is revealing that Baldwin finds in Fonda's performance a veritable identification with racialized minorities. Not merely does Fonda's character, Tom Joad, choose to strike out on his own at the film's end (no bridal suite here, no romantic couple) but he does so from a position of Left commitment in which isolation is in the service of greater commonality (an image of imagined and not yet achieved collectivity).

Again, this Leftism and this open-endedness to the protagonist's move into the future are rare. We might, I think, contrast the hard knocks that Fonda faces in *You Only Live Once* and *The Grapes of Wrath* to the political optimism on exhibit in another of his 1930s roles, namely *Young Mr. Lincoln*. Like Joad, Lincoln at the end of this 1939 film is seen going on up the road alone but it is the road of assured civic integration and reconciliation, and it matters that the subject here is the "young" Lincoln: we know the future, we know what's ahead on this road, and the film serves, as biopic, to illustrate accomplished history rather than to suggest that history remains to be made—or, as in the case of *The Grapes of Wrath*, to be fought over with the outcome still in question.

At the same time, we might contrast *The Grape of Wrath*'s Leftism—social conditions may force you to strike out on your own but you do so in hope of building collectivity at some point down the road—with the even more fully individualized dead-endedness of 1932's *I am a Fugitive from a Chain Gang* where isolation from society is in the service of no higher good and simply has to do with its protagonist (Paul Muni) finding no place within human relationship to thrive and having simply to keep on the run in a desperate attempt at survival. Like *You Only Live Once*, with its couple excluded from the social, *I am a Fugitive from a Chain Gang* offers a bleak depiction of a social order that simply refuses to offer sustenance and let certain social subjects find their way. In a rich discussion of the biopic in his *The Persistence of Hollywood*, Thomas Elsaesser astutely, and wonderfully, notes how the genre (especially at Warner Bros.) emerged from the gangster film (both forms are chronicles of a life) but as a means of reforming the earlier genre in the direction of uplift insofar as the life chronicled in the biopic is one of positive accomplishment, not lawless rise-and-inevitable fall. In this respect, it is worth noting that *I am a Fugitive from a Chain Gang* was adapted from a real-life autobiography. Like the biopic, the gangster film here makes an appeal to real history. But, *unlike the biopic*, it does so to portray a limit version of history—one that fails (or, to put it more immediately, and pointedly, one that fails *the individual*, whether as part of a hoped-for couple or not).

I am a Fugitive from a Chain Gang is, again, a limit case, a rare case that speaks critically from the edges of boundedness to the privileges that lie within. Within, the situation appears much more benign: Hollywood films here acknowledge isolation—in this case, they depict characters who live for or by themselves, eschewing larger bonds of human relationship *but* finding personal existence to suffer for that isolation in a manner that only a conversion to greater good can overcome. On the one hand, there is the hedonist who thinks only of his or her own pleasure (and turns other people into mere objects for pleasure): from 1938, an example would be gangster Rocky Sullivan (James Cagney) in *Angels with Dirty Faces*, who uses criminality to lead a high life of cheap thrills (or not so cheap as he likes the high life of clubs and well-dressed molls). On the other hand, there's the hermit-like cynic, often wounded by human relationship, who turns away from pleasures into self-lacerating isolation: the extreme would be Rick (Humphrey Bogart) in 1942's *Casablanca*.

To live solely for oneself, such Hollywood films suggest, is to live incompletely. One narrative solution allows the monadic hero to go it alone but *only insofar as isolation and separation from society becomes a way to help that society* (again, *The Grapes of Wrath* would stand as the rare, leftist example). Hence, the curious genre of the aforementioned historical biopic where a Great Man (and, much less often, a Great Woman) has so to commit himself to his cause that he often has no place for personal relationship (or has to fight it as when Emile Zola [Paul Muni, again] has to turn his back on his overly possessive wife in order to realize his greatness as freedom fighter) and becomes a monumental figure embalmed in visual tableaux that, like stations of the cross, set out to recreate iconic scenes from the great life. (If I term this genre "curious," it is because this sententious attempt at hagiography often sterilizes the films and deprives them of fun and seemingly typical romantic pleasures we associate with Hollywood. *The Story of Alexander Graham Bell* [1939], in which the ever-cheerful song-and-dance man Don Ameche is cast as the eponymous great man, is an exception. This is a buoyantly romantic comedy as much as a biopic: not for nothing does Alexander Graham Bell's wife Mabel [an etherealized Loretta Young] announce that she is pregnant by responding to Alex's claim that the telephone is his baby that he actually has two babies.)

Hence, too, the fascination in 1930s films with narratives of individualistic *sacrifice*: maternal melodramas like *Stella Dallas* (1937) but also narratives of sacrificial conversion like *Angels with Dirty Faces* itself, in which Rocky feigns cowardice at his execution so as to turn a gang of boys against the gangster life they had so wanted to emulate.

It matters that at the end of *Angels* that it is a bunch of kids who learn of Rocky's (feigned) cowardice and in the last gesture of the film climb a stairway bathed in light (as if religiously redemptive). The sacrifice of the individual serves to benefit the many but many-ness is here presented as generational: it is the mass of youth who will take inspiration and grow, but we don't see that future and the film ends simply on a note of hope and promise. In fact, beyond this vague sense that the children are our future (which I already noted is not shared by all films of the period; pointedly, the boys in *Angels* are not Rocky's own children and we see little of their actual parents), Hollywood films in the period have difficulty imagining collectivity (certainly, they shy away from doing so in class, rather than generational, terms), and especially as imagining it as something that can foster growth and flourishing. Indeed, a converse image of collectivity seems to inhere in 1930s Hollywood films especially: the fear that when people become a mass, they do so under the mark of collective hysteria, the crowd as mob. Take, for instance, Fritz Lang's first U.S. film *Fury* (1936), which suggests how easily everyday American citizens can turn into a lynch mob. It is worth remembering that *Fury* is another one of the films James Baldwin singled out as an exception to cheerful American exceptionalism (although he did find it a bit too Germanic).

If I have insisted so much in this chapter on limit cases beyond the normative, if somewhat diversified, bounds (and bonds) of mainstream Hollywood, and reiterated James Baldwin's recognition of such cases' simultaneous rarity and relevance, it is because of the caution about the risks of potential privilege that I alluded to at the outset to at least some versions of the concept of flourishing. It is not everyone who can afford to flourish, according to some very dominant versions of that concept—or who are afforded by the world they live in the ability to flourish. As Baldwin puts it, "The children of the despised and rejected are menaced from the moment they stir in the womb" (17).

I hadn't known the literature of positive psychology before the invitation to participate *Cinema, Media, and Human Flourishing* and, while I find the positivity that drives it inspiring (as a leftist, I am much enamored of Marxist Antonio Gramsci's suggestion that we need both "pessimism of the intellect" *and* "optimism of the will"; in other words, we can have a cold assessment of our world but not give up hope about working to better it), I do wonder if it doesn't risk downplaying so much that is negative in our world and that we should acknowledge even at risk of seeming pessimistic even though acknowledgement of the worst can be invocation of something potentially better. (A quotation from Theodor Adorno's 1951 *Minima Moralia*, his "account" of life damaged by the American experience of the 1930s and 1940s, nicely captures this necessary blend of pessimism of intellect and optimism of will: "That culture so far has failed is no justification for furthering its failure" [44]).

When, for example, Seligman and Csikszentmihalyi describe in "Positive Psychology: An Introduction" an America that as a "nation—wealthy, at peace, and stable—provides the world with a historical opportunity" and, because "stable, prosperous, and at peace," can turn "attention to creativity, virtue, and the highest qualities in life" (13), I persist in seeing a nation divided; caught in rancorous conflict; driven in very large part (and at the highest levels of governance all the way down to much of what we could call the grassroots) by racism, xenophobia, sexism, deliberate economic deprivations, carceration, immiseration, ecological ravage, and a generalized tone of sheer aggression and thuggishness. (We, of course, need to note that their essay came out in 2000 when much of the depredations of the new century would not have been as apparent.)

Likewise, where Seligman and Csikszentmihalyi inveigh (rightly in many ways) against a psychology that pathologizes but then speak of furthering the cause of the gifted, I worry that such furtherance might itself serve in some cases as a pathologizing of all those who are not deemed gifted: for example, as Baldwin trenchantly notes in his rich analysis of the 1967 film *Guess Who's Coming to Dinner?*, Sidney Poitier is deemed acceptable as a Black marriage mate to a White woman because he is deemed so exceptional (a Nobel Prize winning doctor who wants to help the third world). As Baldwin puts it, "if even the wonder doctor must undergo such trials [of acceptance by both the white parents and his own] in order to be able to touch his lady love, heaven help the high-school dropouts: so many of whom found themselves in Attica, for example, not impossibly for trying to be men" (78).

Similarly troubling are the perspectives on happiness developed and promulgated in the Axial age, as reported by historian Darrin McMahon in an article offered as background reading to participants in our human flourishing project. According to McMahon, the perspective of those offering "recommendations" and "prescriptions" for happiness during this time was that "many—indeed most—will not be up to this challenge." For the Buddha, in particular, McMahon claims, the view is that "Most people . . . live lives of ignorance, illusion, and craving for the ordinary things of this world. They could change this by seeking enlightenment, but, alas, they don't" (5). I worry, especially with that "alas," that we have here a potential blaming of the victim, a chastisement of those deemed not up to tasks that they were never given a chance to deal with. (Much inspired by Theodor Adorno's critique of a conformist world that immiserates everyday subjects at so many levels of experience, I would at the very least rewrite the Buddha's assessment that [in McMahon's words] "Most people . . . live lives of ignorance, illusion, and craving for the ordinary things of this world," as "Most people *are made to* live lives . . . .") Conversely, in a nation productively diversified by ethnicity, race, sexuality, class, lifestyle choices, and so on, and finding richness in that, we need to make sure that assertions like Seligman and Csikszentmihalyi's that " 'normal' people (with 'normal' admittedly, and perhaps usefully, in quotes) also need examples and advice to reach a richer and more fulfilling existence" (10) don't act as coercive normalizations of pointedly specific and socially exclusive modes of behavior.

In this respect, I'm much impressed by the ways my cinema studies colleagues invited to participate in *Cinema, Media, and Human Flourishing* responded to the call with respect and open curiosity *but also*, as other chapters in this book with bear out, with a hard-hitting realism. For instance, there's a recurrent question in a number of the chapters about the political valences of flourishing: internally, does it sometimes impose ideological restrictions on those deemed to offer signs of flourishing, externally is it the case that individual flourishing and independent flourishing in the specific domains of the arts (especially the popular art of cinema) requires, as key positive psychology texts like Seligman and Csikszentmihalyi's imply, a supposedly flourishing, stable society at large? Chapters such as Dudley Andrew's (who also centers, in his contribution, on the 1930s but also as a socially fraught, politically conflictual time) and, among others, Lucy Fischer's (which openly wonders if the arts don't often flourish in the worst—rather than best—of times), Patrice Petro's (which looks at intertwinements of immiseration and, to be sure, resilience in select film and television works), and Patty White's (which reminds us that dominant social arrangements often pointedly and disastrously work against any flourishing for non-normative social subjects) all raise fundamental questions about the idea of propitious social conditions for the flourishing of arts—stable times or conflicted times—and the ability of diverse populations to all be privileged enough to share in any such flourishing.

In my last paragraphs, I have moved to general reflection on culture that may seem to have left cinema behind. But considerations of film are never far from my mind. I take the cinema very seriously as a mode of culture and assume as a scholarly goal to think about the ways it adds to our lives. In particular, I am appreciative of the cinema's inventiveness across history but I am also working to be aware of the bounds or limits to that inventiveness alongside the ways that certain critical works both challenge the seeming inclusiveness within those bounds and require us to see that there's a world beyond cinema that is not as good as we need.

Yet, there's an admitted gap and an absence to my chapter, I must note—and both perhaps are inevitable. The gap comes, as I have just explained, in the last few paragraphs as I move from the specific discussion of narrative possibilities within studio-era cinema to broader, and generally downbeat, thoughts on the world we live in. I think these are horrible times, and I am not sure what it means to flourish in such times, and I am certain we should not characterize the times themselves as good and stable and propitious.

But I am wary of imputing any causality in this situation to film as creative art. We didn't get here because of the arts, and it is unclear to me just what social role—positive or negative—they ultimately play. Increasingly, I'm tempted—as this chapter has shown—to appreciate an inventiveness to Hollywood movie-making but I have no illusions about how consequential might be the inventive or reparative contributions such popular art can make to damaged life (to echo Adorno's phrase for our modernity).

The gap in my chapter comes then—again, perhaps necessarily—from my not explaining how, or even if, we can relate the specifics of film to cultural conditions. Ideological analysis (e.g., Horkheimer/Adorno on the culture industry) of course has an answer: films are in no small part causal of the mental enslavement of modern social subjects. My own interest in Hollywood inventiveness—which Adorno would likely call the pseudo-individualization that he imputed to works of popular culture that pretend to be new while giving us the same old manipulations—is in this respect probably closer to Murray Smith's notion, in Chapter 3, of art as enhancement, as space for creative play.

The absence in my chapter then is hinted at in its beginning: if we are to talk about not only what art is, what are its formal resources, its structures, and so on—but also what it *does*, we need a psychology, a theory of reception—whether social or individual. Ironically, the more I work on film history, the less sure I am what that psychology could be and how we could ever know its workability. I do imagine that the mechanistic psychology that is implicit in ideology critique (in which it is imagined that our only psychological nature is to be manipulated) is not adequate to the task.

What do we take away from the images that flit before us on movie screens? What did audiences at the time take away? We can judge some effects through the memory traces that films leave behind, but it can be a long way from memory to meaningfulness of any socially consequential sort. It is clear to me, though, that we can see—and catalog—the evidence on the screen: Hollywood's inventiveness, as well as the normativities that rein in that inventiveness are there objectively to be enumerated. And here, intriguingly another practice of reception may occur: namely, the one that happens in the classroom where, for all the professor's inability in his or her research to say just what movies have meant to the past, he or she can make them make meaning in the here-and-now of the classroom. The arts don't necessarily speak their meanings, and this gap or absence can beckon to professors of arts and culture in promising and productive ways.

Works Cited

Adorno, Theodor. *Minima Moralia: Reflections from Damaged Life*. 1951. Verso, 2006.

Horkheimer, Max, and Theodor Adorno. *Dialectic of Enlightenment*. 1944. Stanford University Press, 2007.

Baldwin, James. *The Devil Finds Work: Essays*. Delta, 1976.

Bordwell, David. *Reinventing Hollywood: How 1940s Filmmakers Changed Movie Storytelling*. University of Chicago Press, 2017.

Cavell, Stanley. *Pursuits of Happiness: The Hollywood Comedy of Remarriage*. Harvard University Press, 1984.

Elsaesser, Thomas. *The Persistence of Hollywood: From Cinephile Moments to Blockbuster Memories*. Routledge, 2012.

McMahon, Darren M. "From the Paleolithic to the Present: Three Revolutions in the Global History of Happiness." *Handbook of Well-being*, edited by E. Diener, S. Oishi, and L. Tay, DEF Publishers, 2018.

Pawelski, J. O. "Bringing Together the Humanities and the Science of Well-Being to Advance Human Flourishing." *Well-being and Higher Education: A Strategy for Change and the Realization of Education's Greater Purposes*, edited by D. Harward, American Association of Colleges and Universities, 2016, pp. 207–216.

Pawelski, J. O., and L. Tay. "Better Together: The Sciences and the Humanities in the Quest for Human Flourishing." *Handbook of Positive Psychology*, 3rd edition, edited by C. R. Snyder, S. J. Lopez, L. M. Edwards, & S. C. Marques, Oxford University Press, 2018, 108–124. 10.1093/oxfordhb/9780199396511.013.67.

Rice, Elmer. *A Voyage to Purilia*. Cosmopolitan Book Corporation, 1930.

Seligman, Martin E. P., and Mihalyi Csikszentmihalyi. "Positive Psychology: An Introduction." *American Psychology*, vol. 55, no. 1, January 2000, pp. 5–14.

7
Sentimental Miseducation
Women Directors Coming of Age

Patricia White

Contributors to *Cinema, Media, and Human Flourishing* were prompted to address questions such as In what ways do the arts and humanities support flourishing? Do they contribute to well-being in any unique ways in which other endeavors do not? Do some forms of engagement in the arts and humanities support human flourishing more effectively than others? I felt unable to address these questions in the way they were posted. The discipline of positive psychology—and the "eudaimonic turn" toward the study of flourishing, happiness, or well-being—are far from my focus of research in cinema studies, and my training in feminist, queer, and anti-racist critique made me reluctant to approach human flourishing as a universal or abstract concept. Writing on female coming-of-age films that did not line up easily with prescriptive narratives of human flourishing, I also resisted the way the films' reception plotted the contributions of their female makers on a normative developmental path to "success." Yet my interest in these films and in the emergence of a diverse cohort of feminist American independent filmmakers is certainly motived by a conviction that cinema and the humanities enhance public life in troubled times. The critique of the positive—whether of normativity or of a demand for "positive images" that doesn't also entail structural change—has a place in theories of well-being, and vice versa. In this chapter I look at several recent films and filmmakers to reconsider narratives of female flourishing through the lens of queer feminist theory.

In *The Promise of Happiness*, Sara Ahmed interrogates how "happiness is used to describe social norms as social goods" (2). While some humans flourish under existing social structures, many others languish. Ahmed's book critiques positive psychology for perpetuating these exclusions, calling herself a feminist killjoy, unafraid to "expose the bad feelings that get hidden, displaced, or negated under public signs of joy" (65). The figure of the

Patricia White, *Sentimental Miseducation* In: *Cinema, Media, and Human Flourishing.* Edited by: Timothy Corrigan, Oxford University Press. © Oxford University Press 2023. DOI: 10.1093/oso/9780197624180.003.0008 feminist killjoy challenges "the assumption that happiness follows relative proximity to a social ideal" (53) by calling attention to the coercion involved on the turn to and steps on the "path" to happiness. The killjoy, among several figures Ahmed invokes—the unhappy queer, the melancholic migrant—doesn't reject well-being so much as recognize and value experiences that question its social role.

Other queer feminist theoretical concepts challenge eudaimonia as a value: feeling backward (Heather Love), cruel optimism (Lauren Berlant), failure (Jack Halberstam, *The Queer Art of Failure*), and even depression (Ann Cvetkovich). These writers explore the way affect both binds subjects to and offers a way of living through tough times. For such thinkers "ugly feelings" (Ngai) aren't something to be wished away, they are the marks social divisions make on our subjectivities and experiences, and they enable our recognition of historical and structural injustice. As Jack Halberstam puts it, "the negative thinker can use the experience of failure to confront the gross inequalities of everyday life in the United States" (*The Queer Art of Failure* 3). For example, Ellen Scott's chapter in this volume shows how a practice of film criticism that denounces racism can mitigate the damage of Hollywood's legacy of distortion and erasure for Black viewers.

To be clear, none of the thinkers I cite subscribes to what has been shorthanded as the "anti-social thesis" in queer theory, with its all-out embrace of negativity and the death drive (Caserio et al.). Exemplary of that work, Lee Edelman's brilliant reading of Alfred Hitchcock's *The Birds* (1961) links cinema's power to anti- and post-humanist critique; the birds' mysterious attack on children shatters normative society's optimistic belief in "reproductive futurism" (4). In contrast, the feminist philosophers and literary critics I mention are generally in sympathy with Eve Kosofsky Sedgwick's proposition that reparative reading strategies are needed alongside more entrenched "paranoid" ones that privilege the "hermeneutics of suspicion" ("Paranoid Reading" 123–151). Sedgwick takes seriously questions like "how to bring your kids up gay" in a homophobic world ("How To Bring Your Kids Up Gay"). Concepts of liberal selfhood and the dream of the "good life" too often distribute populations into the worthy and the shunned. Those excluded from ideals of self-realizing possessive individualism—women, queers, youth, people of color, people with disabilities, and others—are nevertheless tightly bound to those ideals through cultural values like the happily ever after promulgated in mainstream movies. "A relation of cruel optimism exists when something you desire is actually an obstacle to your flourishing," Berlant begins her influential book of that title (1).

Undeniably, creativity and critique—engagement with the arts and humanities—are necessary to help us imagine the world otherwise. I focus on independent women filmmakers, especially women of color and queer women, who address viewers and experiences historically neglected by Hollywood cinema. *Lady Bird* (Greta Gerwig, 2017), *Pariah* (Dee Rees, 2014), and *The Miseducation of Cameron Post* (Desirée Akhavan, 2018), for example, challenge normative life narratives, dwelling on obstacles to female flourishing even as they inspire hope. Unequal access to the means of cultural production shapes the form, content, and reception of these films. With limited means, infrequent opportunities, and a restricted legacy, women filmmakers often make work that draws on their own experience. Accordingly, critical expectations of women's work tend to frame filmmakers' achievements in biographical terms, emphasizing identity over artistry. As increased attention to gender inequity in the entertainment industry has forced open the doors to more young women filmmakers, a wave of female-coming-of age films has emerged. Yet, the films' general reception has tended to gloss over their protagonists' deviance and the obstacles to their flourishing and plotted the contributions of their female makers on a clear developmental path toward artistic maturity. My readings look more carefully at the feminist and queer challenge to normative ideas of flourishing that these films pose.

In a memorable scene of mother–daughter squabbling in *Lady Bird*, the high school heroine (Saorsie Ronan) is chastised for lacking a work ethic: "You should just go to City College—and then to jail, and then back to City College—," Lady Bird's mom (Laurie Metcalf) begins to scold. Her daughter responds by abruptly opening the passenger door and exiting the moving car. Lady Bird feels stuck in Sacramento, with an education that is parochial in both senses of the word. Despite what her mom sees as a lack of initiative and the economic strains on the family, Lady Bird is plucky and resourceful, privileged with white skin and blonde hair, a feminist update of the All-American girl (see Figure 7.1). In contrast, the young queer heroines of my other film examples have taken an early wrong turn on the straight path to happiness; the very titles of *Pariah* (2014) and *The Miseducation of Cameron Post* (2018) show a kinship with queer concepts of negativity. Directors Dee Rees and Desirée Akhavan dramatize the costs of familial and societal homophobia and racism, putting their protagonists and their viewers through harrowing emotions while envisioning horizons of change.

Figure 7.1 Saoirse Ronan and director Greta Gerwig shooting *Lady Bird* (2017). A24.

Oppositionality and defeat are acknowledged as part of all three films' ability to access joy and affirmation. Their protagonists are precocious killjoys; their struggles and strategies in some measure echo those of female creators pursuing their craft.

The disparity in the numbers of male and female directors employed in the mainstream film industry remains discouraging—only seventeen percent of 2021's 250 top-grossing films were directed by women, up from nine percent in 1998, when Martha Lauzen began tracking the numbers. As my work and that of many others has documented, women filmmakers have found a foothold working outside of Hollywood in independent features, international art cinema, premium television, documentary production, web series, and other online content (White, "Coming Out in the Middle"; Perkins and Schreiber). While this work encompasses multiple genres, there is a striking emphasis on coming-of-age films. *Lady Bird*, *Pariah*, and *The Miseducation of Cameron Post* are part of a wider corpus of independent feature films by women directors on female adolescence and young adulthood, including *American Honey* (Andrea Arnold, 2016), *Appropriate Behavior* (Desirée Akhavan, 2014), *Booksmart* (Olivia Wilde, 2019), *Diary of a Teenage Girl* (Marielle Heller, 2015), *The Fits* (Anna Rose Holmer, 2015), *It Felt Like Love*

(Eliza Hittman, 2013), *Infinitely Polar Bear* (Maya Forbes, 2014), *Madeline's Madeline* (Josephine Decker, 2018), *Mississippi Damned* (Tina Mabry, 2009), *Never Rarely Sometimes Always* (Eliza Hittman, 2019), *Night Comes On* (Jordana Spiro, 2018), *The Tale* (Jennifer Fox, 2018), *Tiny Furniture* (Lena Dunham, 2010), and *White Girl* (Elizabeth Wood, 2016). Among these, more than half are inspired by the director's or writer's own life, nearly all are dramas, and most are by directors under forty years of age.

The wave has its precedents in such 1990s landmarks as *All Over Me* (Alex Sichel, 1997), *But I'm a Cheerleader* (Jamie Babbit, 1999), *Gas Food Lodging* (Allison Anders, 1992), *Incredibly True Adventures of Two Girls in Love* (Maria Maggenti, 1998), and *The Slums of Beverly Hills* (Tamara Jenkins, 1998). Like those earlier works, the preponderance of films in the recent cycle are debut or sophomore features. New opportunities for women directors owe much to shifts in independent film culture since the 1990s, including the successful cycle of films known as New Queer Cinema, which featured key women producers like Christine Vachon and Andrea Sperling. While the filmmakers vary in background, most came of age during third-wave feminism, and many are film-school trained. While the majority are straight, white, and cis-gendered, queer and non-white directors are among the most successful. This partial list includes only indie films produced in the United States, but there are many films from elsewhere that fit these categories (for a narrative of global women filmmakers' emergence in the twenty-first century, see White, *Women's Cinema, World Cinema*). Since 2017, the #MeToo movement, catalyzed by revelations of movie mogul Harvey Weinstein's pattern of egregious sexual misconduct, has extended an urgent invitation to women tell their own stories, share their rage, and bring their perspectives to the screen. The woman arthouse auteur has a newly powerful, if still precarious, position.[1]

[1] Campaigns for gender and racial equity in filmmaking underway since the 1970s have gained momentum with recent initiatives around the globe and protests at international film festivals. The Swedish Film Institute under Anna Serner achieved a target of fifty percent funding of women's projects in 2014, and similar policies were soon adopted in Australia, the UK, and Canada. In the United States, which lacks meaningful government support for filmmaking that could be shaped by policy, Martha M. Lauzen's yearly studies of top-grossing films have shown the percentage of women directors increasing by only eight percentage points since 1998. Looking more closely at independent screens, Stacy L. Smith at USC Annenberg conducted a study with Sundance Institute and Women and Film Los Angeles that showed that women faced significant obstacles showing their work at festivals and sustaining their careers (Sundance Institute and Women in Film Los Angeles Women Filmmakers Initiative). Smith went on to lead the Annenberg Inclusion Initiative, which tracks statistics on race and gender employment and depictions across platforms and budgets (Smith et al.). The 2014 #OscarsSoWhite social media campaign pushed the Academy of Motion Picture Arts and Sciences to diversify its voting membership; after the addition of several thousand members,

Although I would classify many of the films I have cited as feminist, they are rarely stories of collective struggle, assaults on dominant codes of representing women's bodies, or explicit engagements with feminist theory, politics, and culture. Indeed, they are often resolutely focused on the individual. This preponderance of coming-of-age tales can be frustrating—by definition, such stories eschew political and collective frameworks. Besides, shouldn't women's cinema have come of age decades ago? At the same time, the cycle makes room for, even demands, new narratives—the stories of queer and gender-nonconforming people, women of color, and immigrant women. Such films speak to the feminist tenet that the "personal is political," while departing from postfeminist scripts of "having it all" to probe the contradictions of gender and agency in neoliberal times.

As I have suggested, these films speak to the way the role of the woman director in Indiewood is itself structured around a coming-of-age narrative. The impressive rise of independent film during the 1990s, the era of mini-majors like Weinstein's Miramax, banked on the reputation of maverick male directors. While women filmmakers of the era like Allison Anders were sometimes put forward to balance the attention accorded male visionaries (she was one of the filmmakers invited to make the 1995 omnibus film *Four Rooms*, for example), they were too rarely accorded their own vision. Industry assumptions that women are more suited to certain genres than others—romance, domestic drama, films about children and youth—remain pervasive, although films from Ida Lupino's *The Hitchhiker* (1953) to Kathryn Bigelow's entire oeuvre soundly rebut this assumption. In today's framework of indie authenticity and outrage over the low numbers of women directors in the mainstream industry, the woman director is called to *tell her own story*. Her debut feature is naturalized as a rite of passage rather than an aesthetic statement in its own right. Identified with coming of age as a filmmaker, debut works don't qualify the director as an auteur, which requires a complete oeuvre for the critic to decipher. The assumption that women only write themselves (carried over from biases in fiction writing) may actually contribute to the stark difference in female and male directors' time to realizing a second feature—what more does she have to tell? Plenty, of course, is my contention, and some of this talking back is conveyed in the very ways debut features respond to the autobiographical imperative.

membership was thirty-two percent female and sixteen percent people of color in 2019. #MeTwo has catalyzed celebrity-led initiatives for equity like #TimesUp and #5050by2020.

The films I have named explore the quotidian, the uncertain, and the marginal, a female self at odds with social expectations. Appropriate to the times, nearly all of them depict their heroines seeking to flourish in proximity to precarity and trauma. *American Honey*'s rootless protagonist is on a cross-country ramble with no destination. *Diary of a Teenage Girl*, *It Felt Like Love*, and *The Tale* relate bad choices around teenage sex. In these films of sentimental miseducation, the protagonists resist being drawn-out—the etymology of education—along a well-trod female developmental path; they take a wrong turn or never leave home. This refusal is a generic response to neoliberal times and its emphasis on female capacity (which, Sarah Banet-Weiser argues, has been incorporated into a popular performance of feminism). The films engage the desire and discontent that roil traditional women's genres like romance and melodrama while offering no easy outcomes.

Lady Bird, Greta Gerwig's loosely autobiographical directorial debut about the senior year of an odd duck California teen, is both the most successful and the most feelgood of the three narratives I'm taking up in this chapter. Gerwig was already known as an indie star, lauded for her writing and acting in a range of films, including several directed by her partner Noah Baumbach. This, her first solo outing, earned her a best director Oscar nomination, only the fourth in history to go to a woman. The film's pitch-perfect account of (pre-Instagram) aspirational teen female selfhood (white, cis, straight, middle-class, smallish town) both emulates and diverges from the senior-spring teen comedy genre (paving the way for 2019's *Booksmart* by Olivia Wilde). Gerwig describes her film as a mother/daughter romance and a love letter to her hometown of Sacramento. Lady Bird—it's her given name, as in, a name she has given to herself—yearns to leave Sacramento, where she butts heads with her equally stubborn mom. She makes some stupid choices—loses her virginity with the wrong guy, betrays her best friend (Beanie Feldstein)—but attempts to repair them, ditching the prom for her friend and symbolically reconciling with her mom.

Channeling Adrienne Rich's claim that "the cathexis between mother and daughter—essential, distorted, misused—is the great unwritten story," Gerwig plots her rom com moments around this central pair (226). The film ends with Lady Bird going away to college in New York, seemingly the self-actualizing postfeminist heroine. Except instead of situating her in ivy-covered halls, the film shows her in the hospital, where she lands after binge-drinking at one of her first parties. The ending is in keeping with the mumblecore genre where Gerwig first emerged. A representation of (at least temporary, temporalizing) failure is a shift away from narrative closure that also leaves an opening for the director's own story to be written differently. Gerwig may be acclaimed for telling her own story more than for her craft, a typical construction of female authorship. But a crucial part of that story is the emergence of the author, the very conditions of authorship, in the telling.

While Lady Bird is not depicted as an aspiring writer, she "wants to go where writers are"; and her college entrance essay is singled out for praise by her teacher Sister Sarah Joan (Lois Smith) for vividly conveying her love for Sacramento. The film ends as Lady Bird, now content to be called by her given name, Christine, leaves a conciliatory voice message for her mom. As she speaks of the pleasure of driving around Sacramento, images of her hometown taken from the car window flow by, as if the content of that admissions essay has been rendered by the filmmaker that Gerwig became. Like a "diary of a teenage girl," this scene insists on a public space in independent cinema for a private female voice, redefining the markers of the good life insofar as it is her distance from the town that underwrites her future, her missteps that characterize her path.

With its spunky heroine, primary female friendship, maternal rule, and girls' school setting, *Lady Bird* resonates with the nineteenth-century tradition of sentimental fiction. Nina Baym details in her classic study *Woman's Fiction* the hundreds of mid-century American novels (written by what Hawthorne famously called the "damned mob of scribbling women") that formulaically trace the story of an unfortunate young woman who finds her own way in the wide, wide world. It's fitting, then, that Gerwig's follow-up to *Lady Bird* was her adaptation of Louisa May Alcott's *Little Women*, that quintessential text of nineteenth-century white American female self-reliance and a precursor to the young adult (YA) genre. The 1994 version of the classic, directed by Gillian Armstrong and produced by Robin Swicord and Denise Di Novi, already brought forward the text's feminism, with Jo's coming into writing (and writing what she knows best) as a narrative climax honored over the marriage plot (which nevertheless prevails, in contrast to Armstrong's own 1976 debut film, *My Brilliant Career*, which remains true to its historical subject's marriage refusal). In killjoy fashion, Gerwig's adaptation crosscuts the sisters' diminished fates as young women (*Good Wives* is the title of Alcott's second volume) with the promise of their childhood. Yet in its final scene, *Little Women* includes a vision of anti-racist feminist flourishing conditioned upon female economic independence; Jo sets up a progressive school in the large home she has inherited from her aunt. The American individualist narrative of white female achievement is offset by a collectivist politics of production, an example of the kind of "creative community" that Dudley Andrew in Chapter 4 argues is central to cinema.

In contrast, the queer youth of *Pariah* and *The Miseducation of Cameron* encounter trauma for their challenges to normative choices: in the former, Alike (Adepero Oduye) is cast out by her mother, and in the latter, the orphan Cameron (Chloë Grace Moretz) is sent to a gay conversion camp. *Pariah*, Dee Rees's semi-autobiographical debut feature, wields its very title as a powerful badge of stigma. But from the film's first scene set in a raucous African American lesbian bar, the film's teenage protagonist, Alike, is depicted in community, even as she needs to find her own way. As I have detailed in an essay on the film, *Pariah* makes an appeal to the indie marketplace through classic coming-of-age beats, but it also opens a new space through the rich lifeworld it creates for its protagonist and viewers.

As Jack Halberstam argues in *In a Queer Time and Space*, queerness develops, "at least in part, in opposition to the institutions of family, heterosexuality, and reproduction . . . [and] according to other logics of location, movement, and identification" (1). Alike faces the cruelties of the promise of happiness in her heartbreaking conflict with her Christian mom and the betrayals of friends and lovers. Like *Ladybird*, *Pariah* concludes with its protagonist poised to start college across the country. In this ending, the

Figure 7.2 Adepero Aduye in *Pariah* (2014). Focus Features.

integration of self through maturation as a writer, only implied in Gerwig's semi-autobiographical screenplay, is explicit. While Alike's poem of metamorphosis resolves the narrative on the soundtrack—"I am free!" her voice-over concludes the film—the final image does not offer closure. Lingering in a queer time and space, Alike is again alone on a bus, waiting to leave Brooklyn (see Figure 7.2). *Pariah* gestures to stories and subjects still on the horizon, refusing to represent what Ahmed calls the "happy objects" of normative life narratives.

The Miseducation of Cameron Post (2018), a Sundance film festival grand jury prize winner, is a modest tale of a teenager's time spent at a Christian conversion center for youth suffering from SSA, or "same sex attractions." The film's title explicitly thematizes the function of education, which, Ahmed points out, is described by Plato as "the art of orientation" (54); Cameron is turning the wrong way. Another coming-of-age-on-fragile-ground story, the film is independent filmmaker (and web and TV producer) Desirée Akhavan's sophomore effort. Her first, the autobiographical *Appropriate Behavior*, in which she stars, skewers her identities as an Iranian American, bisexual liberal arts college graduate and an aspiring member of the Brooklyn creative class, alluding to wayward femininity in its title. *Miseducation's* script, co-written by Akhavan and her writing and producing partner Cecilia Frugiuele, is adapted from Emily Danforth's 2012 autobiographical young adult novel of the same title.

The film features an appealing and diverse cast of young actors and a soundtrack of 1990s tunes. The setting in the early 1990s fuels the film's DIY-John-Hughes-meets-New-Queer-Cinema vibe (recalling Jamie Babbitt's similarly themed 1999 comedy *But I'm A Cheerleader*). It is also important because the clock of social acceptance of LGBTQ rights, and awareness of issues facing trans youth, has accelerated remarkably over the past three decades. The blatant homophobia of ex-gay programs would seem to be tied to a past, albeit recent, where gay shame and shaming reside.

Except Cameron is not ashamed. And the film is no progress narrative. In his *New York Times* review, A. O. Scott praises *Miseducation* as, "Neither a glib send-up of a less enlightened era nor a pious reckoning with the bygone injustices of the past." Indeed, the film's reception context during Trump's presidency is defined as much by free-speech protections for conversation therapy and anti-trans "bathroom bills" (Johnson) as by a record number of trans characters on TV (twenty-six in 2018, according to GLAAD). With its low budget, *Miseducation* does not aim to be especially convincing in its period detail. (It also lacks the book's geographical specificity; while the novel is set in Montana, the film was shot in a generic upstate New York summer camp). The myth that things are good now and "getting better," as well as the idea that gay youth have historically lacked emotional resources, are set aside in a skewering of misguided adults who impose belief structures on kids who basically know who they are and what they want.[2] Cam and her friends feel like freaks and misfits because they are teens; being queer just gives the rebels a cause.

The novel's first-person narration clearly aligns the reader with its sensible, sporty, somewhat shy twelve-year-old protagonist who recognizes her attraction to girls early, nurtures it in rentals of *Personal Best* (1982) and *The Hunger* (1983) at the local video store, and conveys her story and surroundings without anguish or rage. She may not have the exuberant confidence of Molly Bolt, the picaresque protagonist of Rita Mae Brown's break-through lesbian novel *Rubyfruit Jungle* (written in 1973 and still not adapted for the screen). But the protagonist of *The Miseducation of Cameron Post*, and its YA readership, represent the "ordinary" youth who have been so central to turning the tides of public opinion around sexual and gender identity in the twenty-first century. Akhavan's film significantly condenses Danforth's novel, opening at a school dance long after the death of the protagonist's parents. Cam is caught making out in the back seat of a car with her best friend and prom queen crush, summarily packed up and sent to God's Promise. As portrayed by the soulfully wholesome Moretz in a sweatshirt and bad 1990s haircut, Cameron is grounded and observant, if not quite butch. She dutifully attends Bible study and group therapy but remains taciturn with her born-again aunt and the staff of God's Promise. She muddles through, like most teens, and even the pot-farming, disaffected crew she falls in with at God's Promise, hippie-child Jane Fonda (Sasha Lane) and two-spirit Adam Red Eagle (Forrest Goodluck) are more grounded than the adults.

Gay conversion therapy is an extreme form of the turn toward "happy objects" entailed by the promise of happiness. In Ahmed's account: "happiness involves a way of being aligned with others, of facing the right way," toward consensus models of the social good (45). In Reparative Therapy, trademarked by Joseph Nicolosi, Sr., spiritual and emotional incentives are used to turn queer subjects to the straight and narrow. The damage inflicted

[2] The It Gets Better Project was started in 2010 by activist and journalist Dan Savage and his partner Terry Miller as a social media suicide prevention campaign for LGBTQ youth and now includes more than sixty thousand online video testimonials.

by "conversion" and "reparative" therapies is dramatically portrayed in *The Miseducation of Cameron Post*'s most shattering scene. Mark (Owen Campbell), whose enthusiastic embrace of the recovery model is scaled to the depth of shame inflicted by his father, attempts to castrate himself. Queer theory uses the term *reparative* to different ends, as a kind of psychic harm reduction in a homophobic world. Against the grim reality and oedipal law of God's Promise, the story converts its very setting to its own reparative purposes. Cam bonds with the other residents, implying that it may well be therapeutic to bring a bunch of queer teens together in a communal living context, if not in the way Rick and Lydia, the brother–sister pair who run God's Promise, intend. Like Ahmed's killjoys, Cam and her friends have become the problem to show where the problem truly lies: with an idea of happiness that violently suppresses their flourishing.

Writing in *The Atlantic*, David Sims astutely notes the film's challenge to narratological norms: "Cameron's hero's journey is that she doesn't need to change." Instead, she "wastes a formative chunk of her youth stuck in a place that's actively trying to transform her." The hero's journey, the narrative model of best-selling screenplay manuals and blockbuster films, is predicated on an autonomous, implicitly male individual who ventures forth to meet his challenges, is aided in his quest, and returns to claim his inheritance and live happily ever after. Some even believe these narrative expectations are hard-wired. The humanist take on this narrative norm would be that the hero could just as well be female, or otherwise other. Queer theory finds this humanist ideal cruelly optimistic. Teresa de Lauretis's "Desire in Narrative" is a magisterial account of how woman is cast not as subject but as narrative goal or landscape to be traversed in the hero's quest; hence the difficulties in resolving a female coming-of-age narrative (1984). *The Miseducation of Cameron Post* offers a narrative interlude instead, a miseducation or undoing, the release rather than the conversion of energy toward a socially sanctioned object, which is arguably an important function of young adult literature.

At the end of the film, Cam and her two friends—not coincidentally, both kids of color, whose astute casting is part of the film's impact—put on their hiking boots and walk right off the property.[3] The film's last shot, frozen in the film's publicity image, is a long take of the trio in the back of a pick-up

[3] Sasha Lane, who plays Jane Fonda, a child of hippies who has a prosthetic leg in which she hides the marijuana stash, debuted in Andrea Arnold's *American Honey* (2016) and came out as gay in the press notes of *The Miseducation of Cameron Post*. Forrest Goodluck, who plays Adam Red Eagle, debuted as the son in *The Revenant* (2015) and is an important role model for Native American youth.

truck, no destination in sight. The trio are traveling toward something else, a Deleuzean line of flight. At one point a biker comes up along the truck and the girls goad Adam on in flirting with him, finding a new promise in the space of the open road. For these kids there *is* no place like home. The film's last shot references the ending of *The Graduate* (1967), in which the hero and his runaway-bride love object breathlessly catch a bus. In that film, the final shot of the seated heterosexual couple is held until the question "what now?" sinks in. It is a reference Akhavan is fond of: her first feature concludes with the hapless heroine on the subway hurtling toward who knows what. This trope of holding on a heroine who's made a choice, without indicating her fate, is shared with *Pariah* and several other women directors' coming-of-age films.[4] In a real-world scenario, the runaway LGBTQ youth of *The Miseducation of Cameron Post* could be heading to the metropolis only to find themselves on the streets. Here, the communitarian aspect is key to their journey and to our enjoyment of it: shame has been repurposed as friendship and world-making. In the last shot of the film, the trio "cruise utopia" (see Figure 7.3) (Muñoz).

In the context of the autobiographical novel upon which the film is based, Cam too may be destined to become an author. Although Emily Danforth's Montana youth did not include conversion camp, she turned the conflict between queerness and her Christian upbringing into a novel that resonated with young readers. The film's address to a youth audience familiar with the book expands its Sundance-branded niche, mobilizing the affect of the YA genre. Digital circulation of independent films and discourse around them likewise delivers many of the films I have discussed to young audiences (including potential filmmakers). Seen in this way, the coming-of-age narrative can be understood as prophylactic rather than normative—the autobiographical protagonists refuse to be properly educated, their narratives refuse closure, and the films' audiences are rerouted. The work of these women filmmakers, like the depiction of quotidian trauma that can be found in

[4] In addition to *Pariah*'s last shot of Alike on the bus, *Never Rarely Sometimes Always* ends with its heroine on the bus back to rural PA after obtaining an abortion across state lines; she finally closes her eyes in rest. Maryam Keshawarz's *Circumstance*, which premiered at the same Sundance edition that launched *Pariah*, leaves its heroine in a cab to the airport, escaping Tehran where she has lost her female lover and her parents' confidence (White, "Changing Circumstances"). *Ava* (Sadaf Foughi, 2018) and *Angels Wear White* (Vivian Qu, 2017) end on freeze frames and tracking shots of their heroines, respectively. The first defies the strictures of Iranian girlhood, the second the vulnerability of a young migrant worker in China. In addition to *The Graduate*, the overdetermined reference is the tracking shot ending in a freeze frame of rebel adolescent Antoine Doinel in François Truffaut's *The 400 Blows* (1959).

Figure 7.3 Forrest Goodluck, Sasha Lane, and Chloe Moretz in *The Miseducation of Cameron Post* (2018). FilmRise.

YA fiction, is a complex response to the injunction to positive images, positive messages characteristic of our current moment's (shockingly belated) attention to diversity and inclusion. In *The Miseducation of Cameron Post*, the adults who think they are promoting flourishing are doing the opposite, while the youth find reparation among themselves. Queer feminist theory attunes us to such projects, as these filmmakers return to the moment of emergence, before the turning points that restrict options for different kinds of flourishing.

Like their protagonists, these films are far from perfect. The "promise of happiness" for independent filmmakers is bound up with the marketplace, and these films make concessions to box office considerations in plotting, casting, and promotion. I think of my work on these texts as reparative—partial, contingent, affirming readings that continue the projects of films that may be limited in budget, execution, experimental vision, or cultural reach. The films associate similar drawbacks with the interstitial state of adolescence, the act of authoring with the act of becoming.[5]

[5] In "Lesbian Minor Cinema," I critique the lesbian coming-of-age feature film for closing down the potential of the minor. Here I am tracking how women directors navigate the contradictions of a political—and market—demand to represent marginalized subjectivities both behind and on-screen.

Despite my vigilance, paranoia even, about the hegemonic content and the structural exclusions perpetuated by the culture industries I study, I remain convinced of the importance of the arts and humanities in public life. My own disciplines—gender and sexuality studies and film and media studies—are interdisciplinary, humanistic inquiries with wide relevance and thus high stakes. Discourse undeniably equals power within globalized information culture, and the humanities are essential to shaping cultural conversations about media, including calls for underrepresented voices that go beyond reflectionism or the insertion of new cultural identities into familiar narratives. Feminist, queer, and anti-racist commitments illuminate the investment that viewers have in particular films and figures as well as the many intersecting issues of power, positionality, access, and embodiment that inform these conversations.

The homologies between coming-of-age films and the casting of the independent woman director as telling her own story reinforce a pervasive cultural investment in female capacity, the "can do," presumptively white, postfeminist girl (McRobbie). I have suggested that emphasizing the imperfect, the queer, and the open-ended resists that normative vision, taps into collectivities through genre and affect, and leaves filmmakers room to maneuver the new media landscape and a public sphere that demands that women speak without making space to hear them. With work by women filmmakers jostling for the indie box office and berths on streaming sites like never before, it would be cruel not to be optimistic.

Works Cited

Ahmed, Sarah. *The Promise of Happiness*. Duke UP, 2010.

Baym, Nina. *Women's Fiction: A Guide to Novels by and about Women in America 1820–1970*. University of Illinois Press, 1993.

Berlant, Lauren. *Cruel Optimism*. Duke UP, 2011.

Campbell, Joseph. *The Hero with a Thousand Faces*. Princeton UP, 2004.

Caserio, Robert L., et al. "Forum: Conference Debates—The Anti-Social Thesis in Queer Theory." *PMLA*, vol. 101, no. 3, 2006, pp. 819–828.

Cvetkovich, Ann. *Depression: A Public Feeling*. Duke UP, 2012.

Danforth, Emily. *The Miseducation of Cameron Post*. Harper Collins, 2012.

De Lauretis, Teresa. *Alice Doesn't: Feminism, Semiotics, Cinema*. Indiana University Press, 1984.

Edelman, Lee. *No Future: Queer Theory and the Death Drive*. Duke UP, 2006.

GLAAD. "Where We Are on TV 2018." https://www.glaad.org/whereweareontv18.

Halberstam, J. *In a Queer Time and Place: Transgender Bodies, Subcultural Lives*. New York University Press, 2005.

Halberstam, J. *The Queer Art of Failure*. Duke UP, 2011.

Johnson, Chris. "Court Strikes Down Bans on Conversion Therapy as Violations of Free Speech." *Washington Blade*, 20 November 2020, https://www.washingtonblade.com/2020/11/20/court-strikes-down-bans-on-conversion-therapy-as-violations-of-free-speech/.

Lady Bird. Directed by Greta Gerwig, Scott Rudin Productions, 2017.

Lauzen, Martha M. "The Celluloid Ceiling in a Pandemic Year: Employment of Women on the Top U.S. Films of 2021. https://womenintvfilm.sdsu.edu/wp-content/uploads/2022/01/2021-Celluloid-Ceiling-Report.pdf

Love, Heather. *Feeling Backward: Loss and the Politics of Queer History*. Harvard UP, 2007.

McRobbie, Angela. *The Aftermath of Feminism: Gender, Culture, and Social Change*. Sage, 2008.

Muñoz, José Esteban. *Cruising Utopia: The Then and There of Queer Futurity*. Duke UP, 2009.

Ngai, Sianne. *Ugly Feelings*. Harvard UP, 2005.

Pariah. Directed by Dee Rees, Focus Features, 2014.

Rich, Adrienne. *Of Woman Born*. W. W. Norton, 1976.

Scott, A.O. "Review: *The Miseducation of Cameron Post* Resists the Straight and Narrow." *New York Times*, 2 August 2018, https://www.nytimes.com/2018/08/02/movies/the-miseducation-of-cameron-post-review-chloe-grace-moretz.html.

Sedgwick, Eve Kosofsky. "How to Bring Your Kids Up Gay." *Social Text*, *29*, 1991, pp. 18–27.

Sedgwick, Eve Kosofsky. "Paranoid Reading and Reparative Reading." *Touching/Feeling*. Duke UP, 2002, pp. 123–151.

Sims, David. "*The Miseducation of Cameron Post* Is a Graceful Coming-of-Age Tale." *The Atlantic*, 1 August 2018, https://www.theatlantic.com/entertainment/archive/2018/08/the-miseducation-of-cameron-post/566366/.

Smith, Stacy L., et al. "Inclusion in the Director's Chair." Annenberg Inclusion Initiative, 2019. http://assets.uscannenberg.org/docs/inclusion-in-the-directors-chair-2019.pdf.

Sundance Institute and Women in Film Los Angeles Women Filmmakers Initiative. "Exploring the Barriers and Opportunities for Independent Women Filmmakers." Research by Stacy L. Smith, Katherine Pieper, and Marc Choueiti. Annenberg School for Communication and Journalism, 2013, https://annenberg.usc.edu/sites/default/files/MDSCI_2013_Exploring-The-Barriers.pdf.

The Miseducation of Cameron Post. Directed by Desirée Akhavan, Film Rise, 2018.

White, Patricia. "Changing Circumstances: Global Flows of Lesbian Cinema." *Global Cinema Networks*, edited by Elena Gorfinkel and Tami Williams, University of Rutgers Press, 2018, pp. 159–177.

White, Patricia. "Coming Out in the Middle: *Pariah*." *Possible Films*, edited by Claire Perkins and Constantine Verevis, Edinburgh University Press, 2015, pp. 133–143.

White, Patricia. "Lesbian Minor Cinema." *Screen*, vol. 49, no. 4, 2008, pp. 410–425.

White, Patricia. *Women's Cinema, World Cinema: Projecting Contemporary Feminisms*. Duke UP, 2015.

8

Learning to Adapt

From Pathology to Splendor

Timothy Corrigan

> Emerson is proposing an anthropology, proposing that there is a splendor inherent in human beings that is thwarted and hidden by a deprivation of the means to express it, even to realize it in oneself. The celebration of learning that was made visible in its spread into the territories and the new states must have taken some part of its character from the revelation of the human gifts that education brought with it. It is interesting to see what persists over time, and interesting to see what is lost.
>
> —Marilyn Robinson, "Save Our Public Universities: In Defense of America's Best Idea"

> Right now I'd be glad to change some growth for happiness.
>
> —Harvey Pekar to Robert Crumb in *American Splendor*.

Over the past seventeen years, I have taught an introductory course entitled an "Introduction to World Cinema, Post-1945 to the Present." The class typically enrolls about seventy students (the maximum for the classroom), and it attracts them from every undergraduate level and from every major across the university, from freshmen to seniors and from the business and engineering schools to the nursing and fine arts schools. No doubt some of them are there simply to fulfill a humanities requirement, some because they (incorrectly) think it will be an easy course, and some because they simply love movies. Why they are there doesn't really concern me, and I always (correctly) assume fifteen percent of them will drop the course once they realize there is considerable reading and writing. More important is what I tell them the first day of the class and then reiterate on the last day: this course should be absolutely crucial to an education and to a future life for two reasons. One is that, in the twenty-first century (and decades before), to be a truly

Timothy Corrigan, *Learning to Adapt* In: *Cinema, Media, and Human Flourishing*. Edited by: Timothy Corrigan, Oxford University Press. © Oxford University Press 2023. DOI: 10.1093/oso/9780197624180.003.0009 educated person you *must* know film history and the films that describe the expanse of world film culture, much in the same way that two centuries earlier an educated person was expected to know the best of what is known and thought in the world (then usually literature and philosophy).[1] The second reason is that, regardless of where their personal and professional futures go, they will inevitably have to deal with media images and will likely have to engage in some kind of analysis of those images as part of their work. Whether that future is as a botanist or a lawyer, a politician or a landscape designer, or a dancer or a chef, they will need to know how to work with moving images and, in many cases, analyze those images as an act of appreciation and understanding, and, in some cases, as ways of determining what is true or realistic.

These goals engage, in turn, larger issues about human flourishing and well-being in the world today. Two issues stand out for my argument here: How do film and media studies address, conceptualize, understand, and promote well-being today? How can films cultivate well-being as a form of learning and as part of an educational project that engages viewers in specific ways?

Doubtless there are many films and film experiences that could be characterized as obstructing or problematizing human flourishing, such as encouraging passive relationships with images of the world or promoting simplified or distorted representations of social life and human beings. At their best, however, those positive questions and goals associated with the film experience can mirror the larger positive values of a personal and social encounter with the cinema today where the intellectual, imaginative, and kinetic ability to engage new worlds, experiences, and realities becomes a distinctive and crucial part of individual and social development and well-being. These multi-layered or multi-tracked engagements can productively blur the lines between critical analysis and psychological pleasure, and, in the best cases, integrate the different experiential values of aesthetics, cognition, and ethics as a sustainable activity that invigorates life beyond the film screen.

The larger interdisciplinary projects devoted to "human flourishing," "well-being," and "the enhancement of the humanities" typically map and evaluate these aims across the activities of immersion, embeddedness, socialization, and reflectiveness, positions entirely relevant to the cinematic.[2]

[1] I realize this is a controversial reference to an Arnoldian idea that poses significant ideological problems in many quarters.

[2] In Louis Tay, James Pawelski, and Melissa G. Keith's "The Role of the Arts and Humanities in Human Flourishing: A Conceptual Model," the authors "propose four mechanisms through which the modes of engagement and the activities of involvement with the arts and humanities may lead to positive effects: immersion, embeddedness, socialisation, and reflectiveness" (4).

Here, however, I will refocus those broader categories on a particular dimension of cinematic adaptation, with all its textual and historical layers and with its implicit pedagogical lessons of "learning to adapt." Although the notion of cinematic adaptation commonly refers, for instance, to the textual and creative activity that binds a novel and its reincarnation on a screen of moving images or to the inverse movement that connects a movie with its reiteration as, for instance, an interactive video game, my focus on adaptive values points to psychological and epistemological possibilities and benefits within the activities of adaptation: as a process whereby viewers learn to negotiate images and sounds according to the emotional, cognitive, social, and even corporeal mobilities that pervade their lives. My touchstone for the pedagogy of these adaptive mobilities will be the 2003 film *American Splendor*, a movie ostensibly about the pathologically misfit cartoonist Harvey Pekar but that is, more importantly, about the flexibilities, enhancements, and values of shifting representational identities in the layered and rapidly moving landscapes of the contemporary world where the place and status of well-being and happiness are increasingly complex and shifting.

As a central part of my reflections on this film, I want to posit a distinction between two commonly overlapped terms used in positive psychology: flourishing and well-being. At least for my focus film (but perhaps with larger implications), human flourishing suggests an active engagement and determination to find fulfillment in life: to flourish is to be actively engaged with positive choices and beneficial relationships with the world. Well-being, in *America Splendor* and elsewhere, is a place or position in life that is more about acceptance than about action, an acceptance that recognizes the circumstantial virtues and values in the life that in many cases already exists. Harvey Pekar never chooses to flourish but he does indeed learn to embrace the well-being that his world offers him.

Adaptive Values and Productive Pathologies

Adaptation studies themselves have flourished in the last two decades, one indication being the variety of innovative models and numerous topics they have generated. Today the different strategies and values informing adaptation practices and theories range from traditional questions about textual fidelity to contemporary debates about intermedial exchanges. Incorporating many of the prominent paradigms, Linda Hutcheon's *Theory of Adaptation* succinctly maps many of the dimensions and angles that energize adaptation studies today through the framework of different formal activities (such as showing versus telling), the various agencies of adapters (involving economic and political motivations), the variations on audience reception (including the differences between knowing and unknowing audiences), and the pressures of different historical and cultural contexts (such as transcultural or indigenous configurations). Most useful for my argument, Hutcheon offers an especially rich way to consider adaptation along a "continuum model" that "positions adaptations specifically as (re-) interpretations and (re-) creations" (172). Along this continuum, adaptation appears, for her, as various forms of "expansion" that begin with a focus on textual fidelities and end with "academic criticism and reviews of a work" (171). At that far end of her spectrum, adaptation includes a broad network of activities, beyond academic work, that may originate in responses to particular texts but which then open up to the wider critical domains of new media where, as Siobhan O'Flynn argues in the epilogue to the second edition, "audiences now claim all aspects of ownership over content that they identify with, immerse themselves in, adapt, remix, reuse, and share," a digital world driven by "porousness, instability, collaboration, and participation" (206).

While Hutcheon and O'Flynn signal the expansive movements that characterize adaptation (especially today), the lingering question here and in many of the discussions about contemporary "convergence cultures" is, I believe, "to what effect?" or, more exactly for my argument, "with what value," here particularly as a value that promotes human flourishing or well-being. Adaptations have always created implicit or explicit values in their processes, products, and receptions, beginning perhaps with its scientific roots in evolutionary models where adaptation implies not just the survival of a species but the flourishing of that species as it grows and develops through new environments. Many of the adaptive values in film culture evolve according to certain textual practices (such as the aesthetic currency of star actors in an adaptation or the added value found in the agency of celebrated auteur-directors). Other adaptations offer ideological, political, and cultural values as the product of their contextual location and resonances (as with Laurence Olivier's patriotic adaptation of *Henry V* in 1944 during the German siege of the UK). Additionally, there are invariably economic and technological values attached to or promoted by virtually all adaptations when they highlight blockbuster budgets, best-selling novels, or special effects technologies like 3D or VR visuals.[3]

[3] See Simone Murray's *The Adaptation Industry*.

Less commonly explored, however, have been the social, psychological, and even physical values invested in adaptive exercises and processes, values which have become especially important in contemporary culture where experiences and identities have become increasingly subject to transformations and mobilizations of both. The ameliorative re-positionings of race and gender within classical adaptations thus become reflections on heritage of those positions and the possibilities of reshaping and redefining them. Less obviously are the contemporary challenges of technological velocities and digital networkings whereby the new platforms of adaptation can elicit new mobilities and subjectivities through changing avatars and experiences. Today learning to adapt increasingly addresses states of crises or simply the intellectual, emotional, and physical challenges of living in a contemporary world with changing identities, geographies, and velocities, where the hybridization and mobilization of selves and subjectivities occur within a network of social discourses, platforms, and screens.

Within contemporary participatory cultures, in short, the security of traditional adaptive values (such as fidelity) has tended to dissipate across networks of porous instabilities, self-performances, and often idiosyncratic and insular collectives. Mobilizing cognitive, emotional, and even physical register across these shifting digital platforms, contemporary fields of adaptation practices and studies often raise key questions about the limits and values of a culture in which adaptation seems to be pervasively and ubiquitous undifferentiated through contending or interchangeable subjectivities. The shadow across the inclination to celebrate this fluidity is what I have called elsewhere digital narcissism,[4] which in turn begs the questions: How do audiences and individuals today learn to adapt within these new frontiers and, more importantly how, as part of these adaptive platforms does one identify, distinguish, and activate values that do not simply affirm subjectivity and private collectivities but offer new sources of human and social development and well-being. How do contemporary adaptations encourage and promote human values and well-being as a new kind of learning within the activity of learning to adapt? In this context, many contemporary adaptations foreground their own critical engagement with the process of adaptation as a way of measuring and opening the terms and possibilities of human and social

[4] I have discussed some of these issues in my essay "Emerging from Converging Cultures: Circulation, Adaptation, and Value."

growth, intelligence, and meaning—beyond the enclosures of converging agencies that promote self-enclosed world building.

A particularly deft discussion of this pedagogical turn within contemporary adaptation, Thomas Elsaesser's "The Mind Game Film" has explored a variety of recent films as examples of what he calls "productive pathologies," pathologies that require their protagonists and the viewers who follow them to adapt productively to rapidly changing worlds and new realities. With films such as Christopher Nolan's *Inception* (2010) and Alejandro González Iñárritu's *Birdman* (2014), Elsaesser argues that these films both describe and demand, as a new hermeneutical aesthetic, a way of learning to see and engage the contemporary digital world through the productive pathologies of paranoia, schizophrenia, and amnesia. In the challenge to understand these films and to adapt to their worlds, "the spectator's own meaning-making activity involves constant retroactive revision, new reality checks, displacements, and reorganization not only of temporal sequence, but of mental space" (21). Reflecting the new communication technologies and mobilities that increasingly define contemporary subjects and societies, these films "make 'mind games' out of the very condition of their own (im) possibility: they teach their audiences the new rules of the game, at the same time as they are yet learning them themselves" (37–39). They teach, in short, increased subjective efficiency in navigating and executing the new representational orders of a digital world. And with that efficiency come the pleasures, satisfactions, and contentments of learning to adapt.

A broader and more expansive model for developing this perspective on adaptive pedagogy is Francesco Casetti's essay "Adaptation and Mis-adaptation," an essay which retains an awareness of the technological mobility of adaptation today, but which also provides a framework for investigating the human and social values elicited within that mobility. Reformulating the process of adaptation as the movement between different "communicative situations," Casetti argues that adaptations should be considered as "sites of production and the circulation of discourses; that is, as symbolic constructions that refer to a cluster of meanings that a society considers possible (thinkable) and feasible (legitimate)" (82). An adaptation is a "reappearance in another discursive field": as a "*recontextualization of the text*, or . . . *reformulation of its communicative situation*" (82–83, author's emphasis), whereby "a text appears as an event within the world" (84) and as a connection with other social discourses. Here, adaptation works to "re-program" reception as a "second life of reception" (85). The common adaptation interaction between cinema and literature thus becomes about two large "construction sites" "where every society experiments with its values, meanings, and system of relations—in other words, what it deems visible, thinkable, shareable," where "society challenges itself and to some extent the destiny of its members" (90).

What is most significant for me about Casetti's formulation (and my adaptation of it here) is its emphasis on the larger social and historical significance of adaptation as a subjective and social activity and process that productively measures and debates cultural and historical formations and discourses about human and social value. As an active negotiation and renegotiation of the encounter between different discourses, adaptations become sites where individuals can re-conceptualize, rethink, and re-imagine themselves as social agents, where choices and actions can delineate possibilities and potentials for growth, change, and happiness. I am particularly interested in Casetti's notion of mis-adaptation where the misfit of an adaptation can become a revealing learning lesson and where the values that emerge from these "construction sites" appear as the critical products of learning how and what to adapt.

Beyond the Pathological: *American Splendor* (2003)

One of the corrective moves in recent well-being studies has been to shift the psychological and social focus from interventions in pathologies to reenforcement and shaping of positive psychological and social abilities and skills. Coincidently perhaps, many modern adaptations gesture toward those earlier models by featuring psychologically or socially troubled characters at their center—especially the more reflexive films that call attention to the process of adaptation as its subject matter. Jean-Luc Godard's *Contempt* (1963), R. W. Fassbinder's *Berlin Alexanderplatz* (1980), Jon Amiel's *The Singing Detective* (1986), Spike Jonze's *Adaptation* (2002), Alejandro González Iñárritu's *Birdman* (2014), and Asghar Farhadi's *Salesman* (2016) each, in very different ways, dramatizes the complexity of adaptation through the struggles of characters who are engaged in a crisis to adapt different texts or to adapt to a fraught and troubled world. Shari Springer Berman and Robert Pulcini's *American Splendor* likewise participates in this contemporary tradition but also develops and advances that pathological tendency in adaptation practices toward more productive values, specifically those that align with

Casetti's figures of "reappearance" as a second life, mis-adaptation as part of the "construction sites" of adaptation, and "negotiation" within different communicative situations. Adapting these categories as my flexible touchstones in *American Splendor* highlights the restorative human values and the possibilities of well-being inherent a pedagogy of adaptation. Specifically, these categories become frameworks in the film for the discovery of a social subjectivity within overlapping networks of different contemporary discourses, for an emergence from the pathological binds of digital narcissism, and for the pedagogical value in overcoming that bind within a more productive and empathetic register of social communicativeness.[5]

Based on a series of autobiographical comic books written by Pekar and illustrated by multiple artists between 1976 and 2008, the 2003 film *American Splendor* is an odd biopic and reflexive adaptation about cartoonist Pekar. It recounts his daily life in Cleveland, Ohio, beginning in the 1950s when the young Harvey refuses to join the other children in superhero costumes as they parade across porches on Halloween; Harvey insists that he will not adapt as a superhero and instead appears only as his ordinary, curmudgeon self. The film then proceeds chronologically and episodically through his rather thankless job as a file clerk at a Veteran's Administration hospital, his relationships with somewhat misfit colleagues there, and his marriage to his third wife, Joyce Brabner. Along the way there are the daily inconveniences and miseries that characterize Pekar's life: problems with money, self-esteem, and health, each adding to his constant self-obsession and insular discontent. Played by a constantly scowling Paul Giamatti, Pekar is a classic misanthropist, largely unable to socially integrate, a "nobody guy" whose "perspective is gloom and doom," a "hoarder," and a "social embarrassment" with "obsessive, compulsive qualities." A grumpy everyman, cartoonist Pekar is a cinematic subject who inhabits arenas outside mainstream society and cinema: underground, disaffected, marginalized, and unsociable.

Conventional biopics—from *Young Mr. Lincoln* (1939) to *Lincoln* (2012)—typically concentrate on the singular agency of an individual, who stands out in history, famously or infamously, to drive historical and social events forward through the force of a dominant subjectivity, defining

[5] This foundation in pathologies from which the possibilities of well-being and flourishing might emerge is discussed, in different ways in other essays in this volume. Dana Polan and Patrice Petro, for instance, focus on hoarding as an especially contemporary anxiety from which a social well-being must struggle to emerge. Less directly, Ellen Scott addresses this crisis in racial terms and Patricia White places it in the context of gender politics.

or redefining the social or historical real in terms of that subjectivity. In *American Splendor*, however, that narrative and subjective drive moves and faulters across the shifting registers of different kinds of adaptation, registers which mimic the porous, unstable, and sometimes collaborative world of contemporary new-media adaptations. An extreme version of a narcissistic actor, glued to his or her screen and moving through the digitally interactive platforms within multi-media culture, Pekar inhabits multiple representational levels and social routines, alternating between the befuddled ordinary filmic narrative of Pekar as a file clerk, the comic-book recreation of that life in the book series *American Splendor*, and a third register where the actor Paul Giamatti, the cinematic Pekar, meets the real Pekar (as do other actors who meet their real life counter-parts on film sets). Comic-bubble inserts duplicate film dialogue, and hand-drawn comic-book frames alternate with live action images to create graphic montages not as conflicts or continuities but as different stages for the performance and re-performance of an obsessive self. That these movements occur across relatively old-media, rather than new-media images, forms, and technologies, gestures toward the dynamics of new media while concomitantly de-mystifying and materializing the transformative ease that new media typically promises individuals and their usually romantic avatars. These old-media registers foreground, in short, the representational fabrics and dislocations of new media movements, and subjectivities, now graphically represented, for Pekar and the viewers of the film, as a world of zones, objects, frames, and discourses constructed, deconstructed, and reconstructed by an alienated and self-searching individual.

Across these representational zones, the multiplications of Pekar and his different visual worlds highlight especially the centrality of a body as a mobile identity in the act of refusing to adapt to other people and places. For my argument, this version of social mis-adaptations aligns in the film with the psychological and cultural notion of "the inappropriate" as a revelatory moment that reveals the individual's difficult or impossible ability to adequately adapt to the world. From the opening sequence, Pekar belligerently resists accepting common and acceptable social rituals, codes, and behaviors, embracing instead his insistently marginalized "ordinary" life in Cleveland as an isolated hoarder unable or unwilling to move forward socially or economically. From the beginning Pekar resists inscriptions of most kinds, refusing social mores and expectations and unable to articulate himself (to the extent of losing his voice).

As he adapts and "mis-adapts" himself to various social situations and personal encounters, these movements become formally aligned with that multiplication and serialization of his presences and size of his body across a variety of representational frames (graphic drawings, cinematic reenactments, and off-screen encounters between real individuals and actors). According to Bart Beaty, the central trope of the film, comic-book representations, are essentially distinguished as disruptive systems of figurative co-presences, size differentiations, and serial narratives, all three of which describe formal tactics of *American Splendor* and Pekar's primary forms of resistance, mobilization, and self-expression. In an important sense, these corporeal movements suggest what I would call a repetitiously vertical way of living (through singularity of a resistant self), as opposed to living in a historically horizontal way (as a developing social and historical self). At the beginning of *American Splendor*, the real Pekar's voiceover announces that vertical co-presence of the Giamatti character that permeates the film, as Pekar's voice comments on a shot Giamatti/Pekar walking down a street in Cleveland: "Here's our man. Yeah all right, me. Or the guy playing me." Later, a screen wipes from a conversation in the film diegesis about Pekar's private and obsessively protected jazz collection with his colleague Mr. Boats to a comic frame of that same conversation, and then cuts to the real Pekar addressing the camera, explaining the collection on a cluttered stage scattered with records, against a vacant white backdrop, the accumulations of a manic, self-focused hoarder. As in many scenes throughout the film, this sequence dramatizes the layered and differentiated vertical co-presences of Pekar and their relation to the possessive materiality of identity within distinctive and serialized zones of simultaneity (wryly signaled at a bus stop next to a "Zone Travel" agency). Just as Pekar's series of autobiographical comic books recreate his figure differently according to the different artists who draw him, Pekar adapts to these registers and zones as materially distinctive representational bodies, figures, identities, and subjectivities, as different reappearances as second, third, and fourth lives. This layering and overlapping of material zones and bodies continues later in the film as a particularly disconcerting and deflected mirror image when the filmic Harvey and Joyce watch a Los Angeles stage adaptation of *American Splendor* in which stage actors embody and re-enact their life and at another point when the couple produces a material replica doll of Pekar as a promotional commodity.

Almost needless to say, these repetitions of identity from the real to the figurative to the physical re-adapt and materialize Pekar as vertical layers of various self-representations that also include the film itself (about which Pekar remarks "God only knows how I feel when I see this movie"). While these adaptations provide a remarkable mobility of self-representation, that mobility appears, like the digital narcissism of new media, more like a vertical redundancy that simply adapts while refusing the challenge of horizontal change. Through these shifts and alterations, Pekar and his self-proclaimed "ordinary life" becomes an ironically narcissistic, deconstructed version of contemporary new-media adaptation, at times adapting a self and at other times, being adapted by another framework, with various crucial mis-adaptations along the way.[6]

Across these movements of simultaneous selves and identities, a key confrontation between their alternative subjectivities, discourses, and frames of self foregrounds a critical turning point in the film. While he insists, as he says to Robert Crumb, that "ordinary life is pretty complex stuff," he decides midway through the film to direct that life to "make a mark" on the world by pursuing celebrity fame as another vertical frame of self. That this decision follows a rather sudden awareness of mortality, brought about by his conversations with Crumb and his discovery of the death of the file clerk who preceded him suggests that this particular shift becomes an extreme tactic for expanding into vertical spaces that would lift him above the inevitable temporality of change and loss.

Key sequences at this juncture are Pekar's numerous appearances on the *David Letterman Show* as his fame begins to grow and he now becomes the object Letterman's manipulations and appropriations of his persona. What at first attracts Letterman to Pekar is his odd, unpolished, and occasionally nasty behavior as a man of the people and the streets, but the two

[6] In a different context but clearly related to my model here, Kristen Whissel investigates this tension between verticality and horizontality as it structures contemporary blockbusters and super-hero comic adaptations: "its tendency to map the violent collision of opposed forces onto a vertical axis marked by extreme highs and lows. Specifically, it approaches digitally enhanced verticality as a mode of cinematic representation designed to exploit to an unprecedented degree the visual pleasures of power and powerlessness. Precisely because verticality automatically implies the intersection of two opposed forces—gravity and the force required to overcome it—it is an ideal technique for visualizing power. Verticality thereby facilitates a rather literal naturalization of culture in which the operation and effects of (social, economic, military) power are mapped onto the laws of space and time. Hence, in recent blockbuster films, vertically oriented bodies and objects imply a relation not just to the laws of physics but also to the spaces and times that define a fictional world's prevailing order. Vertical movement thereby gives dynamic, hyperkinetic expression to power and the individual's relation to it—defiant, transcendent, or subordinate" (23). "As the above suggests, verticality's link to gravity and the laws of space and time makes it an ideal aesthetic for dramatizing the individual's relationship to powerful historical forces. Horizontality, in this context, stands for temporal and historical continuity which, when ruptured by the upsurge or fall of a vertically articulated mass, creates a dynamized moment, a temporal–historical break that radically changes the course of events" (24).

personalities eventually explosively confront one another when Pekar realizes that his newfound celebrity is merely a media amusement and hardly a celebrity redemption. At this critical moment, Pekar appears as a caricature of himself: an aggrandized self now suspended between two social, psychological, and representational frames (or, in Casetti's terms, two different "communicative situations"). Mis-adaptation, in this case between the ordinary and the celebrity frameworks and between an enclosed self and exaggerated self, make clear what is at stake and what counts in adapting who you are to whom you want to be: a reconsideration and examination of the self which questions where real meaning and value emerge amidst all the vertical movements of self.

Faced with the realization that the vertical multiplication of self becomes ultimately a *mise-en-abyme* of lost selves, that missing horizontal plane of self-realization rather suddenly begins to emerge in the film, now as a temporal, physical, and mortal movement to be discovered, learned, and engaged as physical and social change. For the co-present figures of Pekar, this ultimately means recognizing and choosing not the vertical axis of self-multiplication on different registers but rather learning, choosing, and adapting to a frame of communicativeness that integrates those selves on a horizontal plane that integrates that self as part of a narrative of awareness, well-being, and potential happiness.

In the final episodes of the film, Pekar finds this move into a horizontal narrative of self specifically as reappearances into two second lives that take him dramatically out of himself as the self-contained actor of his own worlds and learns to re-adapt himself to the world offered him as a physical place. The first is his discovery of his testicular cancer as a clear and real sign of the fragility of his body and his identity: after the initial trauma of this discovery and the crisis of "how to get through this," Joyce urges him to re-adapt and transform the prognosis of self-loss into a narrative triumph of self-removal instead of self-duplication: "you'll make a comic book of the whole thing. Document every detail. Remove yourself from the experience until it's over." The result becomes a new issue of *American Splendor*, titled *Our Cancer Year*, which narrates his successful struggles with a new horizontal form of self-consciousness as self-abnegation. At the crossroads of those two dimensions of self-hood, the multiplied self and the developing self, Pekar reflects for the first time on where his mortal self might find itself in the multiplications of vertical frames: "Am I just a character in a comic book? . . . . If I die will that character keep going? Or will he just fade away?" The film then cuts to an empty white frame in which Pekar walks around line abstract drawings in a world reduced to its bare minimum. Those frames, once able to be filled with multiple versions of self, now become the blank spaces of a mortal self seeking a real body.

Just as Pekar as a child refuses a superhero persona on Halloween, this realization of the graphic emptiness within the mobile and transformative frames of his comic-book life returns Pekar, with some irony, to the call of his real and mortal body. It recalls Scott Bukatman's complaint, in his essay "Why I Hate Superheroes," about contemporary superhero movies adapted from comic books. For Bukatman, those CGI and special-effects movies consistently forsake the physical bodies at the heart of comic-book heroes and so create an abstract "corporality without corpus," a corporeal figuration that "speaks to nothing but its own kinetic effectiveness. By removing the body from space, it removes meaning—lived meaning—from the body," as the "incarnation of electronic technology" (118–119). For him, these adaptations undermine the key dynamic of the original comics where bodies enact a "playful disobedience" highlighting the recalcitrant physicality and corporality of the characters. Or, in terms of my graphics, vertical movements imply a refusal of the physical laws that governs real bodies.

A second turning point occurs shortly after this epiphany about his elided corporality, this time as result of his "unusual name," that illusory sign of a singular identity. Through the 1960s and 1970s, he begins to notice two, then three Harvey Pekars in the Cleveland phone book and then an obituary for one of those Harvey Pekars, and then another. Against a back projection of empty streets in the snow, he reflects on this proliferation of anonymous selves in the phone book that suggest a metaphor that undercuts the singular power of his reproduced subjectivity and, implicitly the stagnant redundancy of vertical adaptations: "I was filled with sadness," he says. "It seemed our lives were linked." As he stares into the camera against a now graphically illustrated background, he begins to consciously recognize and articulate the existential and representational questions that permeate the many redundant, mobile, and narcissistic avatars of himself, reappearing as second and third lives throughout the film. As he disappears into a white background, he poses a series of key pedagogical questions: "Two years later another Harvey Pekar appeared in the phone book. Who are these people? Where do they come from? What do they do? What's in a name? Who is Harvey Pekar?" These redundancies of self thus become a tongue-in-cheek reminder of the proliferations of self that has isolated and secured Pekar in a graphic narcissism which now undercuts itself against a fading backdrop of disappearance and death.

Out of those two critical shifts emerges a different Harvey Pekar within a different communicative register, a self with new lessons about what counts in life and where well-being becomes a profound acceptance of life outside of self. Within the resulting socially and narratively repositioned discourse of a horizontal narrative, at the conclusion of the film, he and Joyce adopt a friend's young daughter, Danielle, as a new and unexpected direction in their own adaptive lives. After constructing and reconstructing himself as worlds built from vertical self-projections, Pekar releases himself as he returns to the streets of Cleveland and into a social subjectivity shared with others over time, where he discovers previously unseen moments of happiness in the different narratives of life as change. At a retirement party for the real Pekar, friends and family mingle in a quiet celebration of what Pekar learns through so many adaptations and mis-adaptations: that the splendor of self appears through the developing narrative encounter with others, not as a possibility to actively flourish but as a meaningful acceptance of where well-being can be found in the world that is his. "But don't think this is some sunny, happy ending. Everyday is still a major struggle . . . . Sure I'll lose the war eventually but the goal is to win a few skirmishes along the way. Right?"

Real Happiness

American Splendor is a film about adaptive choices, lessons, and changes that can transform the pathologies of new-media mobility into a pedagogy of self-aware happiness. Midway through the film, Pekar encounters by chance an old college acquaintance, Alice Quinn, who describes herself as a "plain old wife and mother" in contrast to Pekar's rising fame, and they casually discuss a book she is reading by that master of American realism Theodor Dreiser. Pekar comments, "I hope this book doesn't end like so many of those naturalist novels," where the central character "is crushed to earth by forces he can't control." That of course is the realism Pekar struggles with in his daily life, and the realism that becomes the major thematic and compositional question in a comic-book film which violates most registers of realism: Which realism will you adapt for your life? Which is the will you accept outside your singular and self?

For Pekar and this film, adaptation and mis-adaptation ultimately open the interstices of the real between the platforms of self, as an act of destabilization of the real that extends rather forecloses the self. Far from *American Splendor* in a discussion of Iranian filmmaker Abbas Kiarostami, Jean-Luc Nancy argues that the real resides in "an increased plurality," revealing an "essentially multiple essence" through cinema's "internal multiplicity" of "pictures, image as such, music, words and finally movement" (22–24). Here a film "ceaselessly moves, so to speak, in the film or out of the film in order to reenter it" (24). Here discovering the real becomes, significantly, a kind of education and adaptation, based on the etymology of the word education as "to bring out" the real of the world: "The evidence of the cinema is that of the existence of a look through which a world can give back to itself its own real and the truth of its enigma . . . , a world moving of its own motion, without a heaven or a wrapping, without fixed moorings or suspension, a world shaken, trembling, as the winds blow through it" (24, 44).

Placed in this strangely appropriate framework, *American Splendor* offers a visual morality tale about a world rapidly shifting through different adaptation contexts: as a pedagogical tale about how we negotiate within changing communicative situations and still discover and preserve human and social values. At the conclusion of the film, there is a short episode in which Pekar takes his newly adopted daughter to a school bus (for me, a tongue-in-cheek educational vehicle); as they walk, she asks him not to hold her hand—not, as he initially believes, because it embarrasses her but because he, revealingly, squeezes her hand too tightly. It is an ordinary gesture, but as Gorgio Agamben reminds us about gestures in the cinema, they are often the source of the real. For Agamben, gesture implies "the exhibition of mediality" as well as "the process of making a means visible as such," so that in the world of images, "gesture is the point of flight from aesthetics into ethics and politics" (58, 8). Here, gesture describes the "decreation of the real," or a decreation of facts as part of a larger desubjectivization of reality. In Jean-Luc Godard's work, Agamben tells us that gesture "functions as an unveiling of the cinema by the cinema," which takes us to the realm of mediality where adaptation thrives in the intersection of adaptive encounters (26). Gesture, in the broadest sense of the term, calls forth the interstices in the real in the act of adapting to it, where repetition becomes the salient vehicles for discovering a world beyond the image as potential and possibility: "repetition is not the return of the same but the return of the possibility of what was"; it "realizes the messianic task of cinema" to create "an image of nothing" that no longer recounts a meaning and thus returns the real to the ethical potential of new meanings and new possibilities (25). The positive ethics and value of reality are thus a possibility and potential: a "zone of indistinguishability" or, in Agamben's phrase, "bare life." As Agamben might say, here "repetition is not the return of the same but the return of the possibility of what was" (26). Or, in Pekar's description of his modest well-being, "life seems so sweet and so sad and so hard to let go of in the end . . . Just keep on working and something is bound to turn up."

Works Cited

Agamben, Gorgio. *Cinema and Agamben: Ethics, Biopolitics, and the Moving Image.* Edited by Henrik Gustaffson and Asbjørn Grønstad, Bloomsbury, 2014.

Beaty, Bart. "Comic Studies, Fifty Years after Film Studies: Introduction." *Cinema Journal,* vol. 50, no. 3, 2011, pp. 106–110.

Bukatman, Scott. "Why I Hate Superhero Movies." *Cinema Journal,* vol. 50, no. 3, 2011, pp. 118–122.

Casetti, Francesco. "Adaptation and Mis-adaptations: Film, Literature, and Social Discourses." *A Companion to Literature and Film,* edited by Robert Stam and Alessandra Raengo, Blackwell, 2004, pp. 81–91.

Corrigan, Timothy. "Emerging from Converging Cultures: Circulation, Adaptation, and Value." *The Politics of Adaptation,* edited by Dan Hassler-Forest and Pascal Nicklas, Palgrave, 2015, pp. 53–65.

Elsasser, Thomas. "The Mind-Game Film." *Puzzle Films: Contemporary Storytelling in Contemporary Cinema,* edited by Warren Buckland, Wiley-Blackwell, 2009, pp. 13–41.

Hutcheon, Linda. *A Theory of Adaptation.* 2nd ed. Routledge, 2013.

Murray, Simone. *The Adaptation Industry: The Cultural Economy of Contemporary Literary Adapations.* Routledge, 2011.

Nancy, Jean-Luc. *Abbas Kiarostami: The Evidence of Film,* translated by Christine Irizarry and Verena Andermatt, Yves Gevasrt, 2001.

Robinson, Marilyn. "Save Our Public Universities: In Defense of America's Best Idea." *Harper's Magazine,* March 2016, pp. 1–8.

Tay, Louis, James O. Pawelski, and Melissa G. Keith. "The Role of the Arts and Humanities in Human Flourishing: A Conceptual Model." *Journal of Positive Psychology,* vol. 13, no. 3, 2018, pp. 1–11.

Whissel, Kristen. "Tales of Upward Mobility: The New Verticality and Special Effects." *Film Quarterly,* vol. 59, no. 4, summer 2006, pp. 23–34.

9
Austerity Media and Human Flourishing

Patrice Petro

This chapter explores representations of recessionary culture and impulses to hope in recent television and film. It grows out of an earlier essay I wrote on media and culture in the wake of the 2008 recession, which addressed changing notions of home and homelessness that figure accumulation as loss and clutter as the accretion of memory. That earlier essay from a larger project (first a conference, then a book) was devoted to probing capitalism's limits.[1] Both the conference and the book engaged scholars from a range of disciplines to discuss and debate the ways in which political economy, representational practices, and questions of citizenship are necessary to rethinking capitalism's past and potential futures. Some argued that capitalism would shift and grow as the world changes, while others saw in alternative representations and histories hidden worlds that are already post-capitalist or even outside of capitalism's reach, thereby offering possibilities for new thought and action.

In line with Timothy Corrigan's chapter in this volume, I am interested here in expanding this earlier work by exploring media representations of our contemporary world where "the place and status of well-being and happiness are increasingly complex and shifting." In Chapter 8, Corrigan focuses on *American Splendor* (2003) in an effort to shift the focus from human flourishing (the key prompt for our own disciplinary discussion) to questions of adaptation and well-being. As with several other chapters in *Cinema, Media, and Human Flourishing*, flourishing and well-being here do not spring from open fields of experience, but instead emerge often from rockier fields of social and personal pathologies or crises. Reflecting on theories of literary and filmic adaptation, Corrigan demonstrates the ways in which a film like

[1] The "After Capitalism" conference took place at the University of Wisconsin, Milwaukee in April 2014 and was co-organized by me and Kennan Ferguson. The book, based on the conference, was published with the title *After Capitalism: Horizons of Finance, Culture, and Citizenship*, edited by Kennan Ferguson and Patrice Petro, Rutgers University Press, 2016.

Patrice Petro, *Austerity Media and Human Flourishing* In: *Cinema, Media, and Human Flourishing*. Edited by: Timothy Corrigan, Oxford University Press. © Oxford University Press 2023. DOI: 10.1093/oso/9780197624180.003.0010

American Splendor highlights the possibilities of well-being inherent in what he calls a "pedagogy of adaptation"—a form of learning that maps positive directions for the demands of contemporary subjectivity and which engages viewers in ways specific to the film experience. I also shift from notions of flourishing to focus on resilience and its representation in contemporary media texts. I am aware, of course, that representations of resilience are not anything new in U.S. media or culture. As Dana Polan underscores in Chapter 6, Hollywood films of 1930s, made at another recessionary time, also reflect on the potential and perils of efforts to flourish, even if these sometimes appear as the sole privilege and province of the wealthy.

In the analysis that follows, my examples turn from Hollywood cinema to contemporary media that is itself made on limited budgets, spanning reality television shows about hoarding to recent neo-neorealist narratives, including Sean Baker's *Tangerine* (2015) and *The Florida Project* (2017). These take up questions of dwelling and dispossession and loss, but also reveal, most importantly, impulses to hope and narratives of new possibilities. They are examples of what I have called "austerity media" in that they are cheaply produced (and hence industrially austere), they interact with crises of nonfictional economies (and hence document experiences of austere living), and they render worlds with a distinct and often uncanny aesthetic, from the sublimity of hoarded houses to the color-saturated other-worlds of seemingly familiar places (Santa Monica Boulevard and Highland Avenue in Los Angeles in *Tangerine*, Osceola County in Florida, outside Walt Disney World in *The Florida Project*).

There are, to be sure, many other examples of changing notions of home and homelessness in contemporary film and television—as well as narrative and documentary films that explore possibilities for flourishing in the midst of trauma, precarity, and loss. Shot on a modest budget, Debra Granik's recent film *Leave No Trace* (2018), for example, follows the lives of a father and daughter who live off the grid in the forests of Portland, Oregon. He is a widower and former veteran who, we gradually discover, suffers from post-traumatic stress disorder; almost the sole focus of the film, their mobile and changing home is a campsite deep in the woods surrounded by moss and lush vegetation and isolated from virtually all human or social contact. Indeed, the lush, dense images and profoundly quiet soundtrack becomes a space the two main characters almost seem to disappear into, a bucolic space permeated by a tension between escape and alienation.

When they are apprehended by law enforcement, late in the film, for living illegally in a public park, their unconventional lives are shattered, and they are placed into social services. Contrasting the make-shift encampments that constantly change locations and the more conventional middle-class home where the daughter and father are later placed, the film probes complex issues of what constitutes home and what constitutes homelessness, as both father and daughter defend their former lifestyle from social workers and law enforcement officers who claim that the father has failed to provide his daughter with a proper home. In this film, the symbol of the American dream—a free-standing house replete with a television and toaster oven—is rejected outright as part of the same system that, obliquely but unmistakably, produces a social and ideological conditions that fosters war and post-traumatic stress disorder, as well as unrelieved anxiety and suffering for many far from the traumas of war. As the father tells his daughter, the temporary house provided by social services is not their home and does not contain the objects and comforts they have relied on in the forests. In the end, the daughter decides to stay in a small encampment with other people living on the margins of society; the father, by contrast, slips back into the forest, and the film's only aerial shot follows him into the woods until he disappears.

In the wake of the 2008 recession, several documentaries explored the devastation of the housing collapse and the precarity of notions of home.[2] Perhaps most memorably, the 2012 documentary *The Queen of Versailles* tracks the 2008 financial crisis with a focus on a billionaire family who are in the process of constructing the largest home in America (a 90,000-square-foot private residence, replete with seventeen bathrooms). Faced with the economic downturn and collapse of their time-share business, the billionaire and his wife must readjust their plans, and as the film ends, they are in their "starter" mansion, with the bigger house still on hold. Less than three years later, and in contradistinction to middle-class homeowners, they have recouped all their financial losses and they begin rebuilding the mega-mansion again. A year later, another documentary, entitled *Two American Families* (2013), tells a very different story of home and family, with a focus on families whose reversal of fortune has been several decades in the making. This Frontline documentary features two families from Milwaukee, one black and one white. They work hard, they have children, they dream of owning

[2] Among the many documentary and fictional films that engage the crisis are *Capitalism: A Love Story* (2009), *Wall Street: Money Never Sleeps* (2010), *Too Big Too Fail* (2011), and *Money for Nothing* (2013).

their own homes, and they yearn for success. And yet, no matter how hard they try or how committed they may be, they cannot catch up, they cannot get ahead. While both families suffer decline and losses, only the black family harbors no illusions about the promises of the American Dream (both husband and wife have always worked, neither indulges in the fantasy of the sole breadwinner, and racism and redlining are enduring facts of their life). As their daughter explains, theirs is a struggle, not over life and death, but over light and power.

The specific examples of austerity media that I have chosen to highlight in the rest of this chapter are especially revealing of what Anthony Vidler has identified as "the modern unhomely"—the experience of home or dwelling as the last and most intimate shelter of comfort sharpened, indeed, haunted by its opposite, the disquieting and uncanny abode (Vidler). As Vidler points out, the modern unhomely is itself a result of the resurgent problem of homelessness, made worse by the decline of governmental support in the form of education and living wages, which lends special urgency to the need for reflection on home and the unhomely today. Hoarding shows, by revealing what should have been and what was meant to be hidden, allow us to consider something of the domestic history of austerity narratives; Sean Baker's films, by contrast, propose a dramatic confrontation between home and the unhomely with characters living on the margins of the entertainment industries (*Tangerine*) or the fantasy worlds of theme parks (*The Florida Project*). In approaching austerity media from the perspective of "well-being" and "flourishing," I am interested in exploring recessionary culture from the vantage point of the humanities and film theory, especially feminist film and queer theory, which provide for more expansive views. Although this topic and this angle may not appear to describe or promote notions of well-being or flourishing, the dramatic invisibility of those more actively positive perspectives ironically points toward them through the cloudy lens of hope.

Feminist film scholars Diane Negra and Yvonne Tasker stress the importance of film and media studies to understanding how contemporary economic developments are actually lived, arguing that "media studies offers a unique disciplinary pathway for interpreting recession culture given its focus on the analysis of collective symbolic environments that hold enormous sway in shaping public views" (1). Stories about hoarding on reality TV are particularly interesting in this regard and I have written about them elsewhere (Petro). Here, I simply want to stress that hoarding is not an entirely new or contemporary phenomenon. As historians have pointed out, well before reality TV, depictions of hoarding and hoarders could be found in literary texts, such as Dante's *Divine Comedy* and Charles Dickens' *Bleak House*, and across popular culture (in the sensationalist press coverage of the famous Collyer Brothers who died among their junk in their Harlem brownstone in the 1950s, and of William Randolph Hearst, the inspiration behind Orson Welles's story of excessive accumulation of buildings, objects, and people in *Citizen Kane*).

There is also larger history of scholarly approaches to hoarding that spans several disciplines. In the early twentieth century, for example, psychologists William James and Eric Fromm discussed the problem of hoarding as a pathology of ownership and acquisitiveness. By the latter part of the century, moreover, hoarding appeared in the *Diagnostic and Statistical Manual of Mental Disorders* (DSM)—the handbook of American psychiatry—as a form of obsessive-compulsive disorder (OCD). In 2013, with the release of the newest DSM, hoarding was listed as its own disorder, in need of specific treatment by psychologists (who are regularly featured as experts on the reality TV hoarding shows). In addition to providing hoarders with treatment, which, more often than not, ultimately fails, psychologists work with others in newly founded businesses to repair the material and mental damage of hoarding: vast storage facilities, professional organizers, and new trash collection businesses that specialize in remediating dilapidated and hoarded houses. Most importantly, although hoarding behaviors occur more often among men than women and increase with age, reality TV nonetheless focuses primarily on women as hoarders, returning us to questions about the relationships among dwelling, accumulation, and dispossession, and the linkage of all three to a kind of modern, gendered pathology.

Feminist film scholars have long addressed the ways in which the linkage between "woman" and "home" is rendered in film ("the woman's place is the home"). Among the most enduring of these analyses is Mary Ann Doane's signal essay from the 1980s, "The 'Woman's Film': Possession and Address." In an effort to understand the textual address of films made explicitly for female audiences, Doane explains that in 1940s women's films, "dramas of seeing become invested with horror within the context of the home." Most important to her argument is the way in which looking in these films is despecularized or deflected away from the female body onto objects and a more generalized *mise-en-scene*. Unlike other genres, the woman's film does not configure its female protagonist as mysterious or enigmatic; instead, potential knowledge about her is transferred from the law to medicine. As a result, the erotic gaze becomes medicalized, and the female body is not so much located as spectacle but as an element in the discourse of medicine, "a manuscript to be read for the symptoms which betray her story, her identity." Doane maintains that "the very process of seeing is now invested with fear, anxiety, horror, precisely because it is object-less, free floating" (67–82). As a result of this breakdown in subject/object relations, these films reveal a deeply entrenched identification of women with suffering, hysteria, and paranoia, thereby promoting a disease model of the female body (and that of female viewers). Doane's point is not that this is an accurate or adequate identification, but rather than it is a persistent one in classical cinema that assigns a position or place for women within patriarchal culture. This is true of hoarding shows on reality TV as well, where legal issues (such as threats of evictions or foreclosure) are framed as mental health issues, and older adults, and usually women, come to represent the pathological disease as a whole.

In her book, *Vibrant Matter*, and in a related essay on hoarding, political theorist Jane Bennett similarly explores the breakdown of subject/object relations and related pathologies in contemporary culture. While she is less interested than Doane in questions of gender, she is equally concerned to detect the shape of modern illnesses in material practices. She takes hoarding as a central example but, rather than focus on the psychology of individual hoarders, as reality TV does, she argues that focusing on the things themselves allows alternative material practices to come into view. She theorizes a "vital materiality" that runs through and across bodies, both human and nonhuman, and suggests that recognizing that agency is distributed rather than fixed opens a politics less devoted to blaming and condemning individuals than to discerning the web of forces affecting situations and events. "It hit me in a visceral way," she explains, "how American materialism, which requires buying ever-increasing numbers of products purchased in ever-shorter cycles, its antimateriality. The sheer volume of commodities, and the hyperconsumptive necessity of junking them to make room for new ones, conceals the vitality of matter, which still exists in "trash" which are alive with organisms thriving underground" (5).

Bennett resists locating hoarding as a psychological phenomenon because it puts "things" in the background. In her view, hoarders are not bearers of mental illness but are differently abled individuals who have special sensory access to the call of things. Hoarding may thus not be a deficiency at all but may be a special gift or ability to sense "the somatic effectivity of objects." In Bennett's reading, hoarding is also a coping response to human mortality.

There is an advantage to privileging things over human flesh when it comes to endurance, patience, and waiting it out; whereas human relations are fragile and changeable, things reveal the relative slowness of the rate of change. As Bennett explains, whereas a therapeutic discourse would say that hoarders have lost the ability to distinguish between person and thing, "a vibrant materialist would say that hoarders have an exceptional awareness of the extent to which all bodies can intertwine, infuse, ally, undermine, and compete with those in its vicinity." Vibrant materialists, in other words, resist a medical gaze and are interested in the possibilities for human and nonhuman flourishing (5).

Queer theorist Scott Herring, author of *The Hoarders: Material Deviancy in American Culture*, takes a different approach than Bennett, but with the same intent of moving away from disease models of human behavior. In his book, Herring argues that campaigns against clutter are often barely covert attacks on nonconformity. His two main examples are the mid-century scandal involving the famous Collyer Brothers, whom I cited earlier, and the 1970s fascination with mother and daughter both named Edith Beale, who lived in poverty at Grey Gardens, a derelict mansion in East Hampton. He explains that pathological readings of elderly hoarding are not the proper way to understand aging or hoarding; as a gay, queer theorist, he maintains that unconventional lifestyles should be allowed and not overlaid with disgust and fear. He believes that people have a right to accumulate as much junk as they want, and that campaigns against clutter are more often than not covert attacks on more politicized versions of nonconformity.

To my mind, Herring's most important insight (which he doesn't emphasize himself) is that hoarding has been democratized through media, throughout the twentieth century: the sensationalist press coverage of the Collyer Brothers and of the Beales are just two examples of the popular fascination with hoarding that predate hoarding shows on television. Of course, the Collyers and the Beales had been rich while most of the hoarders on reality TV are not. Herring's point, however, is that before the twentieth century, hoarding referred primarily to the accumulation of wealth rather than trash. Thus, what was previously viewed as a sign of financial greed now functions as a psychopathological diagnosis of late-twentieth-century overconsumption and dispossession, now open for public view. Herring wants to challenge this notion of hoarding as a disease located in a biochemical imbalance and instead treat stories about hoarding culturally and historically;

specifically, he wants to show how deviance is socially constructed and narratively enacted in stories about unconventional lives.

Like Bennett, he therefore traces the ways in which mental illnesses arise in certain times and places; he celebrates nonconformity while Bennett celebrates distributive agency. For my part, I have been interested in hoarding shows and other austerity media texts because they show us how poverty and dispossession are lived today, in complicated and nuanced ways, in the context of planned obsolescence and vast mountains of disavowed waste. As I have pointed out, while most hoarders on TV are women, there is not one but many types of hoarders on reality TV (Petro). There are organized and disorganized hoarders, hoarders who collect storage materials and those who collect junk; there are animal hoarders, who believe they are saving pets that no one else wants, and hoarders of excrement and urine; there are those who hoard to keep people out, fill a void, and cover over a loss. There are hoarders who consider themselves environmentalists, letting nothing go to waste, and hoarders who consider themselves collectors, even artists, as they find beauty and meaning in things no one else wants. There are, finally, proto-feminist hoarders who reject the ideology of "woman's place" and refuse their gendered role as guardians of home, memory, and storage spaces. To be sure, hoarding shows on television are just one example of media that complicate our views of recessionary culture; two recent films by Sean Baker provide another. Indeed, if dwelling in hoarding shows is all about dispossession by accumulation (too much stuff and the literal experience of being "buried alive"), in Sean Baker's recent films, dwelling is all about the merging of people and places, both of which are in constant motion.

Not unlike Bennett and Herring, Baker is interested in telling stories about unconventional lifestyles and nonconformist behaviors. He explains: "When I made 'Tangerine,' I moved to Los Angeles and I thought that Los Angeles was shot out, meaning that there's no other stories to tell. Then I found there's a whole other world south of Olympic that we haven't even seen in film unless it was 'Straight Outta Compton.' You realize who's telling these stories. They're not thinking outside their box, and often their sugar-coated visions of who they are" (Coyle). The same was true of the inspiration for *The Florida Project* and Baker's desire to tell the story of families living below the poverty line, eking out an existence in cheap tourist motels like The Magic Castle, the major setting of the film, located near Disney's Magic Kingdom and surrounded by places like the Orange World supermarket, a Twistee Treat ice cream shop, and a cow pasture. "The issue of the film," Baker explains, "which is the hidden homeless, was something I was unfamiliar with. I didn't even know there was a term—'the hidden homeless.' So it was a topic I wanted to explore myself" (Dry). Both films radiate a candor and immediacy and sense of place that is remarkable in many ways, and not least of all for capturing dream worlds (Hollywood, Walt Disney World) alongside harsh economic conditions.

Like hoarding shows, recessionary culture permeates the economics and aesthetics of Baker's films. *Tangerine* and *The Florida Project* were made on very small budgets with a mix of professional and non-professional actors. Much was made, for instance, of Baker's decision to shoot *Tangerine* on the iPhone 5, which is in fact the least interesting thing about the film itself. The bold sense of color, the pent-up energy of people and places, provide us with a pulsating street view of Los Angeles we rarely see. And unlike hoarding shows, where any movement forward is often revealed as circular and repetitious as people try in vain to navigate their cluttered homes, Baker's films are all about incessant movement: transient and nearly homeless people, moving from place to place, on either coast of the United States, in the shadow of great wealth and the entertainment industries. The remarkable Los Angeles setting for *Tangerine* anchors long sections of the film, which consist of shots of people walking and walking to get anywhere in car culture Los Angeles, sometimes after having waited on a bus that seems never to arrive. In *The Florida Project*, the dilapidated remains of a formerly bustling area on the edge of a theme park provide the setting for unsupervised children to experiment, play pranks, and roam. The palette is dusky purples and green rather than the yellows and citrus colors that define *Tangerine*. But in both cases, Baker is drawn to stories about outsiders striving to get by in recessionary times.

At the center of his films are compelling central characters. In *Tangerine*, first-time actors Kiki Rodriguez and Mya Taylor (Sin-dee and Alexandra), two trans prostitutes, meet at a West Hollywood donut shop on Christmas Eve right after Sin-dee has gotten out of jail for a minor drug felony. *Tangerine* has been described as urban comedy/drama, featuring a cast of recent immigrants and starring two trans women as prostitutes in a series of misadventures on the streets of Los Angeles. But at heart, it is a female buddy movie centered on perhaps the most disenfranchised groups, black trans women. From the opening sequence at Donut Time where the central characters chatter like teenagers to the ending in the laundromat where we witness a nuanced, adult friendship, *Tangerine* is a film that is stylistically beautiful in its rich primary colors, energetic in its pace, by turns incredibly funny and incredibly moving. And despite its orange skies and Los Angeles setting, *Tangerine* is an uncanny Christmas movie, set on Christmas Eve, about unconventional families and friendships. This is brought home in the final sequence, when Alexandra gives Sin-dee the precious gift of her own wig after a stranger in a car drenches Sin-dee with a bottle of urine; and even earlier, when the Alexandra sings "Toyland," made famous by Doris Day, exploring "little girl and boy land" comprising childhood, where borders between genders seem at once clear and obvious fictions as well.

In *The Florida Project*, a mix of unprofessional and professional actors is also in place: non-professionals Brooklyn Prince (Moonee) and Bria Vinaite (Halley) join veteran actor Willem Defoe (Bobby), who keeps his eye on the reckless single mom and her six-year-old daughter. Both films use street casting, with real people who actually live in the worlds depicted on screen. Baker has been asked what drew him to this story of female friendships and mother–daughter relationships, to which he responded: "I think all my films—most filmmakers' films perhaps—are responses to what you don't see enough of," he says. "Maybe I just didn't see enough of this in U.S. film and TV" (Tutt).

Of course Baker is right to stress the need for more stories about recessionary culture, especially those about people living in desperate economic conditions in familiar settings made strange and wonderful. In this chapter, I have endeavored to show that those stories do exist in U.S. film and media, even in the most banal and sensationalized of forms, such as reality TV hoarding shows which, when viewed from the perspective of feminist or queer theory, allow us to see how nonconformity is socially constructed and narratively enacted in complicated and unexpected ways. Baker's films, like Bennett's vital materialism, enact a politics more attuned to the web of forces affecting people and things. In a recent interview, Baker talks about finding an uprooted tree that unexpectedly found its way into *The Florida Project*: "I brought it to my producer, Shih-Ching Tsou, who I co-directed 'Take Out' with, and who played the perfume girl, and she said, 'I love this tree because it's special: it's uprooted but it's still growing.' I was like, that's like the tagline of the movie: 'It's uprooted, but it's still growing" (Tutt). Austerity media at its best reveals that dwelling is not merely a matter of providing shelter or access to things, but of sustaining lives and communities, and in finding hope and resilience amidst the odds.

Works Cited

Bennett, Jane. *Vibrant Matter: A Political Ecology of Things*. Duke University Press, 2010.

Bennett, Jane. "Powers of the Hoard: Further Notes on Material Agency." *Animal, Vegetable, Mineral: Ethics and Objects*, edited by Jeffrey Jerome Cohen, Punctum Books, 2012, 237–270.

Coyle, Jay. "Filmed near Disney, 'Florida Project' Shines Bright Light on Hidden Homelessness." *Orlando Sentinel*, 4 October 2017, https://www.orlandosentinel.com/entertainment/movies/os-florida-project-disney-hidden-homeless-20171004-story.html.

Doane, Mary Ann. "The 'Woman's Film': Possession and Address." *Re-Vision: Essays in Feminist Film Criticism*, edited by Mary Ann Doane, Patricia Mellencamp, and Linda Williams. University Publications of America, 1984, pp. 67–82.

Dry, Jude. "Sean Baker on Perfecting the Artful Issue film in 'The Florida Project.'" *Indiewire.com*, January 2018, https://www.indiewire.com/2018/01/sean-baker-florida-project-video-interview-1201913646/.

Herring, Scott. *The Hoarders: Material Deviance in Modern American Culture*. University of Chicago Press, 2014.

Negra, Diane, and Yvonne Tasker, editors. *Gendering the Recession: Media and Culture in an Age of Austerity*. Duke University Press, 2014.

Petro, Patrice. "Austerity Media: Horizons of Finance, Culture, and Citizenship." *After Capitalism: Horizons of Finance, Culture, and Citizenship*, edited by Kennan Ferguson and Patrice Petro. Rutgers University Press, 2016, pp. 89–105.

Tutt, Louise. "Sean Baker on the Story Behind 'The Florida Project.'" *Screen Daily*, 22 December 2017, https://www.screendaily.com/interviews/sean-baker-on-the-story-behind-the-florida-project-/5125160.article.

Vidler, Anthony. *The Architectural Uncanny: Essays in the Modern Unhomely*. MIT Press, 1992.

Index

For the benefit of digital users, indexed terms that span two pages (e.g., 52–53) may, on occasion, appear on only one of those pages.

Figures are indicated by *f* following the page number

Praise for *End Emotional Outsourcing*

'*End Emotional Outsourcing* is the book that will grab you by the shoulders (gently, with love) and shake loose all the BS that's been keeping you stuck in people-pleasing, perfectionism, codependency, and over-functioning. Béa Albina breaks it down with science, humor, and the kind of wisdom that makes you go, 'Oh sh*t...that's me.' Read this book. Your future self will thank you.'

– ANDREA OWEN, *New York Times* bestselling author of *Make Some Noise*

'This book is a love letter to anyone who was taught that being 'good' means being quiet, accommodating, and endlessly giving. *End Emotional Outsourcing* isn't just about personal transformation – it's a blueprint for collective liberation.'

– DR NICOLE CAIN, founder of the Holistic Wellness Collective and author of *Panic Proof*

'If you've ever felt like you've let your life center around the needs of others, this book is your invitation to return home. It's science, it's soul work, and it's revolution, all braided into one sacred thread. I didn't just read this book, I remembered myself in it.'

– AYESHA OPHELIA, spiritual provocateur and creator of *The Girlfriend Manifesto*

'No more waiting for permission to take up space. No more settling for breadcrumbs. If you're ready to reclaim your power, set boundaries without apology, and stop outsourcing your self-worth, read this book. Now.'

– VASAVI KUMAR, therapist and author of *Say It Out Loud*, and host of the *Say It Out Loud* podcast

'If you've ever felt like your value depends on how much you do for others, this book is more than illuminating – it's liberating. *End Emotional Outsourcing* is a revolutionary guide to breaking free from people-pleasing, perfectionism, and codependency – once and for all.'

– ELLEN VORA, author of *The Anatomy of Anxiety*